The Politics of
Intergovernmental Relations

The Politics of Intergovernmental Relations

SECOND EDITION

David C. Nice
Washington State University

Patricia Fredericksen
Washington State University

Nelson-Hall Publishers/Chicago

Project Editor: Rachel Schick
Copy Editor: Susan Cassidy
Typesetter: Precision Typographers
Printer: Capital City Press
Illustrator: Bill Nelson
Cover Painting: *Shattered Pattern* by Val Berkely

Library of Congress Cataloging-in-Publication Data

Nice, David C., 1952–
    The politics of intergovernmental relations / David C. Nice and
Patricia Fredericksen.
      p.   cm.
    Includes bibliographical references and index.
    ISBN 0-8304-1357-X
    1. Federal government—United States   2. State–local relations—
United States.   3. Federal–city relations—United States.
I. Fredericksen, Patricia.   II. Title.
JK325.N54 1994
320.473—dc20   94-15923
                                               CIP

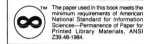

CONTENTS

CHAPTER 1

Federalism: The Setting of Intergovernmental Relations

As passenger rail service in the United States grew increasingly unprofitable in the 1960s, many railroads sought to eliminate passenger service entirely. Others were in serious financial difficulty and did not appear to be able to provide continued service on their own. Without some form of governmental action, passenger trains were threatened with extinction.

That prospect alarmed many observers. Noting the safety of passenger trains, their energy efficiency, and, with electrified track, their ability to function without massive petroleum consumption, many called for action to preserve passenger train service. They argued that the national interest required preserving the service to provide a foundation for a new passenger transportation system that will be increasingly vital as petroleum supplies dwindle.

The national government responded by creating the National Railroad Passenger Corporation, more commonly known as Amtrak, in 1970. It now operates all of the long-distance passenger trains in the United States. While Amtrak owns the trains that it operates and employs the personnel who serve its passengers, much of the track used by Amtrak is owned by private railroad companies, which also run freight trains on the same track. Amtrak's *Southwest Chief*, for example, operates on the track of the Santa Fe Railroad, while most of the track used by the *Crescent* belongs to the Norfolk Southern Railroad.

Although most Amtrak revenues are provided by customers through purchases of tickets, meals, and the like, and subsidies from the national government, a number of states also provide funding for Amtrak services. The state subsidies enable individual states to tailor rail passen-

1

ger service to meet their particular needs. At the same time, state funding enables Amtrak to provide more frequent service on some routes that would otherwise be available and to provide service on other routes that would have no service at all without state support. A number of local governments have also contributed funds to improve passenger stations and to provide coordinated bus service at train stations.

The Amtrak system reflects federalism in action. The national government and the private sector, along with a number of state and local governments, combined their efforts in an innovative solution to a policy problem. By sharing their resources and pooling their efforts, they were able to provide a service that would have been vastly more difficult, if not impossible, for the national government, the states, local governments, or the private sector to provide acting alone.

More than two centuries after the adoption of the U.S. Constitution, Americans continue to wrestle with many of the same issues that faced the Philadelphia Convention in 1787. Many of these issues involve the nature of federalism and the conduct of intergovernmental relations. This chapter will present a basic definition of federalism as well as a number of different views of federalism. In addition, the costs and benefits of federalism will be explored.

Intergovernmental Relations in a Federal System

The American political system is made up of many governments, over 83,000 at last count (*Statistical Abstract* 1990: 272). These governments, including the national government, the states, and a bewildering variety of local units, do not function in isolation from one another. On the contrary, they interact frequently, and these interactions form the basis for the study of intergovernmental relations. The contacts range from harmonious cooperation and assistance to bitter conflict, and from activities as formal as a constitutional amendment or a court hearing to the informality of a cocktail party or a telephone call.

Intergovernmental relations occur when the national government sends disaster relief to a state plagued by floods, when a state government gives financial aid to local schools, and when a city purchases water from a county water plant. When some governors refused to comply with national court orders to integrate their schools, they were engaging in intergovernmental relations, as were the national courts when they issued the orders. States or locales refusing to accept hazardous waste from other states, counties, or cities are also part of the intricate structure of intergovernmental relations. Every major area of governmental activity involves intergovernmental relations to some degree.

Figure 1.1: Basic Political Systems

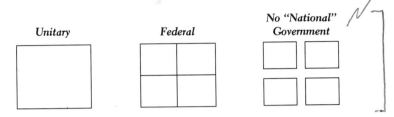

Intergovernmental relations in the United States takes place within our federal system. Although federalism has been defined in many ways, for our purposes a limited definition will suffice. Federalism is a system of government that includes a national government and at least one level of subnational governments (states, provinces, local governments) and that enables each level to make some significant decisions independently of the other(s). The ability to make decisions independently is not absolute; one level may be influenced by another in various ways. Nonetheless, a federal system gives each level the ability to make some decisions without the approval (formal or informal) of the other level (for discussions of this issue, see Macmahon 1972: 3; Riker 1964: 5; Wheare 1964: ch. 1).

Federalism is something of a midpoint on a continuum of political systems. At one extreme is a purely unitary system, in which all decision-making power resides in the national government, and subnational units do not exist or exist only to carry out the directives of the national government.[1] The United Kingdom is a relatively unitary system. At the other extreme is the system in which no national government exists and the "subunits" are independent countries (see figure 1.1). For example, before Italy was united in the 1800s, there was an Italian language, an Italian culture, and an Italian history, but there was no official national government of Italy.

Federal systems can distribute power and responsibilities in many ways, ranging from systems in which the national government is relatively weak and the subunits are dominant, systems that are often called confederations, to systems that give the national government most of the authority and leave the subunits with a relatively minor role. Moreover, the division of power and responsibility in a

1. Bear in mind that a purely unitary system is an abstract concept. National governments in the real world often have great difficulty controlling the activities of subnational governments, even in officially unitary systems.

system can change over time, as it has in the United States, and can vary from one program to another. Responsibilities can be divided, with some given to the national government and others to the subunits, or responsibilities can be shared. The brief definition of federalism lends itself to a variety of possibilities.

A great deal of controversy over the years has centered on the questions of how the federal system operates and how it should operate. In wrestling with these questions, the brief definition is not enough; we need to consider slightly more elaborate interpretations of what federalism is or should be. We will refer to these more elaborate interpretations as models.

Models of Federalism

The term "federalism" conjures up many different images, and when various politicians and scholars use it, they may have different meanings in mind.[2] A model presents a simplified version of reality or of some ideal situation while eliminating unnecessary detail. Of course, if this is not done carefully, important information may be overlooked. Over the years a number of different models of federalism have been widely used. They differ in part because of the spectrum of beliefs and priorities of various observers and in part because some models were developed in different historical eras when the federal system behaved in other ways.

Models of federalism are significant because they direct our attention to important aspects of how a federal system operates. In addition, the models serve to raise questions that we will address later in this book. Competitive models, including nation-centered federalism, state-centered federalism, and dual federalism, emphasize competition among levels of government in the system. Interdependent models, such as cooperative federalism, creative federalism, the various New Federalisms, and row boat federalism, emphasize shared responsibilities, although in varying degrees. Finally, functional models of federalism, including picket fence and bamboo fence federalism, emphasize divisions among different bureaucratic specialists, such as educators and law enforcement personnel.

Competitive Models

To some observers, federalism is essentially a zero-sum game—that is, a game in which there is a fixed amount of some desirable commodity

2. For analyses and discussions of models of federalism, see Adrian and Fine (1991: 95–99), Beer (1978), Dye (1990a: 6–13), Elazar (1984: ch. 3), Grodzins (1966), Leach (1970: 10–17), Sanford (1967: 5, 80, 97), Walker (1981: 46–65, 123–28, ch. 3, 4), and Wright (1988: 36–111).

and in which one player can increase his or her supply of the desired commodity only by taking some away from the other player. Competitive models of federalism generally regard it as a zero-sum game in which two levels of government, national and state, compete for power. One level can gain power only at the expense of the other. The competitive models disagree, however, on the question of the outcome (real or desired) of the competition.

Nation-Centered Federalism. According to the model of nation-centered federalism, the national government is (or should be) the dominant force in a federal system. This model often includes assertions that the national government has a broader perspective on issues, and that the states are backward and poorly equipped to deal with difficult problems (we will examine the latter charge in chapter 4). This model is generally associated with extensive national government activity, a relatively broad interpretation of the powers of the national government, and a fear that leaving problems to the states will result in inaction or a confusing and ineffective response, with different states riding off in different directions without a coherent plan of action.

However, nation-centered federalism is sometimes associated with a fear or dislike of national government power. In this case, national dominance is seen as excessive, undesirable, or even dangerous. National dominance produces red tape, bureaucratic inefficiency, and government that is inaccessible to the citizens and out of touch with problems in the field, in this view. Adherents of this perspective tend to have a second competitive model, to which we now turn, as their ideal.

State-Centered Federalism. With state-centered federalism, the states are seen as the dominant force in the federal system. This model contends that state dominance is desirable because of the danger of concentrating too much power in the national government. The states are seen as closer to the people and able to adapt to variations in problems or citizen preferences from one part of the country to another. In addition, the many states can experiment with different programs to stimulate improved policies. Adherents of this view often contend that the national government was created by the states and is therefore inferior to them, an issue we will discuss in chapter 4.

State-centered federalism is generally not regarded as an accurate description of U.S. federalism today because of the size and influence of the national government. However, many observers have noted the importance of the states in our governmental system. The states participate in many major governmental programs, have grown considerably since the turn of the century, and are often able to exert considerable influence on other levels of government. They have also demonstrated considerable ability to avoid doing things when state officials feel the inclination, regardless of what officials at other levels may want.

Dual Federalism. The third competitive model, which was very influential for many years, is dual federalism, which is sometimes called layer-cake federalism. It holds that each level of government, nation and state, is supreme within its areas of responsibility. According to this model, neither level is dominant in any general sense, and neither level should interfere in the affairs of the other. Dual federalism places a high value on balance; the system needs the flexibility that nation-centered federalism cannot provide and the broad perspective and coherent policies (on some issues) that state activity alone cannot provide. With a clear division of responsibility—the national government handling national functions and the states handling state functions—voters would have an easy time determining who should be rewarded or punished for policy successes or failures.

Dual federalism is a fairly accurate portrayal of the early years of our governmental system (though perhaps not totally accurate—see Elazar 1962). The Supreme Court devoted a great deal of effort to delineating boundaries between national and state responsibilities, and collaboration between national and state governments was less common and less extensive than it is today.

Dual federalism is not without its problems, however. In the process of trying to draw boundaries between national and state functions, some problems may end up on the boundary, with the result that neither level can do anything about them. Dual federalism also ignores the possibility that cooperation between national and state levels might sometimes be more effective than either level acting alone. It assumes that policy responsibilities can be divided so that decisions made in one policy area do not affect other policy areas, a dubious assumption at best. If, for example, education is a state function and defense is a national function, and if the educational system fails to produce mathematicians, physicists, and chemists needed to develop new military technology, what will happen to the defense program? Last, but by no means least, how do we tell a state function from a national one? As we will see in the next chapter, there is no politically neutral way to allocate responsibilities. If civil rights for blacks had remained a state responsibility through the 1950s and 1960s, fewer blacks would have voted or attended integrated schools in the late 1970s. If the state of California had decided to leave provision of passenger train service in the state entirely to the national government, Californians from San Diego to Santa Barbara and San Francisco to Bakersfield would have considerably less service today than they actually do.

Overall, the competitive models tend to ignore the possibility that the national government and the states could both gain power simultaneously, a possibility that is very real. The competitive models also share a serious omission: local governments, such as cities and counties, are typically ignored, although Thomas Dye's (1990a) recent work on competitive federalism is an important exception. Given that local governments spent the most money, hired the most workers, and provided the most services of the three levels of government when the competitive models were most influential, this omission is quite glaring. Local governments were excluded from the competitive models because the U.S. Constitution did not mention local governments and because state constitutions and court rulings tended to treat local governments as creatures of the states and subordinate to them. In practice, however, local governments often function with considerable autonomy.

On the positive side, the competitive models alert us to the fact that conflicts do arise between levels of government in a federal system. Sometimes these conflicts result in a victory for one side or the other, but in some cases the result is a stalemate or truce in which neither side emerges as a clear winner. At times these conflicts are partly for public relations purposes, as when a governor makes a great public display of his or her opposition to a national government action, but in many instances the conflicts are very real and represent differing perceptions of the desirability of government programs or who should pay for them.

Interdependent Models

In contrast to the competitive models, the interdependent models are based on a sharing of power and responsibility, with the various participants often working toward shared goals. Power is not a zero-sum game; all may gain simultaneously. The most famous of the interdependent models is cooperative federalism, which was popularized by Morton Grodzins in 1966.

Cooperative Federalism. Cooperative federalism (also known as marble cake federalism) emphasizes the value of cooperation among levels of government because joint efforts may produce better results than any one level acting alone. Transportation policy, for example, affects the national economy but also influences state economic growth and the local environment, especially with traffic, noise, and the influence of transportation facilities on business location decisions. All these effects are most likely to be recognized and dealt with if all levels are involved, including local governments. The national government has great difficulty keeping track of countless variations in local needs and priorities, yet local governments may lack the resources to cope with their problems alone. A partnership is a reasonable solution. Because no level of government is likely to have a monopoly on good ideas, sharing responsibilities can let the best ideas come to the forefront, regardless of the level from which they originated.

Cooperative federalism accurately reflects the enormous amount of interaction among different levels of government in the United States. With grant programs, technical assistance, mutual aid, and a host of other mechanisms, a great deal of cooperative activity in pursuit of shared goals does occur, and responsibilities for most major programs are shared among all three levels of government. Bear in mind, however, that cooperation is not automatic, nor is it always achieved. When powers and responsibilities are shared, how is cooperation brought about, and what will happen if it cannot be achieved?

Creative Federalism. Creative federalism, a modified version of cooperative federalism, emerged in the late 1950s but reached full flower in the 1960s. It resulted from a sense that many of the traditional government policies designed to attack social problems such as poverty and urban decay were not very successful and that new ideas and solutions needed to be developed. Creative federalism envisioned a partnership of national, state, and local governments as well as the private sector. Together they would develop new solutions and, when necessary, new organizations to attack society's ills. In this view, the private sector could provide new ideas and additional resources, and if existing government organizations proved to be inadequate, new governmental or quasi-governmental bodies could be created.

Creative federalism is a reasonably accurate description of the Great Society era of the mid-1960s, during which efforts were made to apply the model to the real world. The results were not always as expected. Progress was made on some problems (see Schwarz 1988), but high expectations made the progress appear small. Many new grant programs were enacted to stimulate new activity, but confusion over who was eligible for what money and how to apply for it often resulted. Government agencies that existed prior to the Great Society era did not always welcome the new governmental and quasi-governmental bodies that were created, particularly when some of them became controversial. These problems spawned a reaction in the form of yet another cooperative model. Although it may be too early to attach a model of federalism to the Clinton administration, Bill Clinton's emphasis on reinventing government, permitting welfare experiments, and public/private partnerships are consistent with the creative federalism model. An increasing emphasis on the federal deficit may mean that while federal mandates may increase, funding may continue to be the responsibility of states.

The New Federalism (Nixon-Ford Version). The New Federalism (Nixon-Ford version) is largely cooperative federalism but with a dose of dual or state-centered federalism. The New Federalism recognizes the value of sharing responsibilities but contends that the national government has grown too large and too intrusive, particularly through the proliferation of grants for narrowly defined purposes and the regulations that accompanied them. Federal regulations should be streamlined and simplified, and public management at all levels should be improved. State and local officials should have greater discretion to deal with state-local needs. In contrast to the proliferation of grants during the Great Society era, the New Federalism advocated fewer grants but gave state and local governments more discretion over their use to permit a more integrated attack on problems such as crime and community development.

The New Federalism applies fairly well to the efforts of Presidents Nixon and Ford to cut back on federal restrictions and give recipients more leeway in spending federal funds. Both presidents generally believed in a partnership among levels of government and a sharing of responsibilities but with a somewhat smaller role for the national government and more state-local flexibility. We can safely conclude, however, that their efforts did not go as far as they wanted.

The New Federalism (Reagan Version). The New Federalism (Reagan version) is similar in some respects to the New Federalism of Nixon and Ford but places considerably more emphasis on separating national and state functions.[3] In addition, the Reagan administration's New Federalism emphasized reducing national grants to states and localities, in contrast to the growth of those grants during the Nixon-Ford years, and reducing direct contacts between the national government and local governments. The Reagan administration also pressed for reductions in national involvement in domestic policy-making generally. In all of these respects the Reagan version of the New Federalism was closer to dual or state-centered federalism than is the Nixon-Ford version, although Reagan did not always follow the model consistently.

The Reagan administration's proposed "swap" of social programs, with the national government taking full responsibility for Medicaid and the states assuming full responsibility for Food Stamps and Aid to Families with Dependent Children, reflects an application of his New Federal-

3. For discussions of the two New Federalisms, see Conlan (1988), Nathan (1983: 59–68), and Zimmerman (1991).

ism. If the proposal had been adopted, it would have provided more separation of national and state functions. (The proposal failed to gain adoption, in large measure due to opposition from state officials.) The administration did not seem to follow its model of federalism in supporting a variety of national regulations that considerably restricted state discretion in a number of policy areas. The administration seemed to support freeing the states from national government restrictions if that freedom promoted the administration's policy agenda but supported limits on state discretion if state actions did not support administration goals. George Bush generally followed the Reagan administration's lead in intergovernmental relations, although Bush did not seem as interested in intergovernmental matters as was Reagan. Federal mandates tried to influence state and local governments, but federal funding for these programs remained tight. Though the Bush administration, like the Reagan administration, had a tendency to push the costs of federal programs to state and local governments and to encourage nonfederal funding of federally mandated programs, George Bush tended to be less distrustful of civil servants and more willing to employ government in policy delivery (Walker 1991: 114).

Row Boat Federalism. The last of the interdependent models is row boat federalism, which describes the federal system in terms of three people in a boat (Sanford 1967: 97):

> The governments are all in the same boat, tossed by the same waves and dependent on each other's paddles. When any one fails to row, they all move more slowly, and the waves become more dangerous for all.

This is perhaps the purest interdependent model, for while it clearly conveys a sense of shared fate and mutual reliance, it does not make many assumptions about the nature of the relationships among those involved. While the participants might agree on some things, notably the desire to remain afloat (that is, surviving), they may or may not agree on their destination, who should sit where, or how the burdens should be divided. Cooperation is possible, but so is conflict. Power is not *necessarily* a zero-sum game, for by cooperation they may be able to achieve mutual goals more readily than through individual action. Circumstances may arise, however, which create a zero-sum situation, particularly if different participants hold mutually exclusive goals.

Collectively the interdependent models pose some problems, particularly in terms of governmental accountability. If all levels of government participate in a program that fails, how do we determine who deserves the blame? Who deserves credit for a success? If the system is designed on the assumption that the various levels will cooperate with one another, deadlock or waste may result if cooperation is not achieved. Sharing of responsibility creates enormous opportunities for scapegoating, as officials in one level of government seek to blame their failures on officials at other levels. Sharing of responsibilities can also produce delays when action requires consultation with many officials at all levels of government. Negotiations to produce agreement on a plan of action may take months or even years. Meanwhile, a problem may grow larger or cause considerable harm to the country.

On the positive side, the interdependent models, particularly cooperative federalism, do point to some genuine benefits that cooperative action can sometimes produce. In addition, interdependence is clearly a major feature of our federal system, and that feature is likely to persist. Shared responsibilities may also mean that officials at each level have an incentive to keep an eye on officials at other levels to avoid being blamed for the results of their misbehavior. If a function is entirely the responsibility of one level of government, now and forever, what incentive would officials at other levels have to monitor the performance of that program?

Functional Models

To some observers, the most important divisions in the federal system are no longer the horizontal divisions between national, state, and local governments but rather the vertical divisions among government programs such as education, welfare, and transportation. An accurate model of the system must, therefore, consider those vertical divisions.

Picket Fence Federalism. According to picket fence federalism, the main sources of power in the federal system are the various functional bureaucracies, not the national, state, or local governments (see figure 1.2). Program specialists, such as educators, have more in common with their counterparts in other levels of government than they have with other people who work in the same level of government but not in their particular specialty. The bonds among agencies in a particular specialty but at different levels of government (national, state, and local) result from personnel who have had similar training, attend professional conferences together, and move from one position to another in the profession, regardless of what level of government contains that position. Additional bonds result from a set of shared goals and tasks and from grants that channel money to a specific program and cannot legally be spent for anything else. Finally, the functional emphasis is strengthened by the three-way alliance of the bureaucratic agency, interest groups that are

Figure 1.2: Functional Models

A. Picket Fence Federalism

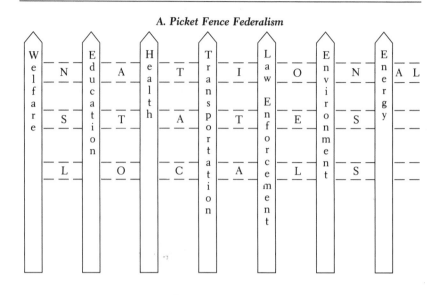

B. Bamboo Fence Federalism

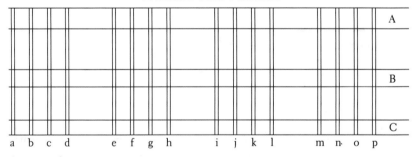

A: national government
B: state government
C: local government
a: primary and secondary education
b: higher education
c: special education
d: vocational education
e: public health
f: Medicaid
g: health research
h: training health practitioners

i: air transportation
j: road transportation
k: rail transportation
l: water transportation
m: unemployment compensation
n: aid to families with dependent children
o: supplementary security income
p: job training

concerned with the agency's activities, and the legislative committees that provide the agency with authority and funding. These three-way alliances, often called subgovernments or iron triangles, form a mutual benefit alliance that is often resistant to outside control (see Cater 1964: 17–48; Freeman 1965).

Picket fence federalism holds that the horizontal components of the fence (the national, state, and local governments) are poorly equipped to coordinate the various functional specialties. Congress, with a committee system organized along functional lines and highly fragmented power, is poorly equipped to serve as a coordinator. Presidents typically find that program implementation and coordination are relatively unrewarding activities that are therefore accorded a low priority. State and local governments are often too fragmented to bring much order out of the chaos.

The picket fence model is valuable in that it draws our attention to the significant divisions that exist *within* levels of government in a federal system. It also alerts us to potential problems. What is likely to happen if the program specialists who administer a grant program have less loyalty to the level of government that employs them than to the program specialists in another level of government that receives the grant? Will the recipients be pressed to comply with requirements they oppose, or will the requirements be softened, downplayed, or even ignored? A number of incidents suggest that the latter possibility cannot be ignored. The Elementary and Secondary Education Act of 1965 is instructive in this regard. When the U.S. Office of Education, which was largely made up of educators, learned that educators in many school districts were not using the funds from the program as the law required, the Office did very little about the situation. The educators at the national level generally sympathized with and agreed with their local counterparts.

The picket fence model also raises the problem of setting priorities and coordinating across policy areas. According to this model, power is largely concentrated in the hands of program specialists, most of whom believe in the importance of their programs, and the various interest groups that benefit from those programs. In that environment, nearly everyone believes that his or her program should be a high priority, and proposals to reallocate funds or alter regulations in order to benefit another program are likely to encounter strong opposition.

The picket fence model probably overrates the importance of functional specialists, however, and probably underrates the importance of national, state, and local governments. The picket fence model implies a great deal of uniformity in a particular program, regardless of the jurisdiction. In fact, many programs vary considerably from state to state and locality to locality, a situation that indicates that the functional specialists are unable or unwilling to create a uniform program everywhere. The picket fence model also assumes a high degree of agreement within program specialties. That agreement is not always present, though, as clashes between teachers and school administrators illustrate.

Bamboo Fence Federalism. A more moderate functional model, bamboo fence federalism, recognizes the importance of both vertical and horizontal relationships in the federal system. Vertical ties among bureaucratic sub-specialists, such as highway transportation officials (as opposed to transportation officials in general), are very strong, regardless of the level of government in which those sub-specialists work. However, broad groups of specialists, such as transportation officials of all types, are far from monolithic. Agency administrators and interest groups may be joined by academic researchers, policy analysts from think tanks, and other participants. Horizontal ties are also more significant than they are in picket fence federalism. National officials can influence the behavior of national program specialists to some degree; state officials influence state program specialists, and so forth. Bamboo fence federalism holds that the functional program specialists are more flexible than the picket fence model implies and are willing and able, at least occasionally, to respond to pressures exerted by national, state, and local officials.

In this perspective, the education profession, for example, is divided by level of instruction (primary and secondary schools versus colleges and universities), clientele served (vocational students, educationally disadvantaged students, and so forth), and bureaucratic position (classroom teachers versus administrators), not to mention differences of opinion on many issues. Administrative reforms, especially at the state level, have improved the prospects for horizontal coordination.

Bamboo fence federalism resembles Hugh Heclo's (1977) work on issue networks, in contrast to subgovernments. Issue networks include an agency, various interest groups, and legislative committees, but the networks are less stable than are subgovernments. Outsiders, such as political appointees of a newly elected president or academic researchers, may be able to penetrate an issue network and bring in new ideas. Changes in public preferences or the emergence of a new problem may disrupt the established relationships within an issue network, making it subject to outside influences.

The functional models alert us to the importance of bureaucratic specialists in policy-making. These specialists and their interest group allies may resist outside control. The research on policy implementation reveals that coordination among different programs is sometimes very difficult at any level of government, a finding that supports the functional models. Moreover, they alert us to some of the considerable differences that exist *within* levels of government.

The functional models, particularly picket fence federalism, tend to overstate the extent of consensus that exists within some functional specialties, however. The picket fence version also seems to underplay the importance of national, state, and local governments. The functional models are valuable in drawing attention to the importance of bureaucratic politics and offer a valuable corrective to the exclusive focus of the competitive and interdependent models on levels of government.

Models of Federalism: A Summary

The different models of federalism all have value: they direct attention to issues and concerns that are important in a federal system. In addition, knowing which model of federalism is held by public officials or scholars can help an observer interpret what they mean. The phrase "proper functioning of the federal system" means one thing if uttered by someone who believes that state-centered federalism is proper but means something else if uttered by a believer in creative federalism.

Knowing a variety of models is also helpful when a federal system changes. As noted earlier, a model that accurately captures the functioning of a system at one point may be inaccurate if the system changes in a significant way. Finally, when people are unhappy with governmental performance, a common phenomenon in American politics, the various models of federalism point to some potential causes of problems and present some different strategies for improving performance.

The Benefits of Federalism

Controversy has long raged over the issue of what federalism does to the functioning of a political system. Regrettably, little systematic analysis has been presented to enable us to judge the competing claims, and some people disagree over whether some of the benefits are actually benefits. The issue is clearly in need of further research.[4]

Flexibility

One of the most commonly cited advantages of federalism is its ability to permit variations in policies to correspond to variations in local desires or problems. In a purely unitary system, one national policy is established for all, leaving little flexibility to adapt to regional

---

4. See Berkley and Fox (1978: 13–21), Bish and Ostrom (1973: 29–30), Dye (1990: ch. 1, 8), Furniss (1974), Hamilton and Wells (1990: 290–302), Landau (1969), Macmahon (1972: 5–6, 18, 143–44), Neumann (1962), Riker (1964: ch. 6), and Sanford (1967: 54–61, ch. 11).

or local differences.[5] With federalism, different states or localities can tailor their respective policies to match public opinion. This benefit will be produced only if state (or local) policies actually respond to public desires, and there is some evidence that they do (Nice 1983a; Wright, Erikson, and McIver 1987). If, however, a state or locality lacks the resources to support a program the public wants, or if officials ignore or misinterpret public demands, the result may not be adaptation to what citizens want.

Preventing Abuse of Power

A second advantage of federalism is its ability to prevent the abuse of governmental power. Two mechanisms help to produce this effect. First, a federal system (in contrast to a collection of small, independent nations) includes a large and diverse population with many different beliefs and interests. As a result, no single group is likely to be able to gain control of the government and ride roughshod over the rights of others. A system of countervailing power, in which each group is held in check by the opposition of other groups, is created. As James Madison (Hamilton, et al. 1937: 61) wrote in *The Federalist*:

> The influence of factious leaders may kindle a flame within their particular States, but will be unable to spread a general conflagration through other States. A religious sect may degenerate into a political faction in a part of the Confederacy; but the variety of sects dispersed over the entire face of it must secure the national councils against any danger from that source.

A group might be strong enough to achieve a position of dominance in a single community or even a single state, but the diversity of interests at the national levels serves to limit the power of any single group.

Federalism also helps to prevent abuse of power through the mechanism of redundancy. If a political system has only one government, and that government malfunctions (in the sense of becoming tyrannical), the citizens would be extremely vulnerable. The federal system, with its many governments, will be less affected if one malfunctions; other governments can step in and correct the situation. Note that dual federalism, with its emphasis on separation of national and state governments, provides little opportunity for one level to intervene

5. Of course, a formally unitary system may, in practice, grant subunits discretion to adopt different policies. In the process, however, this makes the system more federal in operation. Conversely, a system that is officially federal may, in practice, permit little or no subunit discretion, as in the case of the former Soviet Union. Formal provisions and actual practice do not always match.

if the other level fails to protect citizen rights. It is probably not coincidental that when dual federalism was the dominant model of federalism employed by the Supreme Court, the national government conspicuously failed to protect the rights of African-Americans who were being abused by state and local governments. Interdependent models of federalism, with their acceptance of interactions among all levels of government, undoubtedly make the redundancy mechanism more effective in preventing abuse of power by recognizing the propriety of one level trying to influence others.

Some observers have expressed doubts regarding the ability of federalism to prevent abuse of government power. In the United States federalism clearly did not succeed in protecting the rights of African-Americans in the period from 1880 to 1940 nor the rights of Japanese-Americans in the 1940s. Other countries have not had any greater luck in protecting the rights of citizenry with federal systems as in the case of Germany in the 1930s and 1940s. Given the relatively limited evidence, the safest conclusion is that federalism may help to protect established freedoms somewhat but is far from foolproof.

Encouraging Innovation

Federalism has been praised for its ability to stimulate innovation. With approximately 83,000 subnational governments in the United States, we have many arenas in which new policies can be developed and tested. As a result, we can try many different policies at once and learn about their effects more quickly than we could by trying one policy at a time nationwide. For example, the modern income tax was developed by Wisconsin but then spread to other governments. Moreover, many national government programs were initially adopted at the state or local level. Trying a new policy in a few limited areas is much less expensive than trying it nationwide, and if the policy fails to perform as expected or has undesirable side effects, we will do less damage testing it in a few localities rather than nationally.

Bear in mind that new policies can also be tried in limited areas in unitary systems, a practice that enables them to enjoy some of the same advantages. However, the many decision-making arenas in a federal system improve the likelihood that an idea overlooked or rejected in one arena may be adopted in another and, therefore, given a chance to prove itself. In this respect federalism may help to encourage development and testing of policy innovations to a greater degree than do unitary systems. Once a new approach has been tried and proven effective, national adoption or incentives to encourage state or local adoption can spread the improvement to other parts of the country.

Competition: Responsiveness and Efficiency

To some observers, federalism stimulates a healthy sense of competition among governments, a situation that fosters responsiveness and efficiency. Having only one government gives it a monopoly on public services, a situation that may lead to waste and unresponsiveness. With a multiplicity of governments, citizens in different jurisdictions can compare the services they receive and the costs they pay. Those who are receiving less and paying more will bring it to the attention of their officials and, if necessary, relocate. Officials have an added incentive to meet public demands. With cooperative federalism, competition within levels is complemented by competition among levels; people who are not satisfied with the performance of one level can turn to another level. We will return to that phenomenon in the next chapter.

Preventing Management Overload

With the growth of government responsibilities and functions has come another benefit of federalism. In a large and complex society, the task of operating all government activities is much too large for a single unit to manage. Piling too many decisions and too much information on the central government can lead to paralysis and deadlock or to some problems being crowded out by others. By parceling out the burden of administration over many governmental units, federalism prevents any one unit from being overwhelmed by the enormity of the task.

Coping with Conflict

Federalism has been praised for its ability to help political systems cope with conflict. Part of this ability results from allowing different states or localities to have different policies, with the result that they do not have to engage in political combat with one another—assuming that they are willing to tolerate the variations in policy. Federalism also aids in the management of conflict by creating many centers for resolving conflict. In a purely unitary system, all political tension is focused on the single, central government. It must bear all the anger, resentment, and frustration that are brought to bear on the political system. A federal system disperses those tensions over many jurisdictions, thus helping to keep them at a more manageable level. In addition, by having many decision-making arenas, a federal system may reduce the pain of defeat in any one arena. If I lose a battle in my state, I can try again at the national level or local level or even in another state. No loss is ever final.

Fostering Participation

The existence of many subnational governments gives the public many arenas for participation. Numerous elections, public hearings, referenda, and officials who may be contacted directly help to open up the system to citizen involvement. For citizens who prefer more active involvement, federalism creates many offices with limited powers and responsibilities that enable people to gain political experience (and enable the public to judge their performance) before moving on to higher offices with greater responsibilities and powers.

Encouraging Self-Reliance

Federalism has been credited with promoting a sense of self-reliance in the public. Instead of passively waiting for an all-powerful national government to solve all of society's problems, citizens at the state and local level have incentives to mobilize and deal with their own problems directly, and they have organized governments ready to assist them. Evidence in support of this viewpoint is relatively thin, although we will shortly see one mechanism of federalism that may encourage a form of self-reliance that some observers find troubling.

Military and Diplomatic Strength

Two other major advantages of federalism are revealed by contrasting a federal system with a situation in which the "subnational" units are independent nations, e.g., if the fifty states were fifty separate countries. First, a federal system produces far greater military and diplomatic strength than would be the case if the subunits functioned as independent nations. A federal system pools the resources of many people and can support a large military apparatus, as well as being able to act with a degree of unity that fifty independent nations could hardly match. One of the most powerful reasons for the shift from the Articles of Confederation to the Constitution was the belief that a strong national government was needed to handle military and diplomatic tasks.

Economic Benefits

In contrast to a large number of small nations, a federal system also facilitates free trade and economic growth (see *The Federalist,* no. 11). For example, ordering something by mail from another state is a routine matter in our federal system. Imagine, though, that the national government does not exist; the other "state" is now another country. Its currency is different from yours. Your state may have levied a tariff on its goods, which will increase their prices. If you want to move there to get a better job, you might have to apply for permission to move there and wait years to become a citizen. A federal system eliminates those problems over a large area, fostering economic growth and competition. The recent movement toward greater integration in Europe reflects the belief that a quasi-federal arrangement will yield economic benefits for a great many people.

The Costs of Federalism

Economists are fond of saying that there is no such thing as a free lunch. Everything of value has a price that someone must pay. While some of us might think of exceptions to that rule, the benefits of federalism are clearly accompanied by a number of significant costs.

Neglect of Externalities

First among the costs is the problem of externalities or spillover effects. When people in one jurisdiction make a policy decision, it may affect people who live in other jurisdictions and who have no voice in the policy decision. Negative externalities are undesirable effects, such as pollution, which could result from lax pollution controls in one community but drift or flow to others. Positive externalities are desirable effects, such as clean air, which result from policies in one community but flow to surrounding communities. In the case of negative externalities, federalism encourages people in one community to ignore the harm they do to others because they are not represented in that community's decision-making process. In the case of positive externalities, federalism may lead to underproduction of desirable things because some of the benefits flow to outsiders who do not pay for them. That tendency is more pronounced if subnational governments play a larger role, as in state-centered federalism.

Bear in mind that different jurisdictions may decide to cooperate in order to correct for externalities. Several communities may join forces to combat a traffic problem that is primarily centered in one community but that affects all of them, for instance. As we will see in later chapters on interstate and interlocal relations, a fair amount of cooperation takes place to deal with some types of externalities. Unfortunately, the spirit of cooperation is not always present, and when it is lacking, externalities may not be corrected.

Coordination Problems

Federalism has also been criticized for creating a host of coordination problems. With over 83,000 units of government in the United

States, duplication of effort and working at cross-purposes are unavoidable. With the growth of government responsibilities, the sharing of program responsibilities, and occasional differences of opinion over what should be done, the task of getting all the participants pulling in the same direction at the same time is often staggering and sometimes impossible, particularly when the various participants have relatively little control over one another.

Unresponsiveness

To some observers, federalism carries the risk of unresponsiveness because of the dispersal of power over so many units of government. The multiplicity of decision centers creates enormous capacity for delay and obstruction. Even if a policy is favored by a substantial majority of the public, opponents may control a number of subnational governments and effectively hamper action. The mechanisms by which federalism obstructs tyranny also serve to frustrate the efforts of everyone else. The dispersal of political conflict may exhaust and dissipate support for change. Some evidence indicates that federal systems display slower growth of the public sector and small social welfare programs (Cameron 1978; Wilensky 1975: 52–53), a finding that supports this argument. Of course, views of government activism vary, and this could even be a way to promote self-reliance! When problems demand action, however, federalism may serve to slow the response.

Localistic Biases

Some critics charge that federalism biases a political system in favor of local interests at the expense of national interests. When a number of public officials from Nevada and Utah with strong prodefense records announced their opposition to deployment of the MX missile (to be based in Nevada and Utah), they were voicing local, not national, concerns. Speaking for local concerns is not necessarily bad, of course. Few of us want our own community's interests to be ignored when policy decisions are made. The problem, as some critics see it, is that federal systems tend to pay too much attention to local interests and too little attention to national ones. With all but two of the nation's 500,000 or so elected officials chosen by subnational constituencies, sensitivity to subnational viewpoints is in fact considerable.

Inequality

Some of the most intense criticisms of federalism stems from the fact that it can produce enormous inequalities in services and even in the protection of basic rights. Public funding for education in the United States varies considerably from state to state and also from district to district in most states. Should a child's prospects in life be influenced by where he or she happens to live? Poor people have more access to medical care in some states than in others, and the legal equality of women is constitutionally guaranteed in some states but not in others. The flexibility that many see as a virtue of federalism can produce situations in which program benefits and fundamental rights enjoyed by some people are denied to others who, by any standard except location, are equally deserving.

Bias

The interjurisdictional competition created by federalism, noted earlier as a spur to responsiveness and efficiency, has also been charged with creating a systematic bias in favor of the affluent (Berkley and Fox 1978: 27–29; David and Kanter 1983). State and local officials must always be concerned about the possibility of losing jobs, investment, and wealthy taxpayers to other jurisdictions, for those losses will erode the tax base. These same officials often devote considerable effort to attracting new wealth in order to boost the tax base. Poor people, by contrast, contribute little to the tax base and require expensive government services. As a result, state and local officials generally do not fear losing them and often do not want to attract them. At the local level in particular, officials in some communities have devised a number of mechanisms for excluding the poor. The result of these incentives: officials at the subnational level have more to gain from being sensitive to the needs and desires of relatively prosperous people than to the desires of poor people, and the smaller the jurisdiction, the stronger the tendency.

Loss of Accountability

The complexity of government in a federal system creates major problems for citizens who wish to hold public officials accountable for their actions. With so many units of government and so many officials, how do we determine who is responsible for the results? If we include where a person lives, works, and shops, he or she could be served by several dozen units of government run by several times that many officials (the typical metropolitan area has over ninety separate local governments in it). Particularly when responsibilities for programs are shared among national, state, and local governments, citizens will have great difficulty deciding who deserves the blame or credit for the performance of individual programs or the system as a whole.

Evasion of Responsibility

A closely related problem is the many opportunities that federalism creates for officials to evade responsibility for dealing with controversial issues and responsibility for how those issues have been handled. The president discusses a report on the crisis in American education and concludes that the solution is largely up to the states. The governor complains that the state highway system is in poor condition because of inadequate federal funding. A mayor blames the city's financial problems on the state government. The buck, it seems, stops somewhere else. Many of these claims often have an element of truth in them, but sorting out the claims and counter-claims is a difficult task for elected officials and program managers alike (see Kettl 1988). This problem is more common when program responsibilities are shared among different levels of government, for then all the participants can easily blame one another when things go wrong.

Bear in mind that a number of the advantages and disadvantages of federalism are partially a matter of one's point of view. The obstacles that federalism creates to abuse of government power can also hamper desirable actions. The responsiveness to variations in opinion from state to state can produce localistic biases and inequality. Whether the benefits outweigh the costs is in part a reflection of individual priorities.

Summary

Federalism is a system of government that includes a national government and at least one level of subnational government(s). In addition, each level is able to make some decisions independently of the other. Each level may be equally powerful, or one may be more powerful than the other(s).

Some observers regard federalism as a competitive enterprise, with the different levels contending for power. In this view, one level can gain importance only by reducing the importance of another level. Other observers emphasize the interdependence of federalism, with powers and responsibilities being shared by national and subnational governments. This perspective contends that much activity in a federal system involves various governments working together to reach common goals. Finally, functional models of federalism place primary emphasis on divisions among functional specialists, such as educators, social workers, and transportation officials, rather than divisions between levels of government.

Advocates of federalism contend that it produces many social benefits, including responsiveness to varying needs and opinions, reduced risk of abuse of power, greater innovation, and increased military and economic strength. Critics charge, however, that federalism encourages neglect of externalities, inaction, localism, and inequality in services and basic rights. The relative importance of these various effects is, to some degree, a matter of personal values.

CHAPTER 2

Intergovernmental Politics

Some years ago, a group of homeowners learned that a developer planned to build a multistory medical building in their neighborhood. The residents appealed to the developer to abandon the project in order to preserve the residential character of the neighborhood, but the developer rejected their pleas. The residents then turned to the city zoning board, which had previously zoned the neighborhood for residential use only. The zoning board agreed with the residents, but the developer appealed to the city council, which overruled the zoning board. The council amended the zoning ordinance to permit construction of the medical building. The residents then filed suit in state court and succeeded in blocking construction of the building for a time. Eventually, however, the developer succeeded in gaining approval for construction of a smaller medical building at the same location.

A great many of the activities that constitute intergovernmental relations occur because someone is trying to influence the behavior of someone else. A city official who wants to regulate an activity may need to win the approval of the state legislature. A presidential candidate who wants to win an election may seek the support of a mayor or governor. Private citizens who want to preserve a scenic area may urge the state and national governments to declare the area a state or national park. While the attempts to influence others assume a bewildering variety of forms, several important tendencies and relationships can be identified.

In this chapter, the scope of conflict will be discussed and explored. The roles of political parties and interest groups in intergovernmental politics will be assessed. The influence of Congress and the electoral college will be analyzed, and a detailed example of intergovernmental lobbying will cast light on the dynamics of the process.

The Scope of Conflict: The Most Important Principle of Intergovernmental Relations

When a policy decision is made in a federal system, particularly one in which powers and responsibilities are shared by different levels, the question of which level should make the decision often arises. The answer to that question can affect the outcome of the policy decision because of the phenomenon known as the *scope of conflict* (Schattschneider 1960: 2–11). The scope of conflict is simply the size and extent of a conflict, including the number of people and private organizations and the number, type, and level of government actors involved. As the scope of conflict expands or contracts, the balance of power among the various combatants may change. A group may have few allies in its home town but many allies in other parts of the state. State officials may be hostile to the group's objectives, but national officials may be sympathetic. State legislators may be too busy with other issues to respond to the group's concerns, but a state judge might be willing to hear a case brought by the group. Consequently, contestants in intergovernmental politics seek the scope of conflict and the decision-making arena that are most likely to produce the desired policy decision (see also Anton 1989: 75, 97; Wood 1991).

Take the case of a homeowner who lives next door to a factory that operates day and night and is extremely noisy. The homeowner complains to the factory owner and is told that the cost of equipment and competition from other firms require the factory to run at night and make sound-proofing impossible. At this point the conflict is at a very limited level; no unit of government is involved. The homeowner loses.

Undaunted, he expands the scope of conflict by rousing the neighbors and calling on the city government. Under pressure from the neighborhood, and citing a city noise ordinance, city officials order the factory owner to maintain quiet at night, either by installing soundproofing or by shutting down from 10:00 P.M. to 8:00 A.M. By expanding the scope of conflict to include sympathetic neighbors and a sympathetic city government, the homeowner has turned defeat into victory.

The factory owner, having failed to keep the conflict private and fearful that the city's directive will reduce profits, rallies business groups across the state and appeals to the state legislature. The scope of conflict expands again and in this case the state legislature sides with the factory. A state law is enacted to restrict local governments' authority over factory noise. The factory continues its noisy nighttime operations.

The homeowner, who is now extremely irritable due to lack of

Table 2.1: The Scope of Conflict and Political (or Policy) Outcomes

Scope of Conflict	Result
Private (homeowner meets with factory owner)	Homeowner loses
Local government	Homeowner wins
State government	Homeowner loses
National government	Homeowner wins

sleep, seeks the help of national environmental and health groups. Together they turn to the national government for help. Joining with the AFL-CIO, which is concerned about the effects of factory noise on workers' hearing, they push stricter legislation through Congress in order to control factory noise. Note that the homeowner has simultaneously gone to a different decision-making arena and brought in allies rather than acting alone. The scope of conflict has again changed, and the result is a change in policy.

The case of the homeowner and the factory owner is depicted in table 2.1. Note that the outcome of the conflict is heavily affected by the scope of conflict. If one of the participants could control the scope of the conflict, he or she could control what the outcome would be. While our story is only hypothetical, we will examine a number of actual cases in later chapters to illustrate the importance of the scope of conflict in affecting policy choices.

Most people have little interest in debates over which level of government should be responsible for a given task in some abstract sense. What most people care about is getting the policies they want. How, then, can we account for the bitter debates over which level of government should handle a particular problem? The answer: those debates are actually debates over the scope of conflict and, therefore, over *policy*. To return to our hypothetical example, the factory owner might try to avert national involvement by claiming that the issue was a state matter, not a national one. Would she make that claim because she is a political philosopher and a student of theories of federalism? No. The claim would be rooted in the belief that a state-level decision would produce a policy beneficial to the factory's financial prospects and a national decision would not.

In other words, debates about federalism are often debates about policy in disguise. This is so because arguments about federalism are usually arguments about the scope of conflict. If my opponents have many allies at the state level and I do not, I can strengthen my position by extolling the virtues of local, grass-roots decision making or national involvement. On another issue, if I have many allies at the state level and my opponents do not, I may gain tactical advantage by denouncing national meddling in state affairs and demanding state action because of the obvious inadequacies of local programs. The art of intergovernmental politics is in trying to reduce, maintain, or increase the scope of conflict to produce the desired policy decision. Failing to consider the scope of conflict could result in defeat of policies in one arena when another arena might have been responsive.

Note, however, that expanding the scope of conflict to statewide or nationwide levels can require substantial time, effort, and money. Individuals and groups lacking these resources often have a difficult time expanding the scope to those levels. Also, the process of taking an issue from one decision-making arena to another (and perhaps another and another) can continue for years, a phenomenon that gives great advantage to groups that are able to maintain their efforts over the long haul.

Is it possible that someone could adhere so strongly to a view of federalism that he or she would rather lose a policy battle than deviate from that view? Could a person believe so strongly that a particular issue was, for example, a local matter, as to endure an undesirable policy rather than call for state or national action? It is indeed possible but does not appear to be common. Even the vocal states' rights advocates of the lower Mississippi saw virtue in national government intervention when it produced policies they desired, such as more effective flood control (see Leach 1970: 38).

Political Parties and Intergovernmental Politics

Intergovernmental politics in the American system is shaped by a number of structural factors that have profound implications for the way the system behaves.[1] One of the most important of these is the political party system, which is influenced by the federal system but affects the operation of the federal system as well. For present purposes, the political party system involves several major characteristics of the political parties: the extent of their unity, the legal regulations they face, their performance, and their ability to survive over time.

The Effects of Federalism on the Parties

One of the most prominent effects that federalism has on the parties is encouragement of party disunity. The existence of federalism

---

1. This section draws on many sources, including Agranoff (1972; 1976), Asher (1992), Bibby (1987), Bibby, Cotter, Gibson, and Huckshorn (1983), Calvert and Ferejohn (1983), Crotty (1984), Deckard (1976), Eldersveld (1982: 118–36, ch. 12), Grodzins (1966: ch. 12), Key (1955; 1956: 29–36), McGregor (1978), Polsby and Wildavsky (1980: 108–10), Riker (1964: 129–30), Simon, Ostrom, and Marra (1991), Truman (1962), and Wildavsky (1967).

means the existence of a number of subnational governments with significant decision-making power. These subnational governments present something of a dilemma to the parties: if the national party program is unpopular in a particular state, should the state party remain loyal to the national party program and lose the state election or deviate from the national program in hopes of winning?

The magnitude of the forces generated by those subnational units can be illustrated simply: of the hundreds of thousands of elected officials in the U.S., only two are chosen on anything resembling a national basis. All the rest, including members of Congress, governors, state legislators, and all local officials, are chosen on a state or substate basis. A party that refuses to adapt to local preferences risks losing many important offices. Federalism, then, tends to create internal divisions within the parties and makes party unity difficult to achieve.

American parties are also shaped by a variety of laws and regulations, most of which have been enacted at the state level. The variations in the laws from state to state create additional obstacles to party unity as well as massive headaches for candidates seeking their parties' presidential nominations. They must try to comply with fifty sets of state rules and regulations, as well as national party rules and national laws.

The legal environment of the parties includes the nearly universal (in the U.S.) primary as a nominating device. With the primary, nomination of candidates is controlled by the voters who show up at the polls, not the party organization and especially not the national party organization. Aspiring politicians must therefore be very sensitive to whatever views are held by the state or substate primary electorate. If the electorate disapproves of the national party program, candidates who hope to be nominated have a strong incentive to deviate from the national party program. The national party organization can do little about it.

The legal environment of the parties has also contributed to party disunity by shaping the party organizations. Party officials at one level are typically chosen by officials in the level below or independently of other levels. Officials in higher levels rarely have much authority over lower party officials, and rewards and penalties are few. Internal party communications are often undependable as well, which means that people in different party organizations may be unaware of one another's plans and activities. As a result, power in the American party organizations resembles a *stratarchy*, in which each level of the party organization—national, state, congressional district, city, county, and so forth—has considerable autonomy. No centralized chain of command exists to promote unity and enforce discipline.

In short, the legal environment of the American party system is more conducive to a fragmentation of power and party disunity than to the creation of parties that develop national party programs supported faithfully by every unit of the party. These tendencies are compounded by the separation of powers between executive and legislative branches nationally and at the state level. Under a parliamentary system, the party with a majority in the legislature chooses the chief executive. If that chief executive loses a vote on a major proposal, the government typically falls and members of the legislature must face a new election, which brings the risk of electoral defeat. Party disunity is, therefore, hazardous to legislators' careers. With separation of powers and fixed terms of office, party disunity carries no such risk.

In recent years the decentralized structures of the parties have changed somewhat. A wave of reforms, especially in the Democratic Party, established national party rules governing selection of national convention delegates. States that did not follow the rules risked exclusion of their delegates. National Republican Party organizations have expanded the services they provide to candidates, services that include funding and technical assistance. These centralizing forces have been offset, however, by new campaign technologies, including television, direct-mail fundraising, and public opinion polling, which enable individual candidates to run campaigns independently of the party organizations. Further fragmentation of the parties has resulted. When members of a party are able to work together, it is typically because of shared beliefs rather than fear of party discipline.

While federalism affects the parties by creating incentive for party disunity, other effects deserve mention as well. By creating a great many offices covering a variety of jurisdictions, a federal system provides bases in which a party that is out of power nationally can survive. In the period from 1860 to 1928, for example, the Democrats lost fourteen out of eighteen presidential elections and never received a majority of the total popular vote. By continuing to elect many state and local officials, as well as U.S. senators and representatives, particularly in the South, the party was able to survive until a time when its popularity increased.

The survival of an opposition party is critical if a system is to provide voters with an alternative to the party in power. In addition, the party that is out of power nationally is able to maintain a corps of experienced officials (in subnational offices) who are prepared to assume national office if the public desires rather than having to rely on inexperienced candidates, with the risks and uncertainty they bring.

Federalism shapes the parties through the interplay of national and subnational political tides. As V. O. Key (1956: 18–19) noted, states do not operate as completely "autonomous political entities." Rather, they are affected by national political movements in various ways. In the short run, a boost in the popularity of a party at the national level can improve the prospects of its candidates for state and local offices. An attractive and popular presidential candidate can generate coattail effects that help other members of the party farther down the ticket. A decline in the popularity of the national party due to a scandal or an unattractive candidate can serve to drag down state and local candidates as well.

The short-term effects of coattails appear to have weakened somewhat in recent years. Much of that change is due to increasing ticket splitting by voters and campaigns conducted through the mass media rather than parties. When the electorate judges state and local candidates separately from national contenders, as ticket splitting indicates, national political tides will have less influence on subnational races. Some of the weakening of short-term influences results from changes in the timing of elections. In the presidential election year of 1944, thirty-three states held gubernatorial elections, but in 1980, only ten states held them at the same time as the presidential race (excluding Alaska and Hawaii). The increasing tendency to avoid electing governors in presidential election years serves to further separate state and national politics. While that may be pleasing to governors, it also means that subnational officials have less incentive to care about the popularity or behavior of national officials and candidates (Polsby and Wildavsky 1980: 108, 110). The incentives for party unity are further reduced.

Even in nonpresidential election years, however, national political currents are present. For all but one of the midterm elections years from 1950 through 1982, the party in the White House lost governorships, and the average loss was six governorships (Bibby 1987: 64–65). When voters are unhappy with the president, gubernatorial candidates of the president's party suffer the consequences (Simon 1989; Stein 1990).

National political forces may also produce more lasting changes in state party systems. Realignments, which produce new and enduring party loyalties in the electorate, generally result from national political issues and national political forces. Slavery and the Civil War produced a realignment, as did the Great Depression and the New Deal. The party loyalties created by realignments affect citizen behavior in state and local elections as well as national elections, however. The traditional strength of Republicans in New England and of Democrats in the South grew out of national realignments. While realignments do not occur very often— generally every thirty to forty years—their effects are profound and lasting.

As a result of these national political forces, state and local parties function in an environment that is in some respects beyond their control. A Republican gubernatorial candidate in the Deep South in the 1940s could be intelligent, trustworthy, hardworking, and a tireless campaigner but could not overcome party loyalties shaped by national events. In a similar manner, the rise of Republican strength in the South began at the presidential level and gradually trickled down to state and local races.

The Effects of the Parties on the Federal System

If federalism shapes the parties, the parties also influence the conduct of intergovernmental politics in the federal system. If subnational governments are to have any genuine autonomy in a federal system, the party system must somehow provide room for differing opinions and different policies. To take an extreme case, the former Soviet Union appeared to be a federal system on paper, but its single, highly disciplined and centralized party gave little room for subnational units to make important decisions on their own.

The parties may provide leeway for subnational units in several ways. First of all, interparty sectionalism, with one party stronger in one part of the country and the other party stronger elsewhere, can help protect subnational autonomy. The simple fact of different parties in power in different states and localities permits some variation. In addition, the party out of power nationally must be at least somewhat sensitive to the need to protect the importance of the only jurisdictions that it does control, states and localities. The limited unity of the parties at the national level in the U.S. requires many national policy initiatives to draw at least some support from both parties, a situation that gives the out-party ample opportunity to protect the importance of its subnational bases.

The parties can also provide subnational autonomy through intraparty sectionalism. If each of the parties has significant internal divisions—Southern Democrats being more conservative than Northern Democrats, for example—jurisdictions controlled by the same party can nevertheless enact a wide variety of policies. Moreover, these internal divisions mean that neither party can change the system very much without the help of the other party. Party disunity enables members of a party to advocate and defend the positions of their respective states and localities, regardless of which party is in power nationally.

Many studies have found evidence of intraparty sectionalism in the American parties. Both parties have internal divisions that help to maintain subnational autonomy, and those divisions show no signs of disappearing.

Parties in a competitive setting have an incentive to maintain the importance of subnational jurisdictions because of the protection they provide in the event of national defeat, as noted earlier. Party politicians have displayed considerable ingenuity in creating all sorts of devices to help their parties survive, from campaign finance laws to rules governing access to the ballot. Preserving federalism is yet another tactic for helping the party to endure.

In seeking to establish a coalition large enough to build a national majority for selecting presidents and passing legislation, however, a party must try to balance national and subnational perspectives. If it overemphasizes subnational concerns, it will have great difficulty uniting behind a presidential candidate or legislative program. If the party overemphasizes national concerns, by contrast, it risks losing congressional and state-local elections. The task of balancing national and subnational interests is often difficult and sometimes impossible.

Interest Groups and Intergovernmental Politics

As is the case for political parties, interest groups are affected by federalism but also shape the politics of intergovernmental relations. For present purposes, an interest group is any group, whether of private individuals or public officials, that might influence governmental decisions. One of the most important things that federalism, particularly in its interdependent versions, provides for interest groups is a great many opportunities and arenas for exerting influence—what Grodzins (1966: 14–15, 274–76) called "the multiple crack." A group may plead its case before city officials, county officials, governors, state legislators, members of Congress, judges at all levels, and bureaucrats. If one official, agency, or level does not respond favorably to a group's demands, the group can seek a more positive response elsewhere, as the principle of the scope of conflict indicates (see also Anton 1989: 75, 97).

The multiple crack emphasizes the fact that in the American federal system, public policies typically emerge in a sequence of decisions made in different arenas. A group learns of a presidential proposal and lobbies the White House to change the proposal in some fashion. If the group is unsuccessful, it may turn to lobbying Congress as the president's proposal is discussed and revised in committee or on the floor. If legislation is eventually passed, the group may then lobby the federal agency responsible for implementing the program nationally and also try to influence the state or local government participants in the program. The group will have a number of chances to make an imprint on the policy.

Bear in mind that this situation can create problems for a group because its opponents may be doing exactly the same thing. A group may finally achieve a positive response from the national government, for example, only to find the results eroded by offsetting actions of state or local governments responding to other groups. Groups that have trouble staying mobilized for extended periods or that lack effective access to some officials may find themselves outmaneuvered as a result.

The size and diversity of the federal system (as opposed to a group of small, independent nations) create a multiplicity of groups, a situation that limits the influence of each at the national level (see *The Federalist*, no. 10). Generally, as we move from national to state to local levels, size and diversity decline, and a given group is therefore less likely to encounter effective opposition locally. The Rajneeshis in Oregon exerted substantial influence in local politics where they lived (for a time), but their influence was limited at the state level and virtually nonexistent nationally. Indeed, national government action led to the deportation of their leader.

In a related vein, governments compete with one another in seeking to attract jobs, investment, and affluent citizens. This competition is most acute at the local level because of the smaller geographic reach of local governments. An individual or company wanting to locate in a given area can typically select from several local governments in that area. Moreover, relocating from one local government to another is relatively easy for affluent families. As we move from local to state to national governments, the difficulties associated with relocating from one jurisdiction to another increase. As a result, competition among governments for wealthy residents, business investment, and jobs is most acute locally and least acute nationally. More affluent groups are, therefore, likely to be particularly influential at the local level.

The preceding analysis implies that interest groups, particularly affluent ones, are more likely to benefit from local than national policy-making, other things being equal (see McConnell 1966: 109). Other things are not always equal, however; groups can shape the functioning of intergovernmental politics in a number of ways to achieve their policy goals in various arenas—national, state, and local.

Consider the case of an interest group that is defeated at the local level. The principle of the scope of conflict tells us that the group might gain from expanding the conflict to the state or national level and mobilizing suitable allies in the process. The group that is dominant locally can be expected to oppose that expansion because it threatens the group's dominant position.

Some rather peculiar situations may result. Truman (1962: 123) notes the case of national organizations taking the position that a given issue is a state matter rather than a national one. Why, might we ask, is a national organization interested in the issue if it is really a state matter? The answer is twofold: first, a group will seek the scope of conflict most likely to produce the policies it desires. If a national group feels that the states are more sympathetic than the national government, advocating state action, rather than national action, is a logical response. Second, a group that prefers resolving an issue at the state level may need a national organization to oppose groups seeking national government intervention.

While smaller jurisdictions may enhance group influence in general, this advantage may be offset by the limitations of small jurisdictions. Some are too poor to finance costly projects, such as freeways or major universities. Some are too small to cope with problems covering large geographic areas. A group may find, therefore, that local officials are sympathetic but lack the means to do what the group wants (on this point, see Dahl 1980). The group desiring large-scale, expensive programs or uniformity across the country or state may have little choice but to turn to higher levels of government. Note, too, that the receptivity of local governments to group influence in general does not assure receptivity to every group. Taken together these considerations help to explain the considerable growth of the national and state governments in the U.S. since the turn of the century.

Interest groups, like political parties, have a stake in maintaining the autonomy of subnational governments, and for an analogous reason. The subnational governments minimize the risk of a complete policy defeat: a group that loses at one level can seek help from other levels of government. More affluent groups also have a stake in maintaining subnational governments because interjurisdictional competition makes them particularly sensitive to the affluent. However, groups desiring costly and/or uniform nationwide programs have pressed for national government expansion and, in the process, have sometimes limited the autonomy of subnational governments.

Intergovernmental Lobbies

One of the most significant developments in the interest group arena in this century is the formation of the intergovernmental lobbies, associations of officials at one level of government organized at least in part to influence officials at another level of government. One indication of the proliferation of these groups can be seen in the increase in the number of associations of state and local officials. Prior to 1900 there were only a handful, but by 1986 there were approximately one hundred, ranging from the National Association of State Budget Officers to the National Association of State Conservation Officers (Penne and Verduin 1986; Walker 1969: 894). Most of these groups have many other functions besides intergovernmental lobbying, but they do lend themselves to lobbying as well.

The development of intergovernmental lobbying was both an outgrowth and a cause of interdependent federalism. As the activities of government became increasingly shared, officials at one level were more and more likely to be affected by actions of other levels of government. Organization was a sensible mechanism for coping with that situation. Once organizations of officials were created, they often served to stimulate more interdependence, as when local educators pressed for more state aid to local schools or when state highway officials lobbied the federal government for more highway programs.

While there are too many intergovernmental lobbies to cover in detail, some of the major ones deserve mention.[2] The U.S. Conference of Mayors, which was formed during the Great Depression, primarily represents larger cities (Haider 1974: 2–20). The National League of Cities, which dates back to the 1920s, contains a much larger and more diverse membership. Both groups have actively advocated urban interests before the national government. State municipal leagues, which are affiliated with the National League of Cities, perform the same task at the state level.

The existence of two urban lobbies has created problems at times. Jealousies, duplication of effort, and frictions between the two organizations led to a number of efforts to merge them, but four attempts failed prior to a partial merger, confined largely to merging the staffs of the two organizations, in 1969–1970. Even that effort was short-lived, however, and then the two organizations went their separate ways (Reed 1983; Stanfield 1976).

The National Governors' Association traces its roots to the presidency of Theodore Roosevelt, who stimulated the organization of governors in hopes of using them to exert leverage on Congress (Haider 1974: 20–31). The association had little impact in its early years, largely because many governors believed in dual federalism and did not believe that they should try to influence national policy-making. The early years of the association were characterized by a concern for returning a variety of national-state programs to the states along with national revenue sources. Those efforts were largely unsuccessful, however, and in recent years the association has come to accept and even support national government action.

One sign of the governors' increasing recognition of the role of the national government and the need to influence it was the 1965 reorganization, which included the opening of a permanent office in Washington, D.C. By contrast, the mayors opened a Washington office in the 1930s. The governors also began to meet regularly in Washington, both as a means for establishing contacts there and as a way of demonstrating their concern for national policy decisions.

The National Association of Counties, formed during the Depres-

2. The following section relies heavily on Haider (1974).

sion, was a relatively ineffective organization during its early years (see Haider 1974: 32–41). Reorganization in the late 1950s produced some improvements, but the association has generally had limited success nationally. A major limitation on its effectiveness is the great diversity of counties—urban and rural, rich and poor, Democratic and Republican. Unity is, consequently, difficult to achieve.

In addition to working with associations of officials or governments, state and local governments also conduct individual lobbying activities. A number of states and localities have their own offices in the nation's capital, and subnational officials often contact national officials to request assistance, express complaints, or otherwise seek to influence decisions in Congress or the executive branch. Officials of a single state or locality, acting alone, can often express their specific views more clearly than they could working through a national association, which virtually always requires compromise among members for reaching a position. Of course, the advantage of individual action may be offset by the limited influence that an individual state or locality is likely to have on members of Congress from other states.

The other group of intergovernmental lobbies worthy of note is the bureaucratic specialists—educators, highway officials, law enforcement officers, and so forth. They are often highly active in lobbying other levels of government, and they have scored a number of successes over the years. As we will see in the next chapter, they have helped to create a grant system that channels funds to their agencies and does not permit much of the money to be shifted to other activities.

The intergovernmental lobbies have a number of resources that enhance their political clout. The governors, mayors, and other elected state and local officials have the legitimacy and respect that result from their positions as elected representatives of the public. When they appear before Congress or other governmental bodies, they speak as people chosen to carry out public responsibilities. They also derive influence from being politicians in their own rights—politicians who serve the same people as the officials they seek to influence. When the mayor of the largest city in a congressional district seeks aid for the city, the member of Congress from that district can hardly ignore the obvious career implications. In a similar fashion, a president who plans to seek reelection must necessarily be attentive to the concerns of governors whose states loom large in the electoral college.

The intergovernmental lobbies also profit from their geographic dispersal. Every senator's state has a governor in it. Every congressional district includes at least a few cities or towns. The intergovernmental lobbies are, therefore, positioned to reach other officials through their home bases. Because of these factors, intergovernmental lobbies have generally enjoyed another political resource: access, the ability to obtain a reasonably respectful hearing. That is not always the case, however. Some observers noted that organizations representing local governments had reduced access to the White House during the Reagan administration (Reed 1983). That situation reflected the similarities between Reagan's New Federalism and dual federalism. First, local governments were not regarded as full partners in the federal system. Second, different levels of government were not to "interfere" in one another's affairs. Local officials continued to enjoy substantial access in Congress during the Reagan years, however.

More recently, in the Clinton administration both local and state governments are perceived to have greater access to the White House. Some observers note, however, that Clinton's commitment to state and local government is limited to policy and political support, not fiscal support. Open communication is dependent upon recognition by state and local governments that with the deficit issue, the administration does not want to hear concerns about a lack of funds but rather about innovation (Walters 1994: 50). Congress still provides access to state and local officials; however, state and local government associations may increasingly be viewed as just another interest group focusing on their issues to the exclusion of the overall national needs (Walters 1994: 53). When funds are scarce, competition for money becomes a much more difficult enterprise for all contestants, public and private.

Another notable resource of the intergovernmental lobbies is social status. Most public officials and agency professionals are well-educated and on the middle to upper rungs of the social ladder. They are, therefore, likely to receive respectful treatment from other officials. In addition, the intergovernmental lobbies in recent years have had the resource of information. Research staffs and well-trained agency professionals can provide analyses and evidence to enhance the credibility of a lobbying effort.

Offsetting these formidable assets is a perennial problem: disunity. Mayors of large cities find themselves at odds with mayors of small towns. Republican governors clash with Democratic governors. Liberals disagree with conservatives. Officials from poor counties have different needs than officials from wealthy counties. Generalists, such as governors and mayors, often have different priorities than specialists, such as educators and social workers. When different components of the intergovernmental lobby are at odds with each other, their ability to influence other levels of government is correspondingly reduced.

The intergovernmental lobby is also limited by the fact that public officials often depend on private interest group support. As a result, the officials may be unable to push for some programs for fear of losing that support. A group of mayors might favor a proposal but hesitate to support it for fear of angering private groups active in their respective communities. Governors are similarly reluctant to publicly advocate positions that anger groups that make large campaign contributions or are otherwise influential in state politics. Concern for adverse political consequences restrains public officials in intergovernmental lobbying as well as other areas.

Benefit Coalitions

As Thomas Anton (1989: 30–32, 67–69) notes, interest groups and public officials often work together in an alliance to support and protect programs that benefit them in some fashion. State and local highway officials join forces with the automobile industry, oil companies, trucking companies, and many other groups to make certain that federal funding for highways continues each year. Parents and teachers unite to demand more state aid to local schools.

Because benefit coalitions generally focus on individual programs or groups of related programs, these coalitions tend to enhance the importance of functional specialties, such as education, regardless of levels of government (national, state, or local). As a result, benefit coalitions encourage the emergence of picket fence federalism (see chapter 1), with its emphasis on vertical (programmatic) linkages. Differences among levels of government are still relevant for benefit coalitions, however; officials at one level may be more sympathetic than are officials at another level, and not all levels are equally well-financed. Nevertheless, benefit coalitions are primarily concerned with obtaining program benefits and only secondarily concerned with which level of government provides them.

Congress and Intergovernmental Politics

Many important decisions that affect the conduct of intergovernmental relations are made by Congress or at least involve congressional participation.[3] Congress helps determine how much federal money will be given to state and local governments and what restrictions will be placed on the use of that money. Congress shapes national policies in many ways, and it monitors program implementation in the bureaucracy, though

3. Various aspects of intergovernmental politics in Congress are explored in Fenno (1978), Grodzins (1966: 260–70), Hinckley (1988: 79–87), Keefe and Ogul (1993: 97–121, ch. 9), Mayhew (1974), Beck and Sorauf (1992: ch. 14), and Wildavsky (1974: 45–50).

Table 2.2: Opinions on Whether Members of Congress Should Represent District or National Interests (in percent)

	Members of Congress		
	1969	1977	Public, 1977
District	42%	24%	56%
Nation	28	45	34
Combination of both	23	28	—

Sources: Davidson, Roger. 1969. *The Role of the Congressman.* Indianapolis: Bobbs-Merrill; Keefe, William and Morris Ogul. 1993. *The American Legislative Process,* 8th ed. Englewood Cliffs, NJ: Prentice-Hall.

not always as effectively as some observers would prefer. The functioning of Congress has, therefore, enormous implications for whether state and local viewpoints are reflected in national politics.

As a general rule, Congress is quite receptive to state and local influences. This does not mean that all localities get what they want—that is often impossible. Rather, members of Congress are generally willing and able to speak for and protect the interests of their states or districts, and a number of features of Congress enhance that ability.

One of the key factors enhancing congressional receptivity to subnational interests is the American party system. The use of the primary as a nominating device assures that if a member of Congress encounters a disagreement between national party leaders and the voters at home, the voters, not the national party leaders, have the ability to control nominations. When the nominee runs in the general election, help from national party organizations is relatively limited. This sort of recruitment system is ideally suited to developing a Congress that is sensitive to local concerns and has limited loyalties to national party programs.

As noted earlier, the absence of a parliamentary system in the United States means that members of the majority party can break ranks without bringing down the government and forcing new elections. The relative weakness of legislative party leaders further enhances the ability of members to go their separate ways when the inclination arises. Members do not have to use that ability to advance state and local interests, nor do they always. Given that most members are interested in being reelected, however, and given that the structures controlling reelection are heavily localistic, members have a strong incentive to respond to subnational viewpoints. Analysis of the areal orientations of members of the House and the public reveals that district concerns receive considerable emphasis (see table 2.2).

Analysis of voting in Congress gives ample evidence of sensitivity to subnational concerns. For example, party loyalty in the House has declined most dramatically among representatives from states where the party has lost voter support in state and national elections, and from states where the state party ideology is at odds with the national party ideology, e.g., states with conservative Democratic parties have shown declining loyalty among Democratic representatives, and states with liberal Republican parties have shown declining loyalty among Republican representatives (Cohen and Nice 1983).

The decentralized recruitment system contributes to a feature of Congress that provides additional sensitivity to state and local concerns: most members of Congress have deep roots in the state that they represent. A study of members of the Ninety-sixth Congress found that more than 70 percent of them were born in the state that they represent. Two-thirds of all senators and three-fourths of all representatives received at least some higher education in the state they represent. Half of all representatives and two-thirds of all senators had held some other elective office in the state (Hinckley 1988: 85–86). Those deep roots encourage members to be sensitive to the problems and desires of their home states and districts.

As if all this did not make Congress sufficiently sensitive to subnational forces, the committee assignment process produces additional leverage for them. Two of the major criteria used to decide committee assignments are: (1) What assignments will help members win reelection, and (2) What assignments members want. Bear in mind that the two criteria often overlap (see Masters 1961; Rohde and Shepsle 1973). Assignments that will help members win reelection typically involve committees working on policies of interest to groups that are powerful in the members' districts. As a result, the Agriculture committees attract members from rural areas; representatives from coastal districts gravitate to committees handling maritime legislation. These committees in turn serve to advocate the interests of districts that are interested in and most affected by the committees' work.

A final mechanism by which Congress protects subnational interests is constituency service work, also known as "casework." Members of Congress receive a steady stream of requests for assistance from their constituents. Many of the requests are for help in dealing with federal agencies, and a reputation for being helpful in dealing with those requests seems to pay off at the polls for members of Congress (Mann and Wolfinger 1980). Members of Congress have enhanced their ability to attract and process casework requests by assigning more of their office staff to their districts (rather than Washington, D.C.), by having more than one district office, and by keeping district offices open all year (Bond 1985). By maintaining well-staffed listening posts in their districts, members are more likely to hear about local problems and to be better equipped to deal with them. A frequent result of casework is the injection of local perspectives into the administration of national programs.

Overall, Congress is well-suited to the protection and advocacy of state and local interests. There are exceptions, of course; Congress does manage to produce national viewpoints at times. Subnational concerns are rarely far from center stage, however, and often they seem to dominate it.

The Electoral College

One of the most peculiar features of intergovernmental politics in the United States—indeed, one of the most peculiar features of the American political system generally—is the electoral college.[4] The electoral college plays a significant role in allocating political influence over the selection of the president, with some fairly clear winners and some fairly clear losers in the intergovernmental political arena.

The most important and obvious effects of the electoral college result from the incentives that it creates for presidential candidates. Because electoral votes are allocated in almost all states on a winner-take-all basis, presidential candidates must focus their attention on competitive states. If you come in first in a winner-take-all state, you receive all of its electoral votes, regardless of whether your margin of victory was one vote or a million votes.[5] If you come in second, you receive nothing, regardless of whether you lost by ten votes or a hundred thousand. Campaigning in states where you are sure to lose or win is, therefore, a waste of precious campaign resources. As a result of this factor, competitive states receive a disproportionate share of the candidates' attention, while states where the outcome is a foregone conclusion are given limited notice.

Not all competitive states receive equal attention, however. Because electoral votes are allotted to the states based on their representation in the U.S. House and Senate, more populous states have more electoral votes than do less populous states. To the candidates, that makes the larger states much more important, for crossing the dividing line between second place and first place in a large state has more impact on the electoral vote total than changing from first place to second (or vice versa) in a small state (see table 2.3).

The electoral college therefore gives political advantage to large, competitive states, such as California, Texas, and New York. A presiden-

4. See Bartels (1985), Bickel (1980), Polsby and Wildavsky (1980: 244–55), and Beck and Sorauf (1992: 21–23).
5. Except in Maine and Nebraska.

Table 2.3: All Votes Are Not Equal: The Popular Vote and the
Electoral College

	Projected Popular Vote for Smith (relative to Jones)	Gains in Final Vote for Smith Over Initial Projection	Change in Electoral Vote for Smith
State A	500,000 votes*	50,000 votes	0
State B	− 500,000 votes**	50,000 votes	0
State C	− 10,000 votes	50,000 votes	+ 3
State D	− 10,000 votes	50,000 votes	+ 30

*Smith leads Jones by 500,000.
**Smith trails Jones by 500,000.

tial candidate who ignores the large, competitive states runs the risk of losing the large blocks of electoral votes they have, a risk no prudent candidate can afford to take.

A second, less important effect of the electoral college is to slightly magnify the voting power of the least populous states. This effect occurs because every state, no matter how small, has two U.S. senators and one representative, for a total of three electoral votes. Most scholars regard this effect as less important than the gains received by the large competitive states, but it does help to account for the opposition of small states to proposals to abolish the electoral college.

One other consequence of the electoral college is its effect on state policies regarding access to the ballot. In the electoral college, a state's influence on the presidential election is a function of the number of electoral votes it has, not a function of how many people vote. Two states with the same population will have the same number of electoral votes, even if voter turnout in one state is twice as high as it is in the other. The electoral college serves as a shield that enables a state to make voting difficult and inconvenient without losing any influence over the choice of the president.

By contrast, a system of direct election of the president would cause states that made voting difficult to lose influence over the presidential election. States would have an incentive to make voting easier and to encourage voter participation, for the more votes cast in a state, the more proportional influence the state would have. Under the electoral college, however, states gain no influence by promoting voter participation, nor is there any penalty for discouraging voter involvement.

Case Study: Lobbying for Federal Aid to Education

While intergovernmental lobbying is an established feature of our federal system, the difficulties that face intergovernmental lobbyists seem to be established features as well.[6] Years of experience have shown that the problems of disunity and dependence on private groups cannot be overcome easily or for very long. A clear example is the battle over federal aid to education, the result of which was the Elementary and Secondary Education Act of 1965.

The national government began providing aid to education in the late 1700s with the Northwest Ordinance of 1787, which gave land grants to support schools. The Morrill Act of 1862 provided land grants to support higher education in agricultural and mechanical sciences. Other programs followed. Some were adopted to improve the educational prospects of particular groups, while others supported particular types of education, such as science or vocational training (Dye 1981: 400–404).

While the national government's involvement in education has a long history, the national role was limited by fears that extensive national participation would jeopardize grass roots control of schools. National involvement was also limited by many disagreements among educators over what form greater national participation in education should take. Supporters of expanded federal aid were divided by the question of racial integration: should federal aid be limited to integrated schools or not? Further disagreements arose over how aid should be distributed: should poorer districts receive additional help or should all districts receive the same amount per student? Finally, there was conflict over the issue of aid to parochial schools. Lobbyists representing parochial schools fought aid bills that gave them nothing, but many public schools lobbyists opposed any aid to parochial schools. As a result of the opposition from groups hostile to any more national aid and the disunity in the ranks of supporters of more aid, lobbying efforts for a general program of national aid failed repeatedly in the 1940s, 1950s, and early 1960s, although some narrowly focused programs were adopted.

A combination of events in 1964 helped overcome the difficulties that frustrated the education lobby, however. First, the various supporters of aid began to iron out their differences. Negotiations among them were stimulated, in part, by the frustration of years of failure and the concern among some lobbying groups that their refusal to compromise was antagonizing other officials. Second, some of the lobbyists came to believe that an aid bill of some sort might actually pass in the near future; to continue refusing to compromise might mean the bill would be written by others with different priorities.

The prospects for more national aid were also improved by the adoption of the 1964 Civil Rights Act, which provided that federal aid

---

6. This discussion relies heavily on Eidenburg and Morey (1969) and Murphy (1973).

to segregated schools could be terminated, a policy that eliminated one of the points of division in the education lobby. Controversies over integration could and did continue, but an education aid proposal no longer needed to face the issue directly. Finally, the 1964 election produced a large increase in the number of liberal Democrats in Congress. As a result, education aid faced a more sympathetic Congress, and the education lobbyists had a strong incentive to work together rather than fight among themselves. They definitely did not want to waste the opportunity that a sympathetic Congress provided.

The divisive question of whether any aid should be given to parochial schools was partially defused by the channeling of national aid through public authorities serving children, whether those children were enrolled in public or private schools. The emphasis on aid to children rather than schools and on aid to poor children especially helped to mute opposition. More than one participant felt reluctant to oppose helping poor children.

As a result of the greater unity among supporters of federal aid, the large Democratic majorities in Congress, and the fact that the racial issue had been addressed in the 1964 Civil Rights Act, the Elementary and Secondary Education Act of 1965 was enacted into law. It produced a modest but significant increase in national aid to education. It also presented educators with a dilemma: many of them had hoped for a program of general aid to education, but much of the money provided by the act was designated for educationally disadvantaged children from poor families. How the educators resolved that dilemma will be addressed in chapter 7.

The education lobbying effort illustrates several important features of intergovernmental lobbying. First, supporters of aid were deeply divided over the issues of race, funding allocation, and aid to parochial schools. That disunity was a major limitation on the lobbying effort. Bear in mind, however, that educators have a common professional background; when a lobbying effort involves state legislators or city council members who come from many different walks of life, the obstacles to unity are often greater.

Second, the public school lobbyists seeking more federal aid were unsuccessful until they reached an accommodation with private school lobbyists. Many intergovernmental lobbies find that their effectiveness is limited without support from private groups as well. Fifty state highway agencies are much more impressive in lobbying for highway aid if they are supported by the automobile industry, trucking companies, oil companies, pavement contractors, and the many other private interest groups favoring highway programs.

Third, the success of the education lobby in 1965 was due in part to circumstances beyond its control. The Civil Rights Act of 1964 helped to reduce the conflict over integration, at least as far as the education lobby was concerned, and the Democratic landslide of 1964 created a Congress more receptive to an education aid proposal. The education lobby could claim little credit for the civil rights law or the landslide. Like all other interest groups, intergovernmental lobbies find that their prospects for success are often influenced by events beyond their control.

Finally, subsequent developments in federal aid to education reaffirm the belief that few victories in American federalism are permanent. During the 1970s and 1980s, criticisms of the performance of American schools and controversies over proposals to give students more freedom in choosing which schools to attend placed the education lobby in a vulnerable position. The Reagan administration's opposition to federal aid programs compounded the difficulty. Not surprisingly, the share of total public school spending covered by federal aid fell from 9.2 percent in 1977 to 7.2 percent in 1982 (*Significant Features of Fiscal Federalism*, vol. 2, 1990: 43, 72). The education lobby was unable to fully protect federal aid programs in the face of a less friendly political environment.

Intergovernmental Lobbying for Revenue Sharing

Other examples of intergovernmental lobbying indicate that the plight of the education lobby is far from unique. General revenue sharing, which gave subnational governments money that they could spend for virtually any purpose, was not passed until years after it was initially suggested. Its adoption was made possible in part by a massive lobbying effort by a number of the intergovernmental lobbies, including those representing governors, legislators, cities, and counties (Beer 1976).

Like the education lobby, supporters of revenue sharing were deeply divided, particularly over how the money should be allocated. In addition, some organizations of state and local specialists, such as highway officials, did not support revenue sharing. They feared that it would draw money away from national grants that could only be spent for specific purposes, such as highways.

After the adoption of revenue sharing in 1972, the program was often under fire, in part because of recurrent budget deficits. National officials who were concerned about national spending exceeding revenues found revenue sharing to be a vulnerable target. The deficits, which were largely beyond the control of state and local officials, significantly undercut the program that they had worked long and hard to create. Moreover, disunity among the intergovernmental lobbies reduced their ability to defend revenue sharing from cuts. During the Reagan administration, revenue sharing was finally terminated altogether. Disunity and forces beyond the control of the intergovernmental lobbies significantly influenced their efforts.

Summary

The conduct of intergovernmental politics is shaped by the structures of federalism but also influences those structures. The most important manifestation of this reciprocal relationship is the scope of conflict. In a federal system, the existence of many decision-making arenas encourages groups to try to expand, maintain, or contract the scope of conflict to a level at which the groups' prospects for success are greater. This process in turn influences the relative importance of each level of government in various policy decisions.

Federalism affects the operation of the political parties by creating numerous forces for disunity and by creating subnational bases where a party can survive when it is out of power nationally. The parties in turn shape the functioning of the federal system. Competitive, sectionally-based parties with regional internal divisions are conducive to subnational autonomy, but a one-party system in which the party has a rigid ideology to which all must adhere is likely to permit little or no subnational autonomy.

A federal system shapes interest group behavior by creating many arenas where groups may pursue their policy goals. At the same time, groups influence the federal system by trying to persuade officials at levels where the groups are most influential to promote group goals and, at times, to encourage officials at other levels of government to do the same. Even public officials have organized in order to influence decisions made by other levels of government. Benefit coalitions, often including both public officials and private groups, seek to promote their policy objectives throughout the federal system.

Congress, which has powerful incentives for representing local interests because of the decentralization of the American political parties, and members' desire to be reelected, shapes the operation of the federal system not only by injecting subnational perspectives into national policies, but also by developing national programs that influence state and local governments. Finally, the electoral college shapes the functioning of intergovernmental politics particularly by creating strong incentives for presidential candidates to be sensitive to interests that are influential in large, politically competitive states.

CHAPTER 3

Fiscal Federalism

In one of the most educational episodes of "Green Acres" ever broadcast, Oliver Wendell Douglas learned that farmers in his area were required to pay a farm tax. No one seemed to know how each taxpayer's tax liability was determined, and further investigation revealed that the Hooterville area had not been represented in the state government when the tax was enacted. As a result of Mr. Douglas' efforts, the state refunded all tax payments paid by farmers in the area since the tax had been adopted, and he became a local hero. His popularity quickly evaporated, however, when the state government sent bills to farmers in the area for all state-financed improvements, including schools and roads, put in place in the years since the farm tax had been enacted.

A basic task facing all governments is amassing the material resources needed to support government programs and operations. In current times the chief resource of concern is money, although in years gone by, land, conscript labor, and many other commodities were used by governments to support their activities. This chapter will examine the growth of taxing and spending by the national, state, and local governments, as well as changes in the relative taxing and spending shares by each level. The growing use of intergovernmental grants, the different types of grants, and the many goals of grants will be assessed. Grants have numerous effects and are supported (and attacked) by complex political coalitions. A number of alternatives to grants have been proposed by some critics. Finally, the problem of coordinating the revenue-raising activities of the various governments in the federal system and the growth of governmental borrowing will be explored.

Table 3.1: The Growth of Government Revenues and Spending

	1902	1988	1991
Total Revenues			
National	$.7 billion	$1,012 billion	$1,200 billion
State	.2 billion	435 billion	516 billion
Local	.9 billion	332 billion	410 billion
Total Expenditures			
National	$.6 billion	$1,095 billion	$1,321 billion
State	.1 billion	333 billion	442 billion
Local	1.0 billion	491 billion	618 billion

Sources: 1902: Mosher, Frederick, and Orville Poland. 1964. *The Costs of American Governments.* New York: Dodd, Mead, pp. 155, 163. 1988: *Significant Features of Fiscal Federalism*, vol. 2. 1990. Washington, DC: Advisory Commission on Intergovernmental Relations, pp. 64, 67. 1991: *Significant Features of Fiscal Federalism*, vol. 2. 1993. Washington, DC: Advisory Commission on Intergovernmental Relations, pp. 50, 51. Revenues for 1988 and 1991 are own-source only and do not include grants from other levels of government. Intergovernmental grants are counted only as expenditures by the final recipient.

A clear grasp of fiscal federalism is essential to an understanding of intergovernmental relations. A government that cannot afford to offer programs that people desire may find those people taking their demands to other governments. A government that depends on another government for financial assistance may become vulnerable to influence by the funding source, and a government that gives substantial financial aid to other jurisdictions may gain influence over how they conduct their affairs. As we shall see, however, things are not always what they appear in the world of fiscal federalism.

Changing Patterns of Fiscal Federalism

As table 3.1 indicates, revenue raising and expenditures by all three levels of government have grown enormously in this century. In 1902, all three levels combined raised and spent less than $2 billion. By 1988, revenues raised exceeded $1.77 trillion, and expenditures exceeded $1.9 trillion. Revenues for 1991 were over $2.1 trillion, with expenditures slightly higher at almost $2.4 trillion.

Although the American economy has grown a great deal since 1902, government revenues and expenditures have grown even faster. At the turn of the century, national, state, and local governments raised and spent sums equal to a little less than 8 percent of the gross national product. By the late 1980s, American governments were raising and spending more than one-third of the GNP (see table 3.2). National revenues as a percentage of GNP grew by more than sixfold. State revenues

Table 3.2: Government Revenues and Spending Relative to the Size
of the Economy

	1902	1988	1991
Revenues as a Percentage of the Gross National Product			
Total	7.8%	36.4%	37.3%
National	3.0	20.7	21.2
State	.8	8.9	9.1
Local	4.0	6.8	7.2
Expenditures as a Percentage of the Gross National Product			
Total	7.7%	39.3%	41.8%
National	2.6	22.4	23.2
State	.6	6.8	7.8
Local	4.4	10.0	10.9

Sources: 1902: Mosher, Frederick, and Orville Poland. 1964. *The Costs of American Governments.* New York: Dodd, Mead, pp. 157, 165. 1988: *Significant Features of Fiscal Federalism*, vol. 2. 1990. Washington, DC: Advisory Commission on Intergovernmental Relations, pp. 15, 64, 67. 1991: *Significant Features of Fiscal Federalism*, vol. 2. 1993. Washington, DC: Advisory Commission on Intergovernmental Relations, pp. 11, 50, 53. 1988 and 1991 revenues are own-source revenues only (that is, revenues that the level raises for itself). 1988 and 1991 expenditures are direct expenditures only.

relative to the size of the economy grew by a factor of eleven, and local revenues grew significantly. Local expenditures grew more substantially than locally-raised revenues.

The figures on the growth of all three levels of government cast some doubt on the competitive models of federalism. They generally assume that the supply of government power is fixed and consequently, one level can grow only by diminishing another. The evidence indicates that all three levels have grown substantially during this century, although the different levels have grown at different rates.

When we examine each level's share of total government revenues and spending, striking changes in the federal system are revealed (see table 3.3). The national government's share of revenues grew from less than 40 percent in 1902 to nearly 60 percent in 1988, declining slightly in 1991 to 56 percent. The state share more than doubled, from 11 percent to 24 percent. The local share fell from 51 percent to 19 percent. While the growth of national revenues has been widely noted, state revenue growth has been proportionally larger.

Changes in government expenditures produce a pattern similar to revenue shifts, although the changes are generally not as dramatic. The national government's share of spending grew from roughly a third of the total to well over half. The state share roughly doubled, but local governments' share fell by more than half, from 58 percent to 26 percent.

In addition to the growth of revenues and spending by all levels

Table 3.3: The Changing Distribution of Revenues and Expenditures

	1902	1988	1991
Own-Source Revenues			
National	38%	57%	56.4%
State	11	24	24.3
Local	51	19	19.3
	100%	100%	100 %
Total Direct Expenditures			
National	34%	57%	55%
State	8	17	19
Local	58	26	26
	100%	100%	100%

Sources: 1902: Dye, Thomas. 1981. *Politics in States and Communities*, 4th ed. Englewood Cliffs, NJ: Prentice-Hall, p. 54; 1988: *Significant Features of Fiscal Federalism*, vol. 2. 1990. Washington, DC: Advisory Commission on Intergovernmental Relations, pp. 64, 67. 1991: *Significant Features of Fiscal Federalism*, vol. 2. 1993. Washington, DC: Advisory Commission on Intergovernmental Relations, pp. 50, 53.

of government and the tendency for national and state growth to have outpaced local growth, another major change in fiscal federalism has taken place. State and local governments, particularly the latter, have grown heavily dependent on grants from higher levels of government as sources of revenue (see table 3.4). In 1902, national grants provided states and localities with less than one percent of their total revenues. By 1991, states received about one-fourth of their revenues from national grants, a slight decline from the high of 28 percent in 1978 but a dramatic increase from 1902. More dramatically, local dependence on grants as a revenue source rose from 6 percent of local revenues in 1902 to 38 percent in 1988, declining slightly in 1991 to 37 percent.

A number of explanations may account for the increasing importance of higher levels of government in raising and spending money and the increase in the financial dependency of lower levels of government.[1] The adoption of the Sixteenth Amendment, which established the national government's authority to enact an income tax, gave the national government a dependable and productive source of revenue. National growth of revenues and expenditures soon followed.

Of course, the states could have adopted their own income taxes, and a few did early in this century, but most did not adopt income taxes until after the national government did. As late as 1948, states raised

1. See Dye (1981: 45), Glendening and Reeves (1984: 69–70), Grodzins (1984: 380–81), and Leach (1970: 197).

only about 16 percent of their revenues from income taxes (Maxwell and Aronson 1977: 42). Consequently, this attractive revenue source, which typically grows rapidly with economic growth, was largely left to the national government.

National growth has also been attributed to national crises, notably wars and the Great Depression. These crises, which clearly exceeded the capabilities of states and localities, stimulated national government growth that did not subside completely after the crises ended. Once programs begin and commitments are made, they are very difficult to terminate.

Subnational revenue growth, particularly at the local level, has been restrained by a host of limitations on state and local taxing powers—limitations that the states have imposed on themselves. Restrictions on tax rates and types have sometimes left states and localities unable to respond to public demands. People unsatisfied with this situation have turned to higher levels of government for help.

Interjurisdictional competition for business, investment, and affluent residents has hampered local revenue raising. Local officials often fear that tax increases will drive businesses and affluent citizens away and discourage others from moving in. As we move from local to state to national levels, interjurisdictional competition grows less severe, for the problems associated with moving from one city to another are typically minor, while changing states is usually more costly and difficult. Moving to another nation is the most difficult of all (but certainly not impossible). As a result, the national and state governments are less constrained in raising revenues.

Table 3.4: Revenue Dependency in American Federalism

National Grants as a Percentage of State Revenue	
1902	*
1988	24%
1991	26%
National-Local and State-Local Grants as a Percentage of Total Local Revenue	
1902	6%
1988	38%
1991	37%

*Less than 1%.
Sources: 1902: Dye, Thomas. 1981. *Politics in States and Communities*, 4th ed. Englewood Cliffs, NJ: Prentice-Hall, p. 50; Mosher, Frederick, and Orville Poland. 1964. *The Costs of American Governments*. New York: Dodd, Mead, p. 162; 1988: *Significant Features of Fiscal Federalism*, vol. 2. 1990. Washington, DC: Advisory Commission on Intergovernmental Relations, pp. 91, 95; 1991: *Significant Features of Fiscal Federalism*, vol. 2. 1993. Washington, DC: Advisory Commission on Intergovernmental Relations, pp. 70, 72.

Another reason for the growth of national and state levels relative to localities is increasing social mobility and interdependence. When pollution generated in one locality pollutes the drinking water of a city hundreds of miles away, or criminal activities in one state are part of a national or even international organization, or economic problems in one region affect the entire nation's economy, pressures for higher levels of government to become involved will be substantial. Moreover, reliance on purely lower-level decision making will often be inefficient in these situations, for people in one community may shift costs (such as pollution) to people in other communities lacking a voice in the decision. A higher level of government may enable all affected people to have a voice.

Higher levels of government have also grown, relative to localities, because of the mechanism of the scope of conflict. Individuals and groups searching for a favorable response to their policy demands have gone from one level to another. Localities, with their limited financial powers and strong interjurisdictional competition, not to mention limited legal powers (see chapter 6) have often been unable or unwilling to respond. Demands have, consequently, shifted to the state and national levels. In some cases the result has been a service provided directly by the higher level, but in many cases the response has been the adoption of one or more grants from higher to lower levels of government.

The Grant System

One of the most striking developments in the American federal system is the growth of grants from one level of government to another. Grants come in a number of forms, largely because different types of grants have different effects.

First of all, some grants give recipient governments more discretion in deciding how to spend the grant than do other types. *Categorical grants* may be spent only for a narrowly defined purpose, such as high school libraries or interstate highways. There are currently almost five hundred categorical grant programs in operation at the national level, and together they account for nearly 90 percent of all national grant funds (*A Catalog of Federal* 1989: 2). *Block grants* are targeted for a broad functional area, such as law enforcement or community development. The recipient can spend the grant for a variety of purposes within that functional area; a law enforcement block grant, for example, could be spent for police training, new communications equipment, formation of an anti-burglary squad, or hiring additional officers. *Revenue sharing* is a grant that the recipient may use for any purpose, from education to law enforcement to tax reduction. It gives the recipient unit maximum flexibility in deciding how to use the grant funds.

Grants also vary in the method used for distributing the funds. *Formula grants* include an established decision rule, generally written in the legislation creating the grant, which automatically determines how much money each recipient jurisdiction will receive. A state education grant to local school districts may be distributed according to a formula stating that each district will receive $1,500 per pupil in average daily attendance, for example. As soon as the grant program is adopted, all recipients know how much they will receive. Needless to say, a great deal of conflict may erupt over what formula should be used. Should the state education grant formula give extra money to school districts that are poor, or those with slow learners, or those that are more productive? Different districts will undoubtedly have different answers, and substantial maneuvering over grant formulas will often result (see Dilger 1983).

A very different approach to distributing funds is the *project grant* system. With a project grant, the legislation creating the grant makes funds available, but potential recipients must fill out an application that describes the project to be financed by the grant. The agency in charge of administering the grant reviews the project proposals and determines which ones will be funded.

Critics complain that project grants often award money to recipient units able to develop impressive project proposals or with special political connections rather than units with the greatest needs (see Derthick 1975; Rich 1989; Wright 1988: appendix B). Indeed, the use of project grants added a new term to the vocabulary of intergovernmental relations: *grantsmanship*. Broadly speaking, grantsmanship involves the ability to determine what funds are available for which purposes and to write a project proposal that will be funded by the granting agency that will enable the recipient unit to do something recipient policymakers want to do. Rural and small town officials often complain that they lack the resources and staff to develop proposals that can compete with those of larger jurisdictions (Hale and Palley 1981: 80–81). Partly as a result of these concerns, some project grants include limitations on how much funding individual states or localities can receive (A *Catalog of Federal* 1989: 1).

Grants also vary in terms of whether a ceiling is attached to the amount of the grant. A *closed-ended grant* has a fixed limit to the amount to be distributed. Once the limit is reached, no more funds are available. An *open-ended grant,* by contrast, does not have a rigid limit on the amount of funds it can provide. An education grant that distributes a certain amount of money per student will have to provide more funds if school enrollment increases. A welfare grant that pays a fixed share of welfare costs will increase if welfare rolls grow.

The distinction between closed-ended and open-ended grants should not be overdrawn. If a closed-ended grant is too small to meet demands, pressures will be exerted to increase the amount of funding available. Conversely, if the cost of an open-ended grant skyrockets, movement to limit outlays is likely to follow.

A final source of variation among grants concerns the presence or absence of matching requirements. A *matching grant* requires the recipient unit to match the grant received with some of its own resources. A highway grant with a matching requirement might require the recipient unit to put one dollar of its own funds into the highway program for every dollar received in grants. The matching requirement need not be dollar for dollar; the Interstate Highway program required recipients to contribute one dollar for every nine dollars received in national grants.

Nonmatching grants, by contrast, do not require the recipient units to contribute resources of their own. Recipients may contribute their own resources if they choose, of course, but the nonmatching grant does not require any fixed contribution by recipients.

The different characteristics of grants can be combined in many ways. One grant could be categorical, distributed by formula, closed-ended, and with a fifty/fifty matching requirement. Another grant might be categorical but of the project variety, closed-ended, and with no matching requirement. A wide range of combinations can be created.

Reasons for Grants

Many types of grants have been developed because the grant system is expected to accomplish many things at once.[2] The public, public officials, and scholars want the grant system to do a variety of things. Some types of grants are suitable for achieving some objectives, but other goals require other types of grants.

One of the most basic goals for grants is to assure that a service is provided at some minimal level everywhere. A service may be inadequately provided in general or may be provided adequately in some places but not others. This objective normally implies a categorical grant in order to assure that the service receives necessary support.

A second major goal is equalization of needs and resources. A basic fact of life in federal systems is that any given problem may be much more serious in some states or localities than in others. Crime, poverty, and a host of other problems vary considerably from one location to another. At the same time, some jurisdictions have abundant wealth to support programs, while other jurisdictions lack the resources to support

---

2. For discussions of the goals of grants, see Break (1980: 76–87), Dye (1981: 49–52), Key (1937: ch. 1), Vines (1976: 25–29), and Wright (1988: 208–10).

even basic services. The grant system can be used to direct resources to states and localities where problems are more serious and financial resources to cope with them are lacking. Studies of how effectively grants target resources to where needs are greatest produce conflicting results. When analyses focus on total needs and total grant funding, grants appear to do a relatively good job of channeling funds to where they are needed most. By contrast, when analyses focus on grants and needs relative to population, targeting appears much less impressive. In any case there are often problems and conflicts involving how needs should be defined and measured (see *Federal Formula Programs* 1990; Pelissero and Morgan 1987; Stein and Hamm 1987; Ward 1981).

A third purpose of grants is correcting for externalities or spillovers. A city that dumps untreated sewage into a river creates problems for other communities downstream. Its residents will resist paying to clean up the water for downstream communities, and those communities are unlikely to voluntarily contribute to the polluting community to help it build a sewage treatment plant. A higher level of government can raise funds from the entire affected area and target them to the source of the problem.

Grants may also be used to increase the progressiveness of government finance. A progressive tax takes a proportionally larger share of a taxpayer's income as his or her income rises. For example, a tax that consumes 2 percent of the income of someone earning $10,000 annually but requires someone earning $100,000 annually to pay 20 percent of his or her income is a progressive tax. By contrast, a regressive tax takes a proportionally smaller share of a taxpayer's income as his or her income rises. A tax that consumes 10 percent of the income of someone earning $10,000 annually but consumes 3 percent of the income of a taxpayer earning $100,000 is a regressive tax.

Most scholars of public finance regard the national tax system as relatively progressive, while state-local revenue systems are more regressive (see Maxwell and Aronson 1977: 109–10; Pechman and Okner 1974). Financing a program from state-local taxes will bear more heavily on people with lower incomes; financing the same program with national grants will bear more heavily on upper-income groups.

A basic goal of all grants, to a greater or lesser degree, is to minimize waste. Many observers have expressed the fear that because officials in the recipient governments do not have to bear the unpleasant burden of raising the money that finances a grant, they may spend it carelessly or frivolously. As a result, in this view, grants must include one or more mechanisms to prevent waste. Because matching rules require recipients to contribute some of their own resources, which they must bear the burden of raising, matching grants may reduce wasteful spending.

Closed-ended grants, with their fixed limit on available funds, may encourage recipients to use funds more carefully; an open-ended grant may encourage recipients to "milk" the program to receive as much money as possible.

Grants may be used to encourage structural reforms of many kinds. A grant recipient may be required to hire personnel funded by the grant based on ability rather than political connections, create an area-wide authority to promote coordination, or develop a comprehensive program plan before receiving any funds. Some observers would like to see the grant system do a great deal more to promote structural reforms (see Reuss 1970).

A basic objective of some grants is to stimulate and encourage policy innovation. A major advantage of federalism is the many areas for developing and testing new programs that the subnational governments provide. Policy innovation is often costly, however, and if a new approach is successful, the beneficial knowledge flows to many jurisdictions—a form of spillover effect. Grants can provide a state or locality with the resources to support program testing and can require other jurisdictions (through the tax system) to share the costs of program testing, the knowledge from which will benefit all jurisdictions.

The goal of stimulating innovation generally calls for project grants because the granting level wants to target funds to new approaches and techniques. To distribute funds automatically by formula risks spending most of the money supporting old, non-innovative activities. An exception to this rule lies in the use of regulations attached to grants; regulations may require recipients to adopt new procedures, techniques, or approaches and, in the process, stimulate innovation.

Some grants are designed to preserve or increase recipient flexibility and adaptability to variations in state or local needs and preferences. Recall that one justification for federalism is its ability to accommodate variations in opinions or problems from one part of the country to another. The grant system can be used to enhance that capability. This objective calls for a grant that gives recipient jurisdictions discretion in how to spend the grant; revenue sharing is the best approach for this objective, and block grants are a second-best option.

Many policymakers want grants to encourage recipient governments to maintain their own efforts to support a program. Officials in the granting level generally do not want the grant money simply to replace the money recipient units would have spent from their own revenues. Matching requirements are sometimes used to require recipient governments to support programs with their own revenues. Maintenance-of-effort provisions, which require recipients to continue to support programs from their own revenues at some specified level, are also used to encourage recipients to maintain program efforts of their own. In times of inflation or substantial economic growth, neither approach is particularly effective over time (see Break 1980: 132–33). A maintenance-of-effort requirement might state that a county must maintain its current level of own-source spending for roads after a state grant program for roads is adopted. A county that continues to spend $10 million of its own money on roads each year fulfills the requirement, but inflation gradually erodes the purchasing power of the $10 million. In effect, the county's effort gradually declines.

In a similar fashion, a state might be planning to increase annual law enforcement spending from its own revenues from $100 million to $500 million over a period of five years. If a national grant with a fifty/fifty matching rate is adopted in the second of the five years, state officials might decide to raise spending from the state's own revenues to only $250 million in the fifth year and match that with $250 million in grant money. Over time, then, the grant reduces state effort, even with a matching requirement.

Many observers, particularly public officials at the recipient level and private citizens, want the grant system to minimize unintended distortions in the budgets of recipient governments. If a large grant for some program requires recipient units to match the grant funds, hard-pressed jurisdictions may be forced to take money away from other programs for which no matching funds are available. A poor county might be able to raise the matching funds for a highway grant only by reducing support for the library, for example. Because the highway grant program is presumably not designed to reduce funding for libraries, the effect is unintended. This problem can be minimized by using matching rules sparingly, varying matching rules according to the wealth of the recipient government (poorer ones would have to contribute a smaller share), and/or having some form of revenue sharing that recipient units could use to meet matching requirements.

A final goal of grants is often ignored in discussions of the grant system but is nevertheless very important. Virtually all grants seek to maintain participation of lower level units of government in programs that they cannot support adequately on their own. State grants to local school districts enable them to continue to play a role in education. National grants to the states enabled them to play a major role in building the interstate highway system. In many program areas a likely alternative to the use of grants is a complete takeover of the function by a higher level of government.

An obvious conclusion emerges from this brief overview of the goals that the grant system is expected to pursue: a number of the goals conflict with one another. Matching rules may help to minimize waste but may also produce unintended distortions in recipients' budgets. Targeting grants to recipient governments with the greatest capacity for innovation often means that relatively prosperous recipient units receive the bulk of the funds (on wealth and innovation, see Walker 1969). This clearly contradicts the objective of equalizing needs and resources.

The most widely recognized conflicts among objectives in the grant system involve recipient flexibility, structural reforms, waste, and establishing minimum service levels. Requiring structural reforms limits the flexibility of recipient governments on those structural decisions. Controls used to minimize waste, beyond some point, may restrict the options of recipients. Matching requirements consume local resources; regulations to prevent misuse of funds constrain recipient behavior. Establishing minimum service levels may override recipient views regarding appropriate service levels in some cases. In short, a number of the goals of grants involve limiting the discretion of recipient officials, a situation that obviously cannot maximize their flexibility. Having many different types of grants helps to accommodate the conflicting objectives to some degree.

The multiplicity of goals, some of which conflict with one another, assures that the grant system will be unable to please all of the people all of the time. The result is likely to be an unending process of criticism, modification, more criticism, and more modification, at the end of which the criticism will be just as intense as it was in the beginning. This is not to say that criticism of the grant system should be ignored, but it should be kept in perspective: no known version of the grant system (and no alternative to it) can simultaneously maximize all the goals the system is expected to pursue.

The Development of the Grant System

While many people have the impression that the use of grants is a recent development in the American federal system, grants have actually been in use for a very long time. The Northwest Ordinance of 1787 provided national land grants to support public schools, and the Morrill Act provided a system of land grants to the states to support agricultural and mechanical higher education in 1862. Grants have been a feature of the system from the beginning.

The long history of the grant system should not obscure the major changes that have occurred in this century. To be precise we should refer to grant systems, for there are fifty state-local grant systems in addition to the national grant system. Together they have greatly altered the operation of the federal system.

At the turn of the century, the national government had a total of five grant programs in operation. Together they distributed $3 million in 1902 and accounted for less than 1 percent of all state-local revenue (Dye 1981: 50; Vines 1976: 21). In short, state and local governments received relatively little financial help from Washington. State aid to local governments in 1902 provided only $52 million and accounted for only 6 percent of local revenue (Maxwell and Aronson 1977: 85).

The grant system has expanded considerably since then. National grants to states grew to approximately $95 billion in 1981, declined slightly in 1982, then began an erratic, gradual rebound. When inflation is taken into account, the purchasing power of national grants peaked in 1978, slowly declined until 1982, then slowly began to grow again (*Significant Features of Fiscal Federalism* 1990: 42). The rate of growth increased considerably in the early 1990s (*Significant Features of Fiscal Federalism* 1993: 13). State grants to local governments have expanded enormously during this century and reached 172 billion in 1988 and provided just over 30 percent of all local revenue (*Significant Features of Fiscal Federalism* 1992: 90).

A major component of the growth of the national grant system occurred during the 1960s, when the number of national grants grew from fifty-one in 1964 to 530 in 1971 (Vines 1976: 21). Many of these new grants were project grants, partly because this was the period of Creative Federalism, which emphasized developing new approaches to solving problems. Simply distributing funds by formula gave no assurance that the money would help to develop new solutions and techniques. Requiring recipients to submit project proposals that specified activities in detail enabled national agencies to target funds to innovative ideas.

Grants proliferated in part because of the operation of the scope of conflict. People who wanted problems addressed and were unsatisfied with state and local responses went to Washington. Responding to their problems through grants enabled officials at different levels to share the credit for fighting crime, combatting poverty, or improving educational opportunities.

The proliferation of national grants and the use of project grants led to complaints that state and local officials could not keep abreast of what funds were available for what purposes. Critics charged that the multiplicity of grants produced vast coordination problems, with many grants working at cross purposes. State and local officials complained of the burdens of developing project proposals and filing reports. Some critics feared the grants were giving the national government too much influence over state and local government.

In response to these complaints, the national government adopted revenue sharing in 1972, although not until a great deal of lobbying by state and local officials had taken place (Beer 1976). Revenue sharing was hailed in some circles as a revolution in fiscal federalism, but, as is often the case with revolutions, the results did not completely meet the expectations. A major limitation on the impact of revenue sharing was that it was a relatively small component of the national grant system from the outset. In addition, inflation steadily eroded the purchasing power of revenue sharing; its growth lagged considerably behind the inflation rate (Peterson 1976: 85–86). The limited time span of the revenue sharing program—it was never made law for more than a half-dozen years at a time—also made state and local officials reluctant to commit it too heavily to ongoing programs. A state that used its revenue sharing funds to support an increase in welfare benefits would be placed in a very difficult position if revenue sharing expired: either benefits would have to be reduced or the state would have to greatly increase its own outlays to compensate for the loss of funds. As a result, revenue sharing funds were generally spent for hardware-oriented programs, such as law enforcement, fire protection, and streets and roads. Very little was spent for social services or health programs (Caputo and Cole 1983: 45).

The Reagan administration came into office committed to altering the national grant system in several major ways. The administration sought to reduce the number of national grants, reduce funding for many grant programs, and terminate revenue sharing. The initial efforts produced some successes: national grant funding declined from $95 billion in 1981 to $88 billion in 1982, and the number of grant programs fell from 539 in 1981 to 405 in 1984. However, a number of the administration's proposals, such as the elimination of national grants for Aid to Families with Dependent Children, were rejected by Congress, partly because of lobbying by state and local officials. Ironically, the Reagan administration's success in terminating revenue sharing meant the loss of the grant program that gave maximum flexibility to state and local officials, a goal often praised (in the abstract) by administration officials. Even the administration's successes left more grant programs in effect than had been the case in 1967, the high water mark of Creative Federalism. The purchasing power of federal grants began to rise again after 1982, and the number of national grant programs also began to grow again, reaching 492 in 1989 and 543 in 1991. (A *Catalog of Federal* 1989: 1–2; *Significant Features of Fiscal Federalism* 1990: 42; 1992: 60). Overall, the results did not match the expectations of many administration officials.

One of the most important points about the development of the grant system is its unplanned nature. Individual grants have been created to deal with individual problems, not because of any grand design. Once a grant program is created, people who benefit from it want to see it continued. Fundamental changes are likely to arouse the wrath of affected groups, as the Reagan administration found when it proposed consolidation of numerous categorical grants into broader block grants that would give states and localities more discretion in spending but fewer dollars.

Effects of Grants

A variety of studies have tried to assess the effects of grants in recent years. A host of different effects have been analyzed, and while not all of the research has produced the same conclusions, a great deal has been learned about the grant system.

Much of the research on grants has focused on their effects on spending by grant recipients. Analyzing the effects on spending is a difficult task, particularly because the amount granted and the amount spent are often simultaneously determined (Gramlich 1977: 219, 227–28). That is, recipient units may, in some cases, influence how much grant money they receive. Recipient officials may lobby for more grant funding for programs they support. In addition, they may revise program guidelines in order to attract more funding for those programs. Does the grant create a desire to spend, or does the desire to spend affect how much grant money is received? Trying to determine how the recipient units would have behaved without the grant is a very difficult task.

A number of studies of the effects of grants on spending have found that grants typically produce higher spending than would have occurred without the grant but that the increases in spending are often smaller than the amount of the grant (see Gramlich 1977; Wright, 1988: 258–60). That is, a dollar of grant money often increases spending but generally by less than a dollar. This indicates that grant money may sometimes replace, in part, money the recipient would have spent from own-source revenues.

Grants stimulate spending in two ways. First, a grant increases the ability of recipients to spend by increasing the revenues they have—the income effect (Break 1980: 98–99). While recipient governments can use grant money to replace locally raised revenues (i.e., reduce taxes), and they sometimes do, the tendency among recipients is to spend the money. Increases in income from grants lead to much greater increases in government spending than do increases in private sector affluence (Break 1980: 98–99). Gramlich (1977: 226) refers to this tendency as the "flypaper effect": money sticks where it hits.

Second, grants may increase spending through price effects (see Break 1980: 95–97). An open-ended matching grant that requires the recipient to match the grant funds dollar for dollar has the effect of cutting the price of a service in half (compared to having no grant). A recipient government, by putting up $1 million of its own funds, becomes eligible for $1 million in grant money. It will, therefore, be able to purchase $2 million of road programs for only $1 million of its own funds. It may, as a result, spend more money in total on the program than it would have otherwise. By the same token, if the grant is repealed or reduced, the program may be vulnerable to cuts at the recipient level because it has become more costly, in effect. When the Reagan administration's cuts in national grants to aid the poor took effect in the early 1980s, most states reacted by cutting benefits to poor people (Nathan and Doolittle 1983: 200–201).

Many analysts also believe the grant system has substantially increased the policy influence of the levels of government distributing the grants, at least partially at the expense of recipients. Some of that influence occurs because the grant funds affect recipient spending, but influence also results from the regulations attached to the grant money (Hale and Palley 1981: 102–104; Wright 1988: 264–67). The national government used grant regulations to induce the states to adopt a fifty-five miles per hour speed limit (later revised), for example.

Although grant regulations have been a feature of the grant system for many years, adoption of grant regulations at the national level accelerated considerably in the 1960s and early 1970s. According to one estimate, the national government adopted over seven thousand new or amended regulations in 1974 alone (*The Question of State Government Capability* 1985: 384). Even revenue sharing, which was adopted to decentralize power, at least in part, brought thousands of local governments into the national grant system and, consequently, made them subject to a number of national grant regulations (Wright 1982: 128–29).

The centralizing effects of grants should not be overstated, however. A variety of factors limit the power exerted by the granting level. First of all, with the proliferation of national grants since the 1950s, recipients are free to choose the grants that most closely reflect their needs and preferences. Grants that are unduly restrictive or burdensome can sometimes be declined, particularly if the amount of money involved is relatively small. In 1984, sixty-four national grants distributed less than $50 million each (*Grant Formulas* 1987: 376–77). In an era of multibillion dollar state budgets, offering a state $1 million is not likely to produce much political leverage.

The centralizing effects of grants are also limited by the phenomenon of *fungibility* (Hale and Palley 1981: 113–16; Wright 1988: 94–95). Fungibility is the ability to use grant money as a substitute for money the recipient planned to spend anyway; the recipient's money can then be spent on some other program. A hypothetical state might have planned to spend $100 million of its own money on each of two programs, highways and education (see table 3.5). The national government announces that $50 million is newly available for highway programs. State officials believe

Table 3.5: Fungibility and Grants

	Highways	*Education*
State's original spending plan (state's own money)	$100 million	$100 million
New federal grant	50 million	—
State's revised spending plan (state's own money)	50 million	150 million
Final spending totals (state's own money plus federal grant)	100 million	150 million

that their state needs to spend only $100 million on highways; as a result, they reduce the amount of state money for highways by $50 million, the amount of the grant, and add the funds taken from highways to the education budget. The highway grant, then, serves to increase education spending, contrary to the expectations of the granting level.

Fungibility greatly reduces the ability of granting levels to shape the spending behavior of recipient governments. While matching requirements and maintenance of effort rules try to limit fungibility, available evidence indicates that they are not very successful (see Break 1980: 132–33; Comptroller General 1980). As noted earlier, state officials who plan to greatly increase spending from their own sources for a particular program could, following the adoption of a new national grant, simply maintain their state's current level of spending from its own revenues (to satisfy the maintenance of effort rule or matching requirement) and use the grant to finance the projected increase. The state's own revenues that would have funded the increase (in the absence of the grant) are then released for other programs.

The centralizing effects of grants are also limited by the bargaining that characterizes much of grant administration. If recipient units do not behave as the granting level desires, the ultimate sanction is the withholding of grant money. This sanction is typically difficult to use. It risks angering supporters of the program—the powerful alliance of interest groups supporting highways would not sit quietly if large amounts of highway grant funds were cut off. State and local officials would also mobilize to block large-scale withholding of grant funds. Members of Congress might respond harshly if the states and localities they represent were to lose large sums of grant money. Agency officials administering grants also hesitate to withhold grant funds because the program objectives of the grant may be jeopardized. If grant funds for antipoverty programs are withheld, for example, the result is likely to be reduced assistance to the poor. Unduly restrictive or burdensome requirements may, therefore, be ignored, watered down, or obeyed only in a symbolic fashion (see Ingram 1977; Lazin 1973).

Finally, the centralizing effects of grants are limited by the sometimes lackluster enforcement of grant guidelines and regulations. With the heavy workloads facing presidents and members of Congress at the national level and governors and state legislators, many administrative matters receive sporadic attention at best. When recipient officials believe that their actions are not being monitored very effectively, they may feel free to pursue their own objectives and disregard grant policies they oppose (see Chubb 1985).

The grant system, with its many separate grant programs, reporting requirements, and applications for project grants, has created a substantial amount of paperwork and red tape for all levels of government (Hale and Palley 1981: 100–101). Various agencies administering grants in the same program area may require different information in different formats. Reporting rules may change from one year to the next; time-consuming changes in information systems will be required for compliance. Reducing the paperwork and red tape was a major goal of the Reagan administration, which made some progress toward that goal but also added new regulations of its own to a number of programs.

Recipient complaints about red tape and paperwork should be interpreted cautiously. Few taxpayers enjoy being audited by the Internal Revenue Service, but most will admit the need for audits in order to control tax evasion. Filing reports is undoubtedly annoying to recipient officials, but an end to reports would risk misuse of funds or an end to the grant system, for few officials at any level would give any other level vast sums without some method for determining how they were to be spent.

The grant system has also strengthened the independence of administrators at the recipient level from their nominal superiors, according to some studies (Brudney and Hebert 1987; Hedge 1983). When a recipient government receives a categorical grant, the money must be spent for the specified program (aside from fungibility). Officials in the state highway department know that they will be able to spend federal highway grants unless the governor and legislature want to return the money to Washington, a decision that would hardly please taxpayers. Elected officials at the recipient level may have less interest in grant-supported activities because the burden of raising money for them is substantially carried by the granting level of government. Administrators at the recipient level may blame the granting government for actions that anger recipient-level elected officials and blame the recipient-level elected officials for actions that anger officials at the granting level.

This criticism of the grant system should be interpreted with some caution. The administrative structures of many states and localities are poorly suited to providing coordinated administration, with or without grants, although that generalization is less true today at the state level than in previous years. Independently elected agency heads, independent special district local governments, and a host of overlapping governments at the local level tend to produce considerable administrative independence and rather poor coordination, regardless of the nature of the grant system.

Political Coalitions and Grants

Decisions regarding what types of grants to use often produce complex combinations of political forces. As the scope of conflict indicates, an interest group that is influential at the granting level generally prefers categorical grants because they target funds to the particular activity the group supports. The group is then partially relieved of the burdensome task of lobbying large numbers of recipient governments in order to be certain that they spend the money as the group desires. Conversely, a group that lacks influence at the granting level but is influential in some recipient jurisdictions generally prefers grants that give recipient units more discretion in spending grant funds, in order to make the most of the group's influence.

Public officials at the granting level can generally be expected to prefer categorical grants for several reasons. First, because they must endure the pain of raising the revenues, officials at the granting level often feel that they have earned the right to have some influence over how the money is spent. In a related vein, when these officials must answer to the taxpayers regarding how their tax dollars were spent, categorical grants may have somewhat greater appeal than revenue sharing. Pointing to support for highways, education, and pollution control may impress more people than simply acknowledging that the funds were given to other governments, which made their own decisions regarding the use of the money. In some instances, officials at the granting level may also have more confidence in their own judgment than they have in the judgment of recipient officials. The preference for categorical grants naturally follows.

The major exception to this tendency exists among granting level officials whose policy views are in the minority at the granting level. They are likely to prefer grants that give more discretion to recipients, some of whom may use the funds in more agreeable ways, as far as those officials are concerned, than would be the case if the granting level allocated funds through categorical grants. This brief review of granting-level coalitions helps explain the popularity of categorical grants among granting levels—forces strong there generally prefer them.

Officials at the recipient level seem to have more divergent views regarding the amount of discretion that grants should allow. Generalists, such as governors, mayors, and legislators, often prefer to have consider-able discretion in spending grant funds. Part of that preference is sym-bolic: they resent being told what to do. Also, recipient officials often want discretion in order to implement their own policy preferences or accommodate the demands placed on them.

Recipient generalists are not fully consistent in their preference for discretion, however. If they support the objectives of a categorical grant, they may welcome it with open arms. Moreover, discretion in spending grant money brings political heat as well as the ability to choose. Groups seeking more funding for their pet programs have a much greater incentive to put pressure on a mayor with $10 million in revenue sharing money to spend than they would if the funds were in categorical grants, which the mayor would have limited ability to reallocate. The influence of these considerations can be seen in the 1970 meeting of the National Governors Conference. A resolution calling for changes in federal high-way aid to give the states the option of spending some highway grant funds for other transportation programs was *defeated* by the governors. In effect they voted against giving themselves more discretion, although the vote was reversed two days later following adverse publicity (Berkley and Fox 1978: 241-42).

Program specialists at the recipient level generally prefer categorical grants. State welfare officials can be confident of receiving federal welfare aid distributed in categorical grants. Revenue sharing, by contrast, in-volves greater uncertainty: a newly elected governor or legislature might decide to spend the funds on libraries or some other programs, leaving the welfare program short of funds.

The major exception to the tendency for specialists to prefer cate-gorical grants occurs in agencies that lack influence at the granting level. These specialists may prefer grants that give recipients discretion in order to make the most of whatever influence they have at the recipient level.

Conflicts over whether to use project or formula grants also produce complex coalitions. Legislators at the granting level often prefer formula grants because the legislation (which the legislators adopt) controls the distribution of funds. A tradeoff is involved, however; trying to develop a formula may engender legislative conflict as each legislator tries to get maximum benefit for his or her constituents. If the amount of funding in a grant program is large, legislators may be willing to endure the wrangling needed to develop a formula. A program with limited funds, on the other hand, may not seem worth the effort; legislators may be more willing to let administrators allocate the money in such a case. This line of reasoning is supported by the tendency for the categorical grant programs distributed by formula to be relatively large, while project grants, which are more numerous, distribute less than one-fourth of all federal grant funds (Hale and Palley 1981: 76–77).

Project grants have provoked controversy because incumbent politicians running for reelection have an amazing ability to produce them just in time for the campaign. Presidents running for reelection in recent years have punctuated their campaigns with announcements of all sorts of grants awarded to key states, leading to charges that project grants are manipulated to help politicians stay in office. Conversely, the threat of grant cuts can be used to discipline state and local officials who are not sufficiently helpful to the president's reelection efforts. Recent research on this charge indicates that the timing of the announcement of project grants and the distribution of grant funds are apparently subject to political manipulation, primarily when programs are new or politically threatened (Anagnoson 1982; Rich 1989).

Project grants are criticized by many officials at the recipient level because of the paperwork that project proposals require, the uncertainty regarding whether any funds will be awarded, and funding delays. Recipient officials who are adept at grantsmanship, however, may prefer project grants because these officials may be able to receive a larger share of the funds than they would under formula distribution.

Complex coalitions also emerge over questions of grant regulations. Many grants include a variety of requirements that recipients must obey (bearing in mind the enforcement problems discussed earlier). Recipients may be required to raise their legal drinking age to twenty-one, refrain from discussing abortion with family planning clients, or file environmental impact statements for construction funded by a grant. Recipients that do not comply face a loss of grant funds, although in practice this is quite rare.

At the granting level, questions of grant regulations often produce conflicts between supporters of the goals of the regulations—highway safety or reducing discrimination, for example—and supporters of the grant program, who may fear that conflicts over the regulations could create opposition to the grant program. Supporters of the grant may also fear that regulations could cause some recipient governments to refrain from participation in the grant program. If many refrain, the grant obviously will not achieve its goals.

At the recipient level, grant regulations can provoke tensions between those who oppose the regulations and those who want the grant money. Indeed, individuals may have both feelings simultaneously. Should they comply with regulations they oppose and receive the funds, or refuse to comply and risk a cutoff of funds? Note, too, that a substantial number of recipient officials may support a given regulation in principle, but they may not admit that support publicly. The regulation can serve as a political heat shield of sorts: the governor can tell irate citizens, "I would love to do what you want, but the blasted federal regulations just make it impossible." This is a politically safer response than saying, "I think that what you want is a ridiculous idea."

This brief overview of grant coalitions underscores a very important point: conflicts over grants rarely involve a completely united granting level battling a completely united recipient level. Differences of opinion over grants commonly exist within levels, and these differences are often as important or even more important than the differences between levels.

Case Study: The State Safety Participation Program

Transportation accidents in the United States kill tens of thousands of people each year, injure hundreds of thousands more, and cause billions of dollars worth of property damage. Most of these accidents occur on the nation's roads and highways, partly because they carry huge amounts of traffic and partly because the automobile is a relatively dangerous transportation mode (compared to traveling by rail or air). The nation's railroads are also involved in thousands of accidents each year; in order to improve railroad safety, the national government established the State Safety Participation Program.[3] It offered the states grant funding on a matching basis to support hiring of railroad safety inspectors. By 1986, the program funded approximately one-fourth of all government railroad inspectors in the United States. However, only thirty-one states were participating in the program by the late 1980s, and some of them participated on a very limited basis.

The decision of a number of states not to participate in the program seems inconsistent with popular images of the grant system. Why would state officials not want "free money"? The answer, at least in part, is that this grant carries a matching requirement; the national grant is available only if state officials contribute some of their own money to the program. In addition, any grant carries a variety of potential or actual costs—compliance with national regulations attached to the grant, possible conflict generated by the grant program's operations, the fear that people will come to expect the services supported by the grant but that the grant will not provide enough funds to satisfy those expectations, and so forth. Finally, the State Safety Participation Program is one of the small grant programs discussed earlier; it distributed just over $2 million nationwide in 1986. The amount of money involved might not seem worth any significant risk for some state officials.

Because the funds are distributed on a project grant basis, the State

3. This section relies heavily on Nice (1993).

Safety Participation Program also raises the concern that funds might be distributed based on the grantsmanship skills of potential recipients rather than the need for the funds. As noted earlier, this complaint has been made regarding many project grants. Does the money go where it is needed most or where the political and bureaucratic skills are?

Available evidence indicates that whether states participate in this particular program and how much they participate can be explained largely on the basis of need. Funding is substantially targeted to states with relatively large numbers of rail accidents, large numbers of rail accident fatalities, and extensive railroad systems. In addition, relatively urban and densely populated states tend to be more involved in the program; consider that a serious railroad accident in a densely populated area could block major traffic arteries and could, if toxic or flammable materials were involved, require the evacuation of enormous numbers of people. With potentially more at stake, urban states have a greater incentive to participate.

The State Safety Participation Program casts at least some doubt on images of the grant system that emphasize centralized control and the insatiable demand of recipients for grant money. While we must be careful not to overgeneralize from a single program, the evidence here and for other small grant programs reveals that recipients do not mindlessly take any and all available grant funding. Instead, recipients shop for programs that seem to be attractive and avoid programs that are not sufficiently rewarding. Even large grant programs are not immune to this phenomenon; the state of Arizona does not participate in the Medicaid program, for which the national government contributes more than $30 billion annually nationwide (Albritton 1990: 435).

Alternatives to Grants: Real or Imagined

Critics of the grant system and of the national grant system especially have periodically called for replacement of grants with other devices that would provide the benefits of grants without the shortcomings. Among the more prominently discussed proposals are tax separation, tax reductions at the granting level, tax credits, and the property tax circuit breaker.

Tax separation and *tax reduction* are based on a common premise. Under the tax reduction approach, the higher level of government reduces its taxes generally; lower levels of government will then be free to raise taxes to increase their own revenues (Glendening and Reeves 1984: 233–34). In a related vein, tax separation would require each level of government to utilize different types of taxes: national income tax, state sales tax, and local property tax, for example (see Break 1980: 35–36).

The basic premise behind both tax reduction and tax separation is that people will tolerate only a certain amount of taxation, either in general or of a certain type. As one level increases its share, less is available for the others. In this view, if one level raises less revenue, other levels will be able to raise more. In the process, those other levels will be raising revenue for themselves and be free to spend it as they see fit, rather than being subjected to the influence of another level of government distributing grant money. The substantial variations in levels of taxation and use of particular types of taxes in the United States over time and from one state to another cast considerable doubt on this premise, however.

The deficiencies of tax reduction or tax separation as alternatives to grants are serious. Lower levels of government might not raise the revenues released by the higher level's tax changes (Glendening and Reeves 1984: 234). Bear in mind that a national tax reduction, for example, would directly increase private incomes, not state or local revenues. The best available estimates indicate that increases in private incomes produce only quite small changes in state and local government spending: for every $1 increase in private income per person, state-local spending rises by only five to ten cents (Break 1980: 98). A $100 billion national tax cut would therefore provide roughly $5 to $10 billion in state-local revenues.

Part of the limited translation of income growth into state-local revenue growth reflects the interjurisdictional competition among states and localities. Because states and localities compete with each other for jobs, investment, and prosperous citizens, officials fear that tax increases will drive business and affluent citizens to jurisdictions where taxes are lower. Even if higher levels of government reduce taxes, lower levels may still be reluctant to act.

Tax reductions or separation cannot overcome disparities between needs and resources. Jurisdictions that are very wealthy might be able to raise enough revenues to make up for the loss of grants (assuming the grants were replaced by tax reductions or separation), but poor jurisdictions would not be so fortunate (Glendening and Reeves 1984: 234). Moreover, while grants can be targeted to recipient governments with the greatest need (although not necessarily easily), tax reductions or separation cannot.

Finally, advocates of tax reductions or tax separation often assert that states or localities could raise revenue for themselves more cheaply than the national government can. As Maxwell and Aronson (1977: 68) point out, however, the national government's revenue collecting costs are actually *lower* than the collection costs at the state level. Shifting responsibility for collection from the national level to the state level would, therefore, produce higher collection costs.

Table 3.6: Tax Credits: An Example

	State A: No state tax	State B: State has tax
Gross national tax	$1,000	$1,000
State tax	0	200
Net national tax (line 1 minus line 2)	1,000	800
Total tax (line 2 plus line 3)	1,000	1,000

Tax credits have also been advocated as an alternative to grants (Glendening and Reeves 1984: 235–36). The higher level of government establishes a tax credit, a reduction in tax liability, based on taxes paid to some other level of government. For example, the national government might provide that, for every dollar a taxpayer paid in state income taxes, the taxpayer could reduce his or her national income tax bill by a dollar (or some fraction of a dollar). If the state did not adopt the tax, its taxpayers would receive no tax credit and would have to pay the full national tax liability (see table 3.6).

From the standpoint of recipient governments, tax credits have the advantage of equalizing tax burdens and reducing interjurisdictional competition. If a state does not adopt the tax, its taxpayers will still have to pay the same amount of taxes, but the proceeds will go entirely to the national government. Lower level officials will feel freer to raise revenues than would be the case with tax reductions or separation.

The chief shortcoming of the tax credit device is its inability to equalize needs and resources (Glendening and Reeves 1984: 236). If a jurisdiction's taxpayers are extremely poor, a tax credit will produce little revenue. Tax credits cannot target resources where problems are most severe, either.

Critics of tax credits also fear that they may give higher levels of government too much influence over the revenue systems of lower levels of government (Break 1980: 43–45). If a tax credit is available for one type of tax but not another, lower levels of government have a strong incentive to adopt the former type of tax rather than the latter. If a general tax credit were adopted, lower level jurisdictions that rely heavily on fees rather than taxes would be under pressure to shift from fees to taxes. In short, higher levels of government could come close to dictating what sorts of revenue systems lower levels could use. Not all observers are comfortable with this prospect.

A third major alternative to grants at the state-local level, although not always presented in that form, is the *property tax circuit breaker* (see Nice 1987a; Peterson 1976: 101–102). The circuit breaker comes in many forms, but most involve a variant on the tax credit. Most states now have

Table 3.7: Property Tax Circuit Breaker: An Example

Family Income	$10,000
State-Defined Reasonable Rate*	5%
State-Defined Reasonable Amount for this Family (line 1 × line 2)	$500
Property Tax Actually Paid	$600
Property Tax Paid in Excess of Reasonable Amount (line 4 − line 3)	$100

*Property taxes paid as a percentage of family income.

some form of state-financed property tax relief, usually a circuit breaker, but coverage varies greatly from one state to another.

Although provisions vary, many state circuit breaker programs begin with a state-defined threshold based on the proportion of family income paid in local property taxes. For example, a state might decide that a reasonable property tax burden would be 5 percent of family income. A family with $10,000 in income would, therefore, be expected to pay not more than 5 percent of its income, or $500, in property taxes (see table 3.7).[4]

If the family actually paid $600 in property taxes, it would be paying $100 ($600 − $500) over the reasonable amount. The circuit breaker would provide state-financed relief to the family based on how much its property taxes exceeded the reasonable amount—in this case, $100. The relief would most probably be only a fraction of the excess amount.

While the circuit breaker appears to be a system of payments to individuals, which it is to some extent, it is also a form of indirect subsidy to local governments. As a local government raises its property taxes higher, more residents are pushed above the reasonable threshold. The state, through the circuit breaker, picks up part of the increase. Moreover, to the degree that the property tax is relatively regressive (there is controversy on that point; see Maxwell and Aronson 1977: 138–40; Pechman and Okner 1974: 59), poorer people are more likely to exceed the reasonable property tax load. As a result, circuit breaker programs generally tend to target relief to localities with large concentrations of poor people and high property taxes (Peterson 1976: 102).

Perhaps the chief drawback to circuit breakers is that they require local officials to raise property taxes to a fairly high level in order to push a substantial number of taxpayers above the reasonable threshold. This process is likely to antagonize individuals and businesses not qualifying for the circuit breaker. They must pay the increase in property taxes out of their own pockets. They may respond by voting the local officials

4. Bear in mind that property taxes are levied on property values, not income.

out of office or by relocating to other localities where the property taxes are lower. Neither prospect is likely to encourage local officials to draw heavily on the circuit breaker. Note, too, that the circuit breaker does not dependably channel funds to where problems are most severe.

All of these alternatives to grants share a common feature: they cannot target resources to particular programs, such as interstate highways or pollution control. That is, in fact, a major reason for their popularity in some circles. Lower level jurisdictions would be free to spend revenues however they preferred. The alternatives are all instruments for reducing the scope of conflict from currently granting levels of government to currently recipient levels.

Because the alternatives to grants cannot target resources to particular programs, none of the alternatives can assure that a particular service is provided at a minimum level everywhere. They cannot readily direct resources where a problem is most severe, nor can they correct for externalities in particular programs. The best available evidence also indicates that neither tax reductions (or separation) nor circuit breakers would provide recipients with the amount of revenues that the grant system does.

Tax Coordination in a Federal System

In a federal system with over 80,000 units of government raising revenue in one fashion or another, the accumulated revenue decisions of the many governments may unintentionally treat some taxpayers unfairly. Some may be taxed out of proportion to any reasonable standard of equity, not because of any deliberate intent but because officials in one jurisdiction are unaware of what other jurisdictions are doing. Businesses operating in many different jurisdictions may be hampered by variations in tax provisions from one state or locality to another. Individuals who live in one locality but work, shop, or visit in others may require costly government services from them but pay nothing in return. These are the types of problems that tax coordination seeks to minimize (for a valuable overview, see Break 1980: ch. 2).

Vertical tax coordination problems arise when two or more levels of government tax the same individuals or businesses. Every year, taxpayers in many parts of the country file national and state income tax returns with noticeable differences in definitions of taxable income, exemptions, deductions, and other provisions. Businesses in many localities must collect state as well as local sales taxes. How can the burdens of multiple taxation be minimized and fairness achieved? A variety of proposals for providing vertical tax coordination have been offered. Their effectiveness varies considerably.

Tax separation is an obvious solution to vertical tax coordination problems, but not necessarily an effective one. Tax separation calls for each level of government to refrain from using the other levels' types of taxes (Break 1980: 35–36). Some degree of tax separation is discernible in current tax policies: local governments raise over 90 percent of all property taxes, the states raise over 60 percent of the general sales and gross receipts taxes, and the national government raises over 80 percent of all income tax revenue. Income taxes provide over 80 percent of all national tax revenue, while property taxes make up roughly 75 percent of local tax revenue. The states have more diverse tax systems: sales and gross receipts taxes provide just under half of all state tax revenue, but income taxes account for nearly 40 percent (*Significant Features of Fiscal Federalism* 1990: 93, 95, 102–103). Some reformers would like to see even greater tax separation.

As an instrument for vertical tax coordination, tax separation leaves a great deal to be desired. Rigid tax separation would deny all three levels of government the freedom to adopt the revenue systems that their citizens and officials prefer. If local governments were assigned the property tax, for example, localities that preferred to use some other tax would not be able to do so (a situation that some already face). States would similarly lose the freedom to devise different tax systems as their citizens preferred. In a related vein, forcing all states or all localities to use a single type of tax might leave jurisdictions where the relevant tax base was limited in dire financial straits (Break 1980: 35). A poor community through which many tourists pass might be able to raise a fair amount of money through taxes which tap the tourist trade, such as sales taxes; restricting that same community to property taxes might leave its treasury fairly empty.

Moreover, if a particular tax is regarded as fair, economical to collect, and free of undesirable side effects, not to mention popular with the public, should that tax be denied to any level of government capable of administering it (Break 1980: 35)? The fact that most local governments were legally restricted to property taxes for raising tax revenues for most of our history made local revenue raising difficult. The unpopularity of property taxes practically assured opposition to increasing local revenues. By contrast, the tendency for income taxes to rise rapidly with economic growth has helped fuel the growth of national revenues and spending. Denying the more popular or productive revenue sources to a level of government would weaken that level's ability to compete financially with other levels.

Probably the most fundamental flaw of tax separation as a means of achieving tax coordination results from the fact that taxes, regardless of their form, are ultimately paid by people. Separating tax sources—a national income tax, state sales tax, and local property tax, for example—provides no assurance whatever that a taxpayer will be treated more fairly than would be the case with national, state, and local income taxes. The taxpayer must still pay taxes to all three levels, and nothing in tax separation assures that the combined effects of the various taxes will be equitable or efficient.

A second method of coordinating taxes is the use of *coordinated tax bases*. If different levels of government use the same tax they can make life simpler for everyone by defining their tax bases in the same way. If a taxpayer has to pay national, state, and local income taxes, using the same definition of taxable income would make filing tax returns much easier for the taxpayer and make enforcement easier for revenue departments (see Break 1980: 37–39).

A number of states have adopted definitions of taxable income that are fairly similar to the national definition, but identical tax bases pose a number of problems. Not all jurisdictions agree on what constitutes a fair or reasonable definition of taxable income, and the definition of a tax base has obvious revenue implications. Some jurisdictions might be able to raise more revenue using a different definition of the tax base. For example, a state with relatively large numbers of single-parent families and families with both parents working will lose much more revenue from a deduction for child care costs than would a state with relatively few of those families, other things being equal. Moreover, if a state defines taxable income based on the national definition, any changes in the national definition may produce large, unexpected changes in state revenue (Break 1980: 38). Use of this approach, then, requires all the levels involved to consult with one another before making major changes in their tax bases.

Tax deductions and tax credits may also be used to improve tax coordination. If, for example, the national income tax is expected to reflect a taxpayer's ability to pay, income that he or she must pay in state and local income taxes is obviously not available for other uses. Permitting the taxpayer to deduct the state and local income taxes from the income subject to national income taxation produces a more realistic indication of spendable income. Without the deduction, and with sufficiently high tax rates, the combined national, state, and local income tax rates might exceed 100 percent—a situation certain to anger taxpayers (Break 1980: 41–42).

As noted earlier, the use of tax deductions and credits sometimes raises fears that a higher level of government may exert undue influence over the revenue systems of lower levels of government. If, for example, the national government allows deductions for local property taxes but not for fees paid to local government or to private vendors providing services that local governments provide elsewhere (such as trash collection), is this effectively favoring citizens in communities that rely heavily on taxes rather than fees for services, and that emphasize government provision of services rather than relying on private vendors?

In 1985, the Reagan administration proposed eliminating the national income tax deduction for state and local taxes paid. The proposal aroused a storm of protest from state and local officials, who correctly concluded that eliminating the deduction would make state and local revenue raising much more difficult. With the deduction, a taxpayer in the 30 percent bracket of the national income tax can save roughly 30 percent of a local property tax increase. Eliminating the deduction would have made the property tax hike much more painful to the taxpayer. The proposal reflected that, in this particular case, the anti-government aspect of Reagan's New Federalism triumphed over the desire to transfer power from the national government to the states. As a compromise, the deductability of sales taxes was repealed, but deductions for income and property taxes survived.

The most drastic method of tax coordination is *centralized tax administration*. In its milder form, a higher level of government establishes a tax base. Lower levels are free to set their own rates on that base; the higher level administers the tax and distributes the proceeds due to the lower level governments to them. Some states, for instance, permit local governments to adopt a sales tax, should they prefer to, on a state-defined base. The state collects the revenues but distributes the localities' shares back to them.[5]

The other version of centralized tax administration involves a uniform tax everywhere in the higher level of government. A specified share of the proceeds is distributed to the lower level of government. This approach gives greater uniformity but reduces the flexibility of lower levels of government.

Centralized administration eases the burdens of taxpayers, who must file only one tax return, and permits lower levels to raise revenues with minimal administrative costs. The chief risk, however, is that the higher level of government may adopt tax code revisions that greatly alter local revenues. If local governments have a local sales tax on a state-defined base, a new state law exempting food and medicine from sales taxation would cause local revenues to plummet.

In addition to problems of vertical tax coordination, federal systems encounter problems of horizontal tax coordination. One of the most

---

5. Break (1980: 39–52) makes a distinction between tax supplements, such as a local sales tax piggybacked on a state sales tax, and centralized tax administration, but in practice the distinction is difficult to make.

prevalent horizontal tax coordination problems arises in metropolitan areas, where someone may live in one city, work in another, and shop and enjoy recreation in several others. This person requires services from many local jurisdictions; how are they to be financed?

One solution is to finance services through user fees when particular beneficiaries can be identified. Parking fees, admission fees to public facilities, and bridge tolls are all examples of this practice (Break 1980: 53–54). Another solution is adoption of local taxes that can generate revenues from nonresidents. A local sales tax or payroll tax can provide revenues from commuters and shoppers as well as residents.

A second major horizontal tax coordination problem arises from taxation (or nontaxation) of interstate sales. Sales taxes are a major revenue source for most states, but problems arise when a company in one state sells a product to a resident of another state. Which state should receive the sales tax revenue? According to the destination principle, the revenue should go to the state that is the destination of the sale—that is, the consumer's state. In this view, the sales tax is essentially paid by consumers and measures ability to pay. The chief problem with the destination principle arises at the enforcement stage: how can a state monitor the countless out-of-state purchases of its many residents (Break 1980: 55–56)?

According to the origin principle, sales tax revenue from interstate sales belongs to the state of the origin of the sale—the location of the seller. In this view, sales taxes are ultimately borne by businesses and reflect either their ability to pay or the benefits they receive from government. Taxation at the origin is also much easier to administer: monitoring a few thousand businesses is much easier than monitoring several million individuals. Unfortunately, taxation at the point of origin creates fears that a state's businesses may be placed at a competitive disadvantage relative to firms operating in states with no sales taxes or no interstate sales taxes (Break 1980: 57–58). In recent years, a number of states have reached agreements to share the revenues from taxation of interstate sales and to share the enforcement burden, but progress has been difficult because of the concerns noted above.

A final major horizontal tax coordination problem involves state corporate income taxes on businesses operating in several states. In trying to determine what share of a corporation's income is subject to state tax, states use different methods. As a result, a corporation may find that the total of all the state shares exceeds 100 percent of the corporation's income. A variety of solutions to this problem have been proposed, such as requiring all states to use the same technique for determining each state's share, but progress has been difficult (Break 1980: 60–71).

The chief obstacle to greater coordination of state corporate income taxes is the revenue implications coordination would have. Some states select allocation methods to maximize revenue; shifting to a different method might reduce revenues. In addition, corporate income tax provisions in at least some states are partly a reflection of the political influence of business groups. Changing these provisions risks provoking a storm of controversy.

Problems of tax coordination are inevitable in any federal system that permits the governments in it to make independent revenue decisions. In addition, when private citizens or governments benefit from a lack of coordination, they are unlikely to support changes. Complete coordination would require either an amazing spirit of cooperation or some organization with the power to dictate revenue policies to all three levels of government. Neither prospect is likely.

Governmental Borrowing in the Federal System

Governments raise revenues in a variety of ways besides taxes. They may charge fees for services, from entrance fees for national parks to building permit charges for construction of a new shopping center. One of the most widely noted phenomena of American fiscal federalism during the 1980s was the dramatic growth of governmental borrowing. Between 1980 and 1990, the national government's debt rose from $914 billion to $3.3 trillion, an increase of nearly 300 percent. Borrowing by states and localities more than doubled in the same period. By 1990, national, state, and local governments combined were spending more than $246 billion annually on interest costs (*Significant Features of Fiscal Federalism* 1992: 244, 96).

The rapid growth of governmental borrowing has been attributed to many sources, from interest groups clamoring for more program benefits and citizens who do not recognize connections between what they demand in services and what they are willing to pay in taxes, to the poor performance of the U.S. economy during much of the 1980s and (at the national level) the Reagan administration's faulty estimates of tax revenues following the 1981 tax cut. One point is clear: the growth of borrowing was not limited to governments. Borrowing by businesses and individuals also rose dramatically, with individual debt virtually doubling between 1980 and 1987 (*World Almanac* 1988: 795). In 1992, personal debt was approximately $809 billion (*World Almanac* 1994: 110).

Governmental borrowing has generally been justified on two grounds. In some cases borrowing is used to finance deficits designed to stimulate a sluggish economy and bring it out of a recession. In other cases, borrowing may be used to finance construction of public facilities that will produce benefits for many years. If a bridge lasts for thirty years, financing it with bonds that are paid off over a period of thirty years will improve the likelihood that the people who benefit from the bridge's services will help to pay for it (see Musgrave and Musgrave 1980, part 6: 710–11).

The rapid growth of the national debt triggered a variety of proposals to reform the national budget process. A number of these proposals were borrowed from the budget processes of state governments in the erroneous belief that the states all balance their budgets. As noted above, however, state borrowing increased dramatically in the 1980s, and studies of state and local mechanisms to restrain spending or borrowing (item vetoes, balanced budget requirements, spending limits, and the like) generally found that they had little or no impact (Lowery 1983; Nice 1991). The struggles over public borrowing are likely to continue throughout the 1990s.

Summary

National, state, and local governments raise and spend substantially more money now than they did at the turn of the century, both in absolute terms and relative to the size of the economy. Growth, particularly on the revenue side, has been particularly rapid at the national and state levels, while state and especially local governments have become significantly more dependent on grants from higher levels of government. Grants come in many forms, with some giving recipients little discretion in deciding how to spend the funds, while other grants permit considerable discretion.

Because the grant system attempts to accommodate many conflicting goals, it is the subject of considerable criticism. Major alternatives to grants, however, lack many of the capabilities of grants. Tax separation and tax reductions by higher levels of government cannot direct resources to jurisdictions with the greatest need, establish a minimum service level for a program, or correct for externalities, for example.

A federal system, with many jurisdictions raising revenues, creates problems of tax coordination, both among levels and within levels. Tax coordination seeks to minimize the risk that individuals and businesses will be unintentionally burdened by the cumulative revenue decisions of various levels of government, and to achieve some degree of equity in the distribution of the costs of government across jurisdictions. Because some governments and individuals may benefit from a lack of tax coordination, however, and because some forms of cooperation may make one government's revenues dependent on the revenue decisions of another, cooperation has remained limited.

CHAPTER 4

National-State Relations

Relationships between the national government and the states have traditionally been at the heart of the study of intergovernmental relations.
The Interstate Highway System was created through the cooperation
of the states and the national government. Conversely, integration of
schools was greatly impeded by conflict between the national government and some states. This chapter will examine various methods for
allocating powers and responsibilities between the national government
and the states. A number of traditional criticisms of state governments
will be assessed. We will see, however, that the states have changed a
great deal in recent years. The issue of civil rights, which has caused
intense conflict between the national government and the states, will
be explored in detail. Finally, some of the major types of national-state
cooperation will be examined.

Allocation of Powers and Responsibilities

Much of the literature on national-state relations addresses the questions
of which level of government should be responsible for which programs,
what rights each level has, and what the nature of relationships between
the levels are and should be. These questions have attracted a great deal
of attention because they are at the heart of the operation of the federal
system. They have also drawn attention because of the wide variety of
answers that have been offered.

Disagreements over these questions arise in large measure because
of disputes over policies. Individuals and groups opposed to national

policies addressing particular issues will often argue that the national government has exceeded its authority. Conversely, groups favoring national policies for those same issues will typically conclude that the national government is acting properly. Changes in the issue or policy may cause groups to reverse their positions. In a similar fashion, views about whether a particular state action is within the proper realm of state authority are often heavily influenced by whether people agree with the action itself. In short, as the scope of conflict principle indicates, perspectives regarding the national-state allocation of powers and responsibilities are colored by beliefs regarding which level is likely to adopt the policy the observers want. This is, in all likelihood, the most important source of disagreement over national-state powers.

Disagreements also arise from the egos, personalities, and even the re-election concerns of state and national officials. State officials resent being pressured by Washington, and national officials resent pressure from the state capitals. A governor may believe that railing against big government in Washington will please the state electorate. In some cases outright defiance and obstruction may seem to carry public relations advantages. When something goes wrong, everyone wants to blame someone else.

A final major source of disagreement is the shortcomings of the various mechanisms for allocating powers and responsibilities. If the federal system had a foolproof mechanism for clearly defining the role of each level, disagreements would be rare. As we shall see, however, the various methods for allocating powers and responsibilities all have notable weaknesses.

The U.S. Constitution

The Constitution provides some guidance regarding national and state roles, but the guidance is far from clear in a number of key respects (Peltason 1991; Pritchett 1977). Some powers are granted exclusively to one level; some powers are shared by both, and some powers are denied to both.

Guarantees to the States. A number of constitutional provisions guarantee the state protection from national abuse or neglect (see Pritchett 1977: 56–59). Article 1, Section 9 prohibits a national tax or duty on the exports of any state, bans the granting of preference to the ports of one state over any other, and prohibits requiring vessels bound to or from a state to clear or pay duties in another port. These provisions reflect state fears that the national government might try to strangle individual states' economies. In theory, the provisions enable the states to compete on equal terms in economic matters.

Article IV, Section 3 provides that no states can be divided or merged without the consent of their respective legislatures. A party in power nationally could not, therefore, merge four states dominated by the opposition party in order to reduce the number of their U.S. senators from eight to two and deprive that party of six likely electoral votes. In a related vein, Article V provides that no state can be deprived of equal representation in the U.S. Senate unless the state consents—and state officials are not likely to agree to a loss of power in the Senate.

Article IV, Section 4 guarantees every state protection against invasion and, on request from the state legislature or governor, domestic violence. Note, however, that the national government also has the authority to act without a request from the state if domestic disorder threatens enforcement of national laws, federal property, or the peace of the country. This provision has occasionally allowed national intervention, which state officials did not want, in situations ranging from the 1894 Pullman railway strike to conflicts over civil rights in the 1950s and 1960s (see Peltason 1991: 152–53; Pritchett 1977: 57–58). Bear in mind that, regardless of constitutional provisions, an invasion of any state by a foreign power would produce enormous pressure for a national response.

Article IV, Section 4 also guarantees every state a republican form of government. Precisely what this means is far from self-evident. Except in a limited number of areas, the federal courts have often been hesitant to address the matter and tend to regard it as a political question—an issue for the executive and legislative branches to resolve (Pritchett 1977: 58–59).

The Second Amendment guarantees the right of each state to maintain a militia. This provision was adopted to assure that the national government would not impair the states' abilities to defend themselves (see Peltason 1991: 226). The Eleventh Amendment guarantees each state immunity from lawsuits in federal courts brought by citizens of other states or foreign countries, unless the state consents to the suit. If state officials act illegally, however—depriving a citizen of his or her constitutional rights, for example—the federal courts may hear suits without the state's consent. The unlawful act is not regarded as legitimate state action under the Eleventh Amendment and therefore is not under its protection (Peltason 1991: 308–309).

Limitations on the States. The Constitution places a number of restrictions on state actions. Many of the restrictions involve international relations in some respect. Article I, Section 10 provides that states may not enter into treaties, alliances, or confederations; levy duties on shipping entering or leaving state ports or navigating state waterways; maintain troops or war ships in peacetime; or engage in war unless invaded or threatened with invasion. While this collection of provisions seem to exclude the states from international relations, the actual practice is somewhat different. State and local governments are involved in a variety of activities designed to bolster international economic ties. According to one estimate, state governments were spending $40 million per year by the late 1980s on international trade and investment programs (Pilcher 1983; Sylvester 1988). State governments have generated international incidents when state (or local) officials have snubbed or otherwise alienated officials of foreign governments. When France refused to allow U.S. bombers to use French air space during a raid on Libya, Alabama's Alcoholic Beverage Control Board voted to suspend purchases of French wines for Alabama's state-run liquor stores. In a related vein, with the exception of inspection fees, states may not tax imports or exports without congressional consent, nor may they coin their own money. While these provisions limit state influence over international economic flows, they also help protect national control over interstate commerce, and encourage free trade among states. The same can be said for the constitutional ban on state laws impairing the obligation of contracts.

Article I, Section 10 also applies to the states' several prohibitions on national government action in Article I, Section 9. States may not enact bills of attainder, which are legislative acts that inflict punishment on named individuals or political groups without trial (Peltason 1991: 99–104). States may not enact *ex post facto* laws, making an action a crime retroactively that was legal when it was performed. States may not grant titles of nobility.

In addition to restrictions that appear in the original Constitution, several amendments limit state authority. The controls primarily address issues of civil rights and individual liberties. The Thirteenth Amendment prohibited slavery, a ban that applies to the national government as well as the states. The Fourteenth Amendment provides that no state may abridge the privileges and immunities of U.S. citizens, deprive anyone of life, liberty, or property without due process of law, nor deny anyone equal protection of the laws. As we shall see, this amendment has been interpreted in a variety of ways over the years.

Several other amendments have restricted state control over access to the ballot. The Fifteenth Amendment provided that the right to vote could not be denied or abridged by the states or national government because of race, color, or previous condition of servitude. The Nineteenth Amendment applied the same prohibition to gender, and the Twenty-Sixth Amendment, to persons eighteen years of age or older. The Twenty-Fourth Amendment provided that the right to vote in a national election could not be denied or abridged because of failure to pay a poll tax or any other tax. All of these voting amendments apply to the national government as well as the states.

Some Ambiguous Provisions. Several important provisions of the Constitution that deal with national or state powers can be interpreted in different ways and have been sources of controversy in national-state relations. First among these is Article I, Section 8, which provides that "Congress shall have the power to lay and collect taxes. . . . to pay the debts and provide for the common defense and general welfare of the United States. . . ." Taken together, the goals of defense and general welfare could encompass an extraordinary range of activities. The federal courts have generally held that the clause permits national spending to affect a wide variety of social conditions. Congress may, for example, attach a regulation to a federal grant even though Congress does not have clear constitutional authority to legislate on the subject of the regulation. Some observers prefer a more restrictive interpretation but that perspective has generally not prevailed (Peltason 1991: 66–68; Pritchett 1977: 177–79).

Article I, Section 8 also provides that the national government has the power to regulate commerce among the states. What activities are to be included under the term "commerce"? At what point does commerce among the states begin and end? If coal is mined in one state, shipped to another state, and used to produce electricity, some of which is transmitted to still other states, which of the activities constitutes interstate commerce? Should the clause be interpreted to include activities that are not interstate commerce themselves but affect interstate commerce? A variety of answers has been offered to these questions, but in recent years the federal courts have generally given Congress considerable latitude to legislate on a variety of matters that may involve some element of interstate commerce (Peltason 1991: 70–76; Pritchett 1977: chs. 12–13).

Further ambiguities are created by the "elastic clause," which provides that Congress has the power "to make all laws which shall be necessary and proper" for executing the powers delegated to the national government. Should "necessary and proper" be interpreted to mean indispensable and essential or simply convenient or useful? Different answers have been proposed (Peltason 1991: 90; Pritchett 1977: 151–52).

Additional disputes have arisen over the supremacy clause (Article VI, Section 2), which states:

> This Constitution, and the laws of the United States which shall be made in pursuance thereof; and all treaties made, or which shall be made, under

> the authority of the United States, shall be the supreme law of the land; and the judges in every state shall be bound thereby, anything in the constitution or laws of any state to the contrary notwithstanding.

The clause clearly provides that the national government's powers are supreme within its scope of legitimate authority (Peltason, 1991: 159). What happens, however, if questions arise regarding whether a national action lies within the scope of legitimate national authority? National efforts to protect the civil rights of blacks led to complaints that the national government had exceeded its authority; those complaints came especially from state officials who opposed black rights. When the national government required a 55 mile-per-hour speed limit as a condition of receiving federal highway aid, critics charged that the national government had no right to set speed limits. Given the vagueness of the general welfare clause, commerce clause, and elastic clause, these questions are unavoidable.

The Tenth Amendment has been a further source of disagreements over the national-state allocation of powers. It provides that powers not delegated to the national government by the Constitution and not forbidden to the states are reserved to the states or the people. Is the amendment simply stating the obvious: powers not assigned to the national government belong to the states or the public unless prohibited? What are those "not delegated" powers, and how far do they extend? Are the powers delegated to the national government to be interpreted strictly or broadly?

As this brief review indicates, constitutional provisions regarding the national-state allocation of powers are considerably less than clear in many respects, prompting disagreements over whether a particular action by national or state governments is permissible (Anderson 1955: 90). Several different methods for resolving these disagreements have been proposed and tried.

The Supreme Court Decides

The Supreme Court has often been placed in the position of resolving disputes over the powers of national and state governments (see Grodzins 1984: 25; Graves 1964: 213–16). A host of landmark Supreme Court cases have tried to clarify constitutional provisions governing national-state relations. The Court's role is plausible in view of its function as interpreter of the law, and its ability to provide consistent guidelines from one end of the country to the other.[1]

1. This is not to say that the Court always behaves consistently but rather to indicate that a single decision-making body has at least a reasonable chance to provide guidelines that are consistent from one state to another. For discussions of major decisions, see Peltason (1991) and Pritchett (1977).

Table 4.1: Laws Struck Down by U.S. Supreme Court

	National	State	Ratio
1789–1860	2	60	1/30
1874–1898	12	125	1/10
1898–1937	50	400	1/8

Source: Walker, David. 1981. *Toward a Functioning Federalism.* Cambridge, MA: Winthrop, p. 55.

The Supreme Court has tried to clarify the national and state roles in regulating commerce in a number of decisions dating back to *Gibbons v. Ogden* (1824). This decision established the principle that the national power to regulate interstate commerce could extend to activities within individual states if those activities were part of interstate transactions. At the same time, the decision laid the foundation for a distinction between *interstate commerce*, subject to national control, and *intrastate commerce*, subject to state control (see Peltason 1991: 70; Pritchett 1977: 181–86).

The Supreme Court attempted to clarify the meaning of the "necessary and proper" clause in the landmark case of *McCulloch v. Maryland* (1819). The Court ruled that the national government has substantial leeway in selecting the methods used to carry out its constitutional responsibilities. This decision played a major role in enhancing the power of the national government (see Peltason 1991: 19–20; Pritchett 1977: 151–52).

The use of the Supreme Court as the "umpire of the federal system" has sparked numerous criticisms, one of which is that the Court, as an agent of the national government, may be prejudiced in its favor, especially when disputes involve previous Supreme Court decisions (Field 1934). When the Court itself is charged with encroaching on state prerogatives, how objective can it be in ruling on challenges to its behavior? When justices are appointed by the president and confirmed by the Senate, can they be equally sympathetic to national and state interests?

The charge of a pro-national bias on the part of the Supreme Court is difficult to assess, but available evidence suggests that the court has not been consistent in its leanings (see table 4.1). In the period between 1789 and 1860, the Court struck down thirty state laws for every one national law overturned. By contrast, the Court struck down only eight state laws for every national law overruled between 1898 and 1937, despite the fact that the number of states had increased considerably. A detailed analysis of Supreme Court decisions in civil liberties cases from 1903 to 1968 found that state governments were more successful than the federal government early in this century (until 1930). From 1930 until 1953, federal and state governments were approximately equally successful in winning civil liberties cases, but from 1953 to 1968, the federal government had a higher success rate than the states—though the gap was much smaller than the gap that existed prior to 1930 (Ulmer 1985: 906–908).

During periods of heightened party conflict, the Supreme Court is particularly likely to strike down state laws in states controlled by the party not in power on the Supreme Court (that is, if more Supreme Court justices were appointed by Republican presidents, laws in Democratic party-controlled states would be particularly at risk). The Court does not, therefore, treat states as a monolithic group but instead separates them according to how much they diverge from the dominant philosophy of the Court (see Gates 1987). This hardly seems consistent with the image of a neutral umpire. The inclinations of the Court seem to vary over time.

One other criticism of relying on the Supreme Court as the final voice in resolving national-state disputes over powers and responsibilities focuses on the question of accountability. Can the Supreme Court, as an appointed body whose members serve for life, be depended upon to give adequate weight to public desires in its decisions? Not all observers believe it can.

The States Decide

From time to time the states have been recommended as the final arbiter of conflicts over the national-state allocation of powers and responsibilities. This possibility was anticipated by the authors of *The Federalist*. They predicted that whenever a national government action created problems for a state, state officials and residents would oppose that action (Hamilton, Madison and Jay 1937: 308–309). When the national government adopted the Alien and Sedition Acts in 1798, critics charged that these acts violated constitutional provisions guaranteeing free speech and a free press. The Virginia and Kentucky Resolutions, drafted by James Madison and Thomas Jefferson, respectively, denounced the acts and called on the states to oppose them. Two remedies were proposed:

> *Nullification.* The states could declare the acts null and void because the national government had violated the Constitution.
> *Interposition.* The states could interpose themselves between the national government and the people. That is, states could obstruct national enforcement of unconstitutional national policies (see Anderson 1955: 117–23; Glendening and Reeves 1984: 55–58).

The Virginia and Kentucky Resolutions were not warmly received by other states (Anderson 1955: 123), but the expiration of the Alien and

Sedition Acts left unclear the question of state review of national legislation.

The issue resurfaced following the adoption of the embargo on U.S. exports in 1807. The embargo restricted U.S. exports and was enormously unpopular in New England, which suffered considerable economic losses. State legislatures and town meetings passed numerous resolutions which echoed the Virginia and Kentucky Resolutions, much to the consternation of President Jefferson (who wrote the Kentucky Resolution). A proposal for a nullification convention in New England was seriously discussed, but repeal of the embargo in 1809 put an end to the discussion (Jones 1976: 171-72; Morison 1972: 101-102). Once again, a definitive answer to whether the states actually had the right to practice nullification or interposition was not provided.

The issue arose again as South Carolina objected to the national tariff during the 1820s. Between 1828 and 1832, tensions escalated as South Carolina tried to nullify the tariff within its boundaries and the national government tried to enforce it. South Carolina asserted that a single state could nullify national policies, but, once again, the issue was deflected rather than resolved when the tariff was lowered in 1833 (Jones 1976: 243-46; Morison 1972: 171-72).

The next major episode occurred in 1859, when a Wisconsin man was arrested for helping a fugitive slave escape. The man was released by an order from the Wisconsin Supreme Court on the grounds that the national Fugitive Slave Law was unconstitutional. The U.S. Supreme Court overruled the state court, whereupon the Wisconsin state legislature passed a resolution nullifying the federal court action (Morison 1972: 372; see also Pritchett 1977: 53-54). The legislature cited the precedent of the Kentucky resolution. In this case the supremacy of national policy was established and the right of a single state to overturn a national policy was not confirmed. However, the Civil War shortly altered the meaning of the decision.

The tensions over slavery and southern fears regarding national policies dealing with slavery ultimately led a number of southern states to attempt secession from the Union. Secession could be regarded as the ultimate assertion of a state's ability to judge actions of the national government (Pritchett 1977: 47-48). The issue of whether states could secede was ultimately settled through force of arms and confirmed by the U.S. Supreme Court in the case of *Texas v. White* (1869): "The Constitution, in all its provisions, looks to an indestructible Union, composed of indestructible states." In short, the states do not have a right to secede. The Court's opinion would have been quite meaningless, however, if the southern states had won the war.

Recall that one of the advantages of a federal system is the greater military and diplomatic strength it creates relative to a collection of small, independent nations (Riker 1964). If secession had been established as an acceptable method of dealing with disagreements, the fifty states of today might well be in seven, ten, or fifteen different countries. The current disintegration of the former Soviet Union shows that this is not merely a theoretical possibility.

The assertion that states are the final judges of national government actions resurfaced in the 1940s as the issue of civil rights for blacks began to gain national attention. Under the banner of States' Rights, a number of southern state legislatures passed interposition resolutions seeking to obstruct national efforts to integrate schools (Graves 1964: 116–17). This doctrine came to represent state opposition to all national civil rights policies.

While the doctrine of States' Rights is often presented as a descendent of the Virginia and Kentucky Resolutions, an important difference should be noted. The Virginia and Kentucky Resolutions had the ultimate objective of protecting citizens' rights as granted by the Constitution, notably freedom of speech and freedom of the press. The doctrine of States' Rights had the ultimate objective of denying citizens' rights granted by the Constitution, particularly the right to vote and the right to equal protection under the law.

In effect, then, the States' Rights movement claimed that the rights of states to conduct their affairs as they pleased were more important than the constitutional rights of their citizens. Activities carried out under the banner of States' Rights did succeed for a time in delaying implementation of national civil rights policy. These activities also did enormous damage to the reputations and images of state governments, damage that has only recently been repaired.

Permitting the states to judge individually the validity of national government actions would be a recipe for considerable confusion. Individual states might nullify the draft in a time of war, or interpose their authority between their citizens and the Internal Revenue Service, or deny women the right to vote. National laws would cease to exist for all practical purposes as they would only be recommendations that states could follow or ignore as they saw fit. The system would resemble what existed under the Articles of Confederation, a system that was replaced by the Constitution precisely because under the Articles, national authority was too weak.

Permitting individual states to choose what national laws they would or would not obey could produce other problems as well. The historical record clearly indicates that the doctrines of nullification, interposition, and the like are utilized primarily at the urging of groups opposed to particular national policies (see Leach 1970: 37–38). If individual state governments began to openly ignore any national law with which state officials disagreed, how long would individual citizens continue to obey laws they opposed? Governments, by their conduct, set examples for people to follow. If state governments set the example of ignoring laws when the practice suits them, they may unintentionally encourage citizens to do the same thing.

A proposal designed to reduce these problems but still give the states the last word in resolving national-state disagreements emerged in the 1960s. The proposed *Court of the Union* would have included the fifty state supreme court chief justices and would have had the power to review decisions of the U.S. Supreme Court (Grant and Nixon 1982: 45). The Court of the Union could have permitted uniform nationwide policies but, as compared with the U.S. Supreme Court, would have been more aligned with state interests.

The reasons for the failure of the Court of the Union proposal are obvious. A heavily populated state would have had the same voting power as a thinly populated one—hardly a pleasing prospect to larger states. Many state chief justices, already staggering under heavy workloads from their state court duties, were wary of assuming additional responsibilities. Some critics objected to adding yet another layer to a legal system that already takes years to resolve some cases, an addition that would cause further delays. Also, because the Court of the Union would have included all states, it raised the specter of "national" policies to which some states might still object. In effect, it still would have produced a national-level, not a state-level, scope of conflict.

Nullification, interposition, and related doctrines are based on the *compact theory of the union,* which holds that the Constitution is a compact among the states. In this view, the states, acting as independent nations, created the national government to act as their agent. Moreover, because the states retained their sovereignty, they have the right to judge whether their agent (the national government) is acting appropriately. This belief is a major component of state-centered federalism. If the states disapprove of a national action, they have the right to overturn or disregard it (see Graves 1964: 116; Morison 1972: 171–72).

The compact theory has been roundly criticized on a variety of counts by William Anderson (1955: chs. 3–4). He notes that the original thirteen states presented themselves as a united group during the struggle for independence and were recognized by other countries as a single country, not thirteen separate ones. Moreover, most of the thirty-seven other states have never functioned as independent nations since they were created by the national government.

Anderson notes that the compact theory has some validity for American government under the Articles of Confederation. The state legislatures sent delegates to draft the Articles, approved the result, and authorized delegates to ratify the Articles. State legislatures in most states selected their delegates to the Confederation Congress and had the power to recall their delegates at any time. In addition, the delegates were paid by their respective states, not the national government. Finally, the national government under the Articles had no power to tax, raise an army, or regulate commerce, nor did it have any implied powers (Anderson 1955: 55–59).

The inadequacies of the national government under the Articles led to demands for a stronger national government. The Constitution, besides creating greater national government powers, also included a number of features that are not consistent with the compact theory. The Constitution provided for a House of Representatives apportioned by population and elected by the voters, both features indicating authority derived from the people. Congress was given the power to make laws applying directly to the people. Unlike the Articles, the Constitution was ratified by conventions representing the public, and members of Congress were paid by the national government and were not subject to recall by their state governments. Finally, as noted earlier, Article IV of the Constitution provided that the Constitution and the laws made "in pursuance thereof . . . shall be the supreme law of the land." Collectively these provisions point to the principle of *popular sovereignty* of the people. Governing authority ultimately resides in the people, and they directly created the national government.

The Constitution is not fully consistent in reflecting direct popular sovereignty, however. Each state received equal voting power in the Senate, regardless of the state's population, and the Constitution originally provided for senators to be chosen by the state legislatures, not the voters. Constitutional amendments are ratified by state, without regard to population, and the mechanism by which states may call for constitutional amendments counts all states equally, regardless of population. These provisions suggest that if the public is the ultimate source of national authority, the grant of authority is channeled through the states. The Constitution, then, sends mixed signals on the issue (see Hamilton, Madison, and Jay 1937: 246–49).

The Public Decides

A very different school of thought holds that neither the national government nor the states should have the last word in resolving disputes over the national-state allocation of powers. In this view, the public should have the final say, partly because democratic government requires that major governmental decisions reflect public views, and partly because governmental authority derives from the people. To ignore public desires is to undermine one of the basic principles on which American government is based (see Hamilton, Madison and Jay 1937: 304–305).

On a more practical level, neither national nor state officials would be able to withstand pressures from a determined public for very long. If the national government were to consider abolishing all national aid to state highway programs, for example, an outraged horde of private groups would descend on Washington and, with little doubt, convince national officials to continue the highway aid. National and state officials cannot afford to ignore public reaction to decisions regarding the distribution of powers in the federal system.

A final advantage to letting the public decide stems from the fact that national and state officials have vested interests in preserving the importance of the positions they occupy. The public, by contrast, has a more neutral position and may, therefore, provide a more objective viewpoint. Of course, private individuals do have policy preferences, but the same can be said for public officials. Officials bring an institutional bias to their decisions as well, a problem that may be less severe for private citizens.

Placing responsibility for resolving national-state disputes in the hands of the public raises some significant problems, however. Public opinion research reveals that a substantial proportion of the public lacks firm opinions on many issues, that public opinion can shift dramatically, and that many people have attitudes that contradict one another—though the last problem may be less extensive than it once was (see Campbell, Converse, Miller, and Stokes 1964: chs. 7–8; Converse 1964; Pierce, Beatty, and Hagner 1982: ch. 7; Nie, Verba and Petrocik 1976: ch. 7). An example of contradictory opinions is presented in table 4.2, which includes responses to three questions regarding national-state relations. Nearly 60 percent of the respondents felt that the states should be strengthened, but 42 percent favored weakening the national government. At the same time, however, citizens were twice as likely to feel that the national government gave them the most for their money as they were to feel the states did, and citizens felt considerably less informed about state government activities than about national government actions. In other words, they favored increasing the power of governments that they felt gave them relatively little for their money and about which they felt poorly informed, and leaned toward reducing the power of the national government, which they believed to be giving them more for their money and about which they felt better informed. Is ignorance bliss?

The transmission of public desires to government also presents difficulties. More than one state electorate has simultaneously elected a governor who has railed against national encroachment on state prerog-

Table 4.2: Public Opinion and Federalism

How strong do you think the following should be made?

	Made Stronger	Power Taken Away	Kept As Is
State Government	59%	11%	22%
National Government	32	42	17

From which level of government do you feel you get the most for your money?

State	18%
National	35

How would you rate yourself on how up-to-date you are on what is going on . . .
   . . . in the federal government in Washington?
   . . . in state government in your state capital?

	Excellent or Pretty Good	Only Fair or Poor
National Government	40%	60%
State Government	27	73

Sources: Glendening, Parris, and Mavis Reeves. 1984. *Pragmatic Federalism,* 2nd ed. Pacific Pali-sades: Palisades, pp. 44, 231; Glendening, Parris, and Mavis Reeves. 1977. *Pragmatic Federalism.* Pacific Palisades: Palisades, p. 103.

atives, and a congressional delegation that supports expanding national powers. Which elections truly reflect public desires, if any?

In a related vein, people may support either a feature of national-state relations or a change in relations in the belief that some desirable result will follow. What if that belief is erroneous? If a resident of a very poor state believes that termination of all national grant programs would yield much more generous funding for state and local services and pro-grams, a belief that is certainly incorrect, should the federal system be shaped by that faulty premise? Few observers would support this.

Living with Indeterminacy

This brief review of mechanisms for resolving disputes over the national-state allocation of powers and responsibilities suggests that no perfect mechanism exists. Moreover, the dispersal of power in the federal system assures that neither the national government nor the states (not to mention local governments) will have an easy time making a binding decision regarding the allocation of powers. Each level of government has many avenues for exerting influence on other levels and for resisting actions by other levels.

While this state of affairs is disconcerting to individuals with a penchant for neatness and order, the indeterminacy has its positive side. If federalism is to help preserve freedom and the rights of the public, each level must maintain the capacity to rein in other levels if they violate citizens' rights. Giving any level the last word in resolving disputes over powers and responsibilities runs the risk of rendering other levels in the system powerless to restrain misbehavior by that level.

Indeterminacy also provides flexibility in national-state relations. If the national government and the states cannot conclusively exclude each other from a given policy area, individuals and groups unhappy with their treatment by one level can look to the other for help. One level's activities may be regarded as intrusion by another level, but the intrusion may nonetheless stimulate responsiveness in government. The situation is similar to the marketplace, where a business executive may be annoyed by the activities of a competitor but may nonetheless be spurred to meet consumer demands more closely as a result (for a valuable discussion of competition as a stimulant of governmental responsiveness, see Dye 1990b).

National-state relations are not exclusively or even predominantly combative, as a great deal of cooperation also takes place. The sharing of responsibilities depicted by cooperative federalism creates the potential for friction, however. For the many policies that have national, state, and local consequences, sharing may well be the most effective way to assure that all consequences receive adequate attention. Once again, this requires all levels to be able to press for their positions. Any level that could conclusively assign responsibilities might be able to slight the concerns of other levels as well.

The Condition of the States: Fallen Arches of the Federal System?

The American states have been assigned a major role in the operation of the federal system, but many observers have expressed doubts regarding the states' capacity to fulfill that role.[2] The weaknesses of the states have been widely discussed, and many problems remain, but a great deal of progress in strengthening state government has taken place in recent years (see Bowman and Kearney 1986; Nice 1983b; Reeves 1982).[3]

2. The term "fallen arches" is from Campbell and Shalala (1970: 6).
3. Criticism of the states can be found in Adrian (1976: 125–26, 247, 281); Grad (1970: 29–30); Grant and Nixon (1982: 278–80); Leach (1970: 118–31); Lockard (1971: 18–22); Martin (1965: 49–50); McConnell (1966: 168–84); *Modernizing State Government* (1967), Reagan (1972: 111–12); Reuss (1970); Rosenthal (1971: 4; 1981: 135–39); Sharkansky (1978: 1–12); Weber (1975); and Zeigler and Tucker (1978:ch. 6).

Table 4.3: Competitive State Party Systems

	1948 to 1962	1956 to 1970	1962 to 1973	1974 to 1980	1981 to 1988
Little Competition[a]	14	10	7	10	4
Moderate Competition	25	22	22	25	32
High Competition	11	18	21	15	14

a. Measured by Ranney's 1965(65), 1971(87), and 1976(61) indices and by Bibby et al.'s 1983(66) and 1990(92) indices. Little competition includes scores of 0 to .1999 and .8001 to 1.000. Moderate competition includes scores of .2000 to .3999 and .6001 to .8000. High competition includes scores of .4000 to .6000. Measure is based on gubernatorial and state legislative elections.

Political Parties

State political parties have been criticized for failing to provide effective interparty competition and for being organizationally weak and ineffective. Without competitive parties, the voters will have essentially no choice in the general election, and the party in power will not have an out-party serving as a watchdog. Without the threat of a competitive opposition party, the party in power tends to disintegrate into a number of squabbling factions (Key 1949), none of which is capable of governing. State party organizations have been denounced for their feebleness and their tendency to disappear after the campaign ends. Weak party organizations are not well suited to sifting the possible candidates to remove the inexperienced, inept, or dishonest, nor are they helpful in mobilizing support for policy making.

The state party systems have grown noticeably more competitive since World War II (see table 4.3). The number of noncompetitive states has fallen dramatically, and the number of highly competitive states virtually doubled until the mid-1970s, when a slight decline occurred. The party in office is more likely to have an effective critic in the opposition party, and voters are more likely to have an alternative to the party in power.

State party organizations have also grown stronger in recent years. Most states now have a permanent party headquarters—a new development in a number of states. Almost all of the state parties now have a full-time chair or executive director, although turnover remains high. Staffing of party headquarters has grown, along with state party budgets. The state party organizations have, in short, increased their capabilities for playing a constructive role in state government, although difficulties remain. Party organizations have a difficult time controlling candidate nominations, and many campaigns are run by candidate organizations rather than the parties. In addition, divided party control of state government is now common; after the 1988 elections only nineteen states had a governor and both houses of the legislature controlled by the same party (Bibby et al. 1990: 101–17).

State Legislatures

The state legislatures have received a large share of the criticism directed at state government. The legislatures have been handicapped by limitations on the amount of time legislators are willing or able to devote to legislative duties. The limitations include biennial (every other year) sessions, limits on the length of sessions, and low salaries, which force legislators to earn most of their income doing other jobs. With little time on the job, legislators have difficulty developing legislative proposals or monitoring the performance of the state bureaucracy.

State legislatures have also suffered from a high rate of turnover among members, much of it resulting from voluntary departures. Without a fairly stable core of experienced members, the legislature has difficulty competing with the experts in the bureaucracy and coping with the complex issues facing state government. High turnover rates also compound the time problems: a large contingent of new, inexperienced members arrives for the legislative session, and by the time they have learned their way around the legislature, the session has ended.

Legislative effectiveness has also been hampered by inadequate staff support and facilities. Solving these problems would provide legislatures with more information sources, allow them to more effectively handle routine matters, and create a working environment freer from distractions. Note that the legislature that lacks its own information sources is heavily dependent on interest groups and state agencies for information on policy issues, and neither source can be depended on to be objective.

Finally, the legislatures have been criticized for failing to give urban areas their fair share of legislative seats. Cities have often found that the state legislatures were unresponsive to urban problems and, as a result, have turned to the national government.

Considerable progress has been made in correcting many of the weaknesses of state legislatures, although the progress varies greatly from state to state. Many legislatures have given themselves more time to do legislative work. In 1946, only five state legislatures met annually, but forty-three now meet annually. Legislative sessions have been lengthened in a number of states, further expanding legislative work time. Legislative salaries have risen in many states (Adrian 1976: 293), enabling members to devote more time to legislative work (see *The Book of the States* 1990: 114–87).

Increases in legislative salaries and more attractive working conditions have helped to reduce legislative turnover. Between 1931 and 1976, turnover in state senates fell from 51 percent at each election to 32 percent. State house turnover declined from 59 percent to 37 percent (Shin and Jackson 1979). Consequently, the legislatures have a larger pool of experienced members to supply procedural and substantive expertise.

Legislative staff support has increased considerably in recent years (Clarke and Grezlak 1975), giving legislatures their own sources of information and more help with routine matters. In addition to helping the legislatures make more informed decisions, expanded staffing helps legislators get more work done in the time that is available. All state legislatures now use computers to help manage the legislative work load. Although applications vary from state to state, legislatures use computers for information retrieval, working out committee scheduling problems, and analyzing financial data, among other tasks (*Book of the States* 1990: 187).

Finally, following years of legal battles, the state legislatures finally gave urban areas their fair share of legislative seats in the 1960s. (We will return to these battles in chapter 6.) Overall the state legislatures of the 1980s are much better equipped to deal with the policy issues facing state governments than the legislatures of the 1940s.

The Governors

In the past, the governor's office in many states was criticized for failing to provide sufficient tenure for the governor.[4] Also, the widespread practice of electing a variety of state executives in addition to the governor caused difficulty. Short terms of office often meant that a governor lacked sufficient time to implement long-range programs or was forced to act hastily given a lack of time for analysis, reflection, and more careful formulation of policies. In addition, formal limits on reelection deprived the electorate of the opportunity to reward a governor for good performance and retain his or her services, or punish a governor for inadequate performance.

Low gubernatorial salaries further limited the amount of time governors were willing to spend in office. A governor considering a reelection bid could be dissuaded by the knowledge that private-sector occupations with similar responsibilities were more lucrative, and low salaries discouraged some able prospects from seeking the office at all. A lack of staff support made getting work done difficult at times and further reduced the appeal of the office.

4. For changes in the office of governor, see Beyle (1989); Sabato (1978; 1983); and Grant and Nixon (1982: 280–84).

Many governors' efforts were further frustrated by the presence of other elected state executives who did not owe their positions to the governor and held very different policy views. Substantial coordination problems resulted, with different state agencies obstructing or duplicating each other's efforts. The limited visibility of many of the elected state executives reduced their accountability to the public and made them more susceptible to interest group influence (McConnell 1966: 184; Froman 1966: 960). As the number of elected state executives increased, voters had a more difficult time keeping informed about the many candidates for office and determining which officials were responsible for state government performance.

Substantial changes in the office of governor have reduced the seriousness of these problems in recent years. The four-year term, which was found in only twenty-five states in 1946, existed in all but three states in 1990. Gubernatorial salaries rose from an average of $11,512 in 1950 to just over $83,000 annually by 1992 (*Book of the States* 1993: 47; Sabato 1983: 86). Even when inflation is taken into account, the increase is substantial. With longer terms of office and higher salaries, governors have in fact been staying in office longer in recent years. During the 1950s, just under 30 percent of all governors stayed in office for five or more years, but fully half of all governors held office that long during the 1970s (Sabato 1983: 103–104). As a result, governors have more time to develop proposals, assess their worth, and execute policies. Staff support has risen substantially from an average of only eleven people in 1956 to approximately fifty by 1990 (Beyle 1989: 36; *Book of the States* 1990: 65).

Some progress in reducing the number of independently elected statewide executives has been made, but the results have been relatively modest. In 1956 there were 709 elected state administrators (other than governors) heading 385 agencies. By 1988, the number of elected state administrators (excluding governors) had declined to 514 officials heading 293 agencies (Beyle 1989: 36). As the number of independently elected executives falls, governors have an easier time controlling the executive branch and the voters have an easier task at the polls.

State Bureaucracies

While the national government's bureaucracy has been roundly criticized in recent years, state bureaucracies have also received substantial criticism. They have been charged with hiring personnel based on political connections rather than ability and with paying salaries that are too low to attract and retain competent workers. Consequently, high levels of expertise are difficult to maintain and turnover is high. These problems are compounded by administrative structures that fail to coordinate related activities, frustrate initiative, and make determination of responsibility difficult (Grant and Nixon 1982: 278–80).

While problems remain, many states have made substantial administrative improvements in recent years. Merit system coverage has been expanded from 51 percent of all state employees in 1958 to 75 percent in 1980 (Sabato 1983: 67). State administrators are now better educated than in the past. In 1964, one-third of all state administrators lacked a college degree, and only 40 percent had a graduate degree. By 1978, all but 14 percent had a college degree, and 56 percent had graduate degrees (Wright 1982: 246). Formal education does not guarantee competence, but state administrators clearly have more training now than they once did.

Administrative salaries have risen as well (Nice 1983b: 374). As a result, state administrative positions are better able to attract and retain qualified personnel. Administrative reorganizations in many states have improved the prospects for coordinated action and clarified lines of authority and responsibility. Overall, state bureaucracies are better equipped for attacking policy problems and providing services than they were in the past, although some are better suited than others.

Revenue Systems

The states have been criticized for relying on inelastic taxes, which grow relatively slowly as the economy grows. As a result, public demands have often outpaced the revenue increases produced by economic expansion. State officials facing this situation have the following options:

- Adopt new taxes.
- Raise rates on existing taxes.
- Refuse to respond to public demands.
- Turn to the national government for aid.

When the political environment is hostile to tax increases, the states may lack the revenues to meet public demands or may become more dependent on national grants.

States have moved to increase their reliance on income taxes, which most observers believe are more elastic than other tax types—although this varies somewhat with different rates and deductions. The number of states with individual and corporate income taxes has risen dramatically (see table 4.4). The proportion of state tax revenues produced by income taxes has risen to more than one-third. The result may well be

Table 4.4: State Use of Income Taxes

	Number of States with Income Taxes	
	Individual Income Tax	Corporate Income Tax
1928–1929	12	17
1990	44	46

	Percentage of State Tax Revenue from Income Taxes		
	Individual	Corporate	Total
1922	4%	6%	11%
1990	32	7	39

Sources: 1922 and 1928–1929 data from Maxwell, James, and J. Richard Aronson. 1977. *Financing State and Local Governments*, 3d ed. Washington, DC: Brookings, pp. 42, 43; 116; 1990 data from *Book of the States*. 1992. Lexington, KY: Council of State Governments, p. 412.

an increase in the ability of the states to meet public demands from state revenues without the trauma of tax increases.

State Constitutions

A fundamental structural problem facing many states is their constitutions. The typical state constitution is much longer than the U.S. Constitution, largely because of the inclusion of all sorts of detailed policy and structural provisions. Since constitutional amendments are more difficult to adopt than changes in ordinary legislation, constitutional detail makes state policy change inordinately difficult. Because many of the provisions are limitations on what state government may do, state officials who want to deal with a policy problem may be unable to act. Critics have called for streamlined state constitutions that contain few restrictions on state officials and fewer policy provisions in order to enable state governments to act more decisively and flexibly.

While some states have made progress in streamlining their state constitutions in recent years, the overall pattern reflects little progress. Between 1944 and 1978, only eight state constitutions grew shorter, while forty grew longer. In 1944, only eleven were 20,000 or more words long; by 1968, fully thirty-five were that large, although the number declined to twenty-eight in 1978.[5] Criticism remains largely valid in this area.

The general lack of progress in streamlining state constitutions reflects the difficulty of adopting major constitutional changes. Legislative majorities of between three-fifths and two-thirds in each house as

5. Derived from various volumes of the *Book of the States*. See also Nice (1988).

well as voter approval are almost always needed. Neither is easy to achieve. In addition, groups that have succeeded in having policies they prefer written into the state constitution in the past generally oppose revisions that would remove those policy provisions.

Forces for Change in State Governments

Improvements in state governments have been stimulated by a variety of factors. A host of reform groups, including the Committee for Economic Development, the Citizens' Conference on State Legislatures, and many others, have agitated for structural reforms for many years. Through persistent efforts ranging from lobbying and research to capitalizing on occasional scandals, reformers have helped enact many changes.

The growth of state governments has also stimulated reforms. At the turn of the century, state governments were relatively small operations (with limited exceptions), employing few people and providing few services. As noted in chapter 3, they have grown a great deal since then. Structures that may have been adequate originally were unable to cope with the increasing powers and responsibilities, and with growth, the deficiencies of state governments became more obvious.

The poor image of state government may have provided additional support for reforms. A series of surveys taken during the 1970s asked citizens which level of government gave them the most for their money. State government typically came in third, well behind the national government and also behind local government (Harrigan 1980: 65). The lackluster image of state government may reflect citizen support for reform and may also have persuaded state officials that changes were needed.

National forces have also stimulated changes in the states. Increasing party competition on the state level has undoubtedly been fostered by declining party loyalty and national civil rights policies. The growth of the national government in domestic policy-making has encouraged the states to put their own houses in order by indicating to the states that if they do not act, the national government may. For example, the state legislatures in many states gave urban areas their fair share of legislative seats only after the national courts ordered the change.

The revitalization of state governments has greatly reduced the problems that have plagued states in the past. In many respects they are better equipped to play a major role in the federal system than they have been at any time in this century. Some states have lagged behind others in the process of revitalization, but the overall trend is clear. As a result, people who seek solutions to policy problems may find the states to be more capable of helping than was previously the case.

Case Study: Unwinding the Federal System

The Reagan administration's New Federalism proposals belong to a long line of efforts to curtail national involvement in domestic policy-making and separate the activities of national and state governments.[6] The first and second Hoover Commissions (1947–1949 and 1953–1955), the Kestnbaum Commission on Intergovernmental Relations (1953–1955), and the Joint Federal-State Action Committee (1957–1959) all attempted to reduce national activities and separate national and state programs. The limited success of their efforts provides valuable lessons for anyone considering following their examples.

The Joint Federal-State Action Committee provided ample evidence of the problems likely to appear whenever major reductions in national domestic programs and elimination of national-state sharing are attempted. The committee's roots lay in a speech that President Eisenhower gave to the National Governor's Conference in 1957. Eisenhower called for the formation of a committee to determine which programs currently involving the national government could be transferred entirely to the states. The committee would determine what changes in national and state revenue systems would be needed in order for states to assume complete responsibility for those programs. It would look to the future to anticipate problems that might require national or state action at some later date and estimate the amount of national or state activity needed. Finally, it would establish deadlines by which time transfers of functions to the states would take place.

The committee began with many factors in its favor. It included members with ample experience in government and considerable competence. Three members of the Cabinet, the director of the Bureau of the Budget, three presidential assistants, and ten governors made up the committee. Virtually all the members agreed on the value of reducing national involvement in domestic policy-making and separating national and state functions, at least in the abstract. The committee had access to a wealth of research, was dedicated to its mission, and, perhaps most importantly, had considerable support from the president. There were many reasons to believe, therefore, that it would be successful.

After more than two years of work, the committee submitted its recommendations, which included termination of national grants to support vocational education and municipal waste treatment plants. National spending on these two programs amounted to just under $80 million in 1957, or a little over 2 percent of all federal grants in that year.

---

6. See Grant and Nixon (1982: 43–44); Graves (1964: 900–903); Grodzins (1984: 307–16); and Wright (1982: 33, 55).

The recommendations seemed to be rather small in view of the amount of time the committee spent developing them. The committee proposed that these programs would be financed by adoption of a tax credit for a state tax on local telephone service. The credit would be against the national tax on local telephone service.

The tax credit proposal was not warmly received by many states because, as tax credits generally do, it would have produced financial losses for poorer states relative to the grants that were to be replaced. Overall, twenty states would have lost money by switching from grants to the proposed tax credit, and the losers included all ten of the poorest states in the country. Wealthier states, by contrast, would have gained money by switching to the credit device (Wright 1982: 55).

The committee responded to the opposition by proposing equalizing grants to poorer states, but further complications ensued when Congress repealed the national tax on local telephone service entirely, rendering the tax credit proposal a moot point. The governors, faced with the prospect of having to fund the programs on their own, began to back away from the committee's efforts. Members of Congress who feared loss of national influence over vocational education and waste treatment policies were joined by agency professionals at all levels of government in opposing the committee's recommendations, and its proposals succumbed to the combined forces of opposition. The committee's inability to achieve major reductions in national domestic programs and greater separation of national and state responsibilities reflects a number of factors beyond the constellation of opponents noted above. Grodzins (1984: 313–16) argues that the fragmented character of American political parties makes planned, comprehensive adjustments in the system extremely difficult. The many interest groups that are active in American politics also make broad, comprehensive changes in the system very difficult (Lowi 1969: 101–88). A general principle, such as a broad-ranging reduction in national domestic programs or separation of national and state functions, encounters opposition from a variety of groups with little interest in the general principle but intense interest in specific programs. These groups fear, often correctly, that an end to national support for a program will mean an overall reduction in the program. Their intense opposition to national cutbacks in specific programs is typically stronger than the support for a broad-ranging reduction in national domestic programs in general.

The committee's efforts were also hampered by the fact that many government programs have effects at all levels. The committee's proposal to terminate national grants to municipal waste treatment plants, for example, reflected a lack of concern regarding the ability of pollutants to travel from one state to another. If a community were to have dumped untreated sewage into a river that flows through several other states, they would have had little recourse had the Committee's recommendation been adopted. Ending national involvement in any program that generates interstate spillover effects is likely to produce neglect of those spillovers. Separating government activities into national, state, and local functions may be attractive for programs that have only national, only state, or only local effects, but few major policies meet this requirement.

Separation of government functions also runs afoul of the warning against putting all the eggs in one basket. If a particular function is entirely the responsibility of one level of government, other levels will not be permitted to correct any deficiencies in the performance of that function. With a system of shared responsibilities, deficiencies in the decision made at one level can be ameliorated by other levels. Individuals and groups can go from one government to another until they find a sympathetic ear.

The responses to the Reagan administration's efforts to curtail national domestic programs and separate national and state functions indicate that the forces that frustrated the Joint Federal-State Action Committee are still powerful. Groups rallied to protect many individual programs from cutbacks, and state officials opposed major reductions in national grants to the states (Conlan 1988: ch. 9). Calls for separation may always be a feature of the political landscape, but the voices for sharing seem to be louder and more persistent.

National-State Relations and Civil Rights

No single issue has produced more intense conflict in the American federal system than the issue of civil rights and blacks. An examination of the historical development of this issue reveals a great deal about how federal systems handle controversial issues, and how altering the scope of conflict can produce changes in government policies.[7]

Compromises in the Constitution

The tensions inherent in the issue of black rights were recognized during the drafting of the Constitution, and the techniques used to resolve those tensions set the pattern for future efforts. One disagreement centered on whether slaves should be counted for the purposes of

7. The historical material in this section is drawn largely from Jones (1976: volumes I and II) and Morison (1972: volumes II and III). Material from 1930 draws on Anderson et al. (1984: ch. 8); Chelf (1981: ch. 13); Dye (1981: 71–75, ch. 13; 1984: ch. 3); Pritchett (1977); and Schattschneider (1960).

apportioning the House of Representatives and, consequently, electoral votes.[8] Free states charged that slaves were not being treated as citizens and were not allowed to vote in the slave states; therefore, they should not be counted. Slave states wanted the slaves to be counted in order to increase the voting power of slave states in the House and Electoral College. Needless to say, the position assumed by the free states would have enhanced their voting power in both arenas as well.

This difficult issue was resolved through an arbitrary compromise, a technique that would be used repeatedly over the years. Article I, Section 2 provided that a slave ("all other Persons") would be counted as three-fifths of a person. The provision had little intrinsic logic: in what sense can someone be three-fifths of a human being? The use of an arbitrary, split-the-difference decision rule reflected an inability to agree on the merits of the issue.

The other point of contention centered on the slave trade, which slave states were anxious to protect. The matter was addressed in a relatively opaque manner in Article I, Section 9: "The migration or importation of such persons as any of the states now existing shall think proper to admit, shall not be prohibited by the Congress prior to the year one thousand eight hundred and eight . . ." In effect, this provision stated that the national government could not ban the slave trade until 1808. It was a pure scope-of-conflict provision: the national government left the issue at the state level. Left on their own, slave states could hardly be expected to ban the slave trade. Scope-of-conflict provisions that involve the national government deciding not to decide were used again to manage the conflicts over black rights, and the consequences for blacks were profound.

The Path to the Civil War

As the nation grew, tensions arose over which new states would permit slavery and which would not. The question was a difficult one because neither side wanted the other to become dominant in the national government. Some mechanism for maintaining a balance of power was sought by both sides. When Missouri sought admission to the Union as a slave state in 1819, opposition erupted in free states. Missouri was farther north than the states where slavery was established and was there-

8. Although the provision does not mention gender, the assumption during this period of our history was that the issue centered upon consideration of male slaves for apportioning representation in the House. An interesting and nontraditional account of the movement toward abolition of slavery and slave suffrage is available in *A People's History of the United States*, by Howard Zinn (1980).

fore regarded as encroaching on free territory. It would have given the slave states a majority in the Senate, rekindling resentment in free states over the approximately twenty House seats and twenty electoral votes that slave states received by counting each slave as three-fifths of a person (Morison, 1972: 138).

After bitter wrangling, the contending sides agreed on the Missouri Compromise of 1820. It admitted Missouri as a slave state but also admitted Maine as a free state. The simultaneous admissions preserved the balance of power in the Senate (twelve free states and twelve slave states). The Compromise also banned slavery in territories north of 36 30' latitude, the line that defines most of Missouri's southern border. An arbitrary line was drawn to regulate the expansion of slavery.

The Compromise managed to resolve the immediate tensions generated by the admission of Missouri, but the underlying problem remained. Thomas Jefferson, among others, recognized the gravity of the situation: "The momentous question, like a fire bell in the night, awakened and filled me with terror. I considered it at once as the knell of the Union" (quoted in Morison 1972: 139).

Tensions erupted again over the admission of western states. The Compromise of 1850 tried to placate all sides by a combination of provisions. California was admitted as a free state, and the domestic slave trade was banned in Washington, D.C. Both provisions pleased free states while a tougher fugitive slave law was added to mollify slave states. Territorial governments were created in Utah and New Mexico without mention of the status of slavery. This last element was a scope-of-conflict provision, as again the national government decided not to decide.

The same technique appeared in the Kansas-Nebraska Act of 1854. According to the Missouri Compromise, slavery could not be permitted in those territories because they were north of 36 30'. Slave states, however, opposed further additions to the ranks of free states. The issue was resolved by permitting the territories in question and new states to decide for themselves whether to permit slavery. Once again, the national government decided not to decide; the issue of whether to permit slavery was handed over to the territories and new states.

The existence of free and slave states side by side produced numerous legal complications, the most noteworthy of which involved Dred Scott. Scott was a slave and had been taken to a state and then a territory where slavery was not permitted. After returning to Missouri, a slave state, Scott sued for his freedom based on the periods he had spent in a free state and a free territory. The case eventually found its way to the U.S. Supreme Court, and tensions surrounding the case and the broader issue of slavery were high.

The Supreme Court attempted to ease the tensions in its ruling in 1857. It ruled that no slave could be a citizen and, therefore, could not bring a suit in federal courts. In addition, the Court held that blacks were not viewed as people when the Constitution was drafted and ratified. Consequently, they were not entitled to *any* constitutional protection of their rights (see Pritchett 1977: 291). The court's decision did not ease the tensions. It did, however, reflect another use of scope-of-conflict decision making. The decision essentially maintained that the issue of slave rights did not exist as far as the federal courts were concerned. Any legal conflicts would have to be addressed in state courts. One did not need legal training to predict the reception a slave would receive in the state courts of slave states.

Ultimately the various compromises failed, and the scope of conflict escalated to a level never reached before or since in American history. During the Civil War, the national government finally decided to establish a national policy, which was the abolition of slavery.[9] In addition, the Fourteenth Amendment to the Constitution effectively made the former slaves citizens and prohibited the states from abridging their privileges and immunities; depriving them of life, liberty, or property without due process of law; or denying them equal protection of the laws. All these protections applied to all people. Finally, the Fifteenth Amendment provided that: "The right of citizens of the United States to Vote shall not be denied or abridged by the United States or by any state on account of race, color, or previous condition of servitude." For a time these provisions were enforced, and blacks were treated as citizens and exercised the right to vote. However, the amendment was notably silent with regard to denying women the right to vote, contrary to the hopes of many women in the Abolitionist movement.

The Rise of Jim Crow

With the disputed presidential election of 1876, a major change took place. Under the so-called Compromise of 1877, southern Democrats

---

9. Two alternative views on the Civil War are that (1) it was fought over the issue of slavery; and (2) it was fought over the issue of the power of the national government. The principle of the scope of conflict tells us that the two explanations are two sides of the same coin: the South was concerned that the national government would assert power to make a policy abolishing slavery. That the issue was not simply national power in the abstract can be seen by asking whether the South would have seceded had the national government asserted the power to establish a policy permitting slavery nationwide. Further evidence can be seen in the support for the Republican Party in the South after the Civil War. Republican strength was strongest in hill and mountain areas where there were few slaves and where, therefore, support for secession had been much weaker (see Key 1949: 280–85).

acquiesced to the selection of Rutherford B. Hayes as president, in return for which the national government agreed to leave the issue of black rights to the states. The scope of conflict was reduced from the national level to the state level, and the result was predictable: the rights that blacks had enjoyed (and that were granted to them in the Constitution) were gradually taken away. Blacks were gradually pushed out of the electorate, in clear violation of the Fifteenth Amendment, and Jim Crow laws required segregation of the races in schools, public accommodations, and many other areas of life.

Legal segregation was challenged in the Supreme Court case of *Plessy v. Ferguson* (1896). The Court ruled that the Fourteenth Amendment made all races equal before the law but did not require social equality, nor did it forbid separation of the races. This case gave rise to the doctrine of *separate but equal,* which was intended to mean that the races could be separated if equal facilities were provided for both. In practice the doctrine meant only separation for most of its history. Little effort was devoted to determining whether the separate facilities really were equal (Pritchett 1977: 490–94). In numerous instances it was very easy to discern vast differences in facilities for different groups.

In the period from 1877 until the 1940s, then, the issue of civil rights for blacks was largely left to the states. Throughout the southern states blacks were routinely denied the right to vote and were the victims of many types of legally sanctioned discrimination. They were treated better in some states, but where they were treated poorly, they could not escalate the scope of conflict to a higher level where they might find a more sympathetic response. The influence of dual federalism as a model of federalism during this period was undoubtedly not coincidental. If each level of government is supreme within its own sphere and neither level is permitted to intervene in the other's activities, governments at one level may be able to deny the basic rights of citizens and, as long as those governments remain in their own sphere, other levels will probably do nothing.

The Civil Rights Revolution

Beginning in the late 1930s, the national government began to move into the civil rights arena again. Part of the national reentry into the issue may reflect the influence of the New Deal of the 1930s. The New Deal did not directly address the issue, but its emphasis on helping the economically disadvantaged could easily be broadened to helping people who were disadvantaged in other ways. The New Deal also created a substantial increase in national grants to the states, a development that would give the national government some leverage on state governments.

During the New Deal era, a number of new justices were appointed to the Supreme Court, and they brought new ideas about the use of national government power to solve social problems. Finally, the New Deal greatly undercut dual federalism, with its emphasis on strict separation of national and state governments.

International events may have prodded the national government into action as well. Blacks served in the armed forces in both world wars, and their contributions led many to feel that blacks deserved better treatment. The tyrannical governments that the United States fought in World War II may have heightened sensitivity regarding violations of citizens' rights at home.

Finally, the national government was goaded into action by civil rights groups. Utilizing a variety of tactics, they drew attention to the issue and repeatedly brought it to a variety of national institutions. Gradually they succeeded.

The national government's return to the civil rights issue was led by the Supreme Court, a situation that was hardly surprising in view of the controversy surrounding the issue. The justices, appointed for life, had less reason to fear the public's response than elected officials. The Court began to tighten up the "equal" requirement of separate but equal; the question of whether segregated facilities truly were equal came under closer scrutiny beginning in the late 1930s. The 1944 *Smith v. Allwright* ruling struck down the *white primary*, a device used to minimize the voting power of the limited number of southern blacks who were allowed to vote. Under the white primary, the Democratic party primary was treated as a private affair—one from which anyone, including blacks, could be excluded. Given the Democratic party's overwhelming dominance throughout most of the South for the first half of the twentieth century, the Democratic primary typically was *the* election; whoever won it would be the next governor, senator, or representative. The Court struck down the white primary for precisely that reason, along with the ample evidence that states did regulate primaries in many ways (see Pritchett 1977: 562–63).

The doctrine of separate but equal received another look in the landmark case of *Brown v. Board of Education* (1954). The Court ruled that the very act of separation implied inequality and that separate but equal was inherently contradictory. Racial segregation in education was ruled unconstitutional, and federal district courts were directed to desegregate schools "with all deliberate speed." The decision provoked a storm of controversy that lasted for years.

Presidential involvement in civil rights issues began primarily with Truman's efforts after World War II, efforts that included desegregation of the armed forces. Congress and the president became more involved with the passage of the Civil Rights Act of 1957. This act was particularly directed toward giving blacks access to the ballot. It authorized the Justice Department to seek injunctions to stop behavior that kept blacks from voting. It was not particularly effective, as indicated by the fact that less than 40 percent of all southern blacks were registered to vote in 1964 (Dye 1981: 72).

These initial efforts by the national government had great symbolic importance, but their actual impact was initially quite modest. Officials in a number of southern states used a combination of legal maneuvering, delaying, and outright defiance to avoid complying with the national policies. Their efforts were often successful, as indicated by the fact that only 2 percent of all black children in the South attended integrated schools by 1964—fully ten years after the Supreme Court ordered an end to segregation "with all deliberate speed" (Dye 1981: 371). What progress was made occurred almost entirely in states that voluntarily complied with the Court's decision. Virtually no integration took place in states that resisted the ruling (see Elazar 1972: 8).

Black voter registration showed greater progress, as noted above, but it was still little more than half the rate for whites in 1964. The record of national civil rights policies during the period clearly indicates the implementation problems that can occur in a federal system. The national government made policy decisions but had great difficulty in translating them into actual results. The limited impact of the early national policies also casts some doubt on allegations that an all-powerful national government can easily force the states to do whatever it wants.

The limited success of the initial national efforts, as well as a growing awareness of the scope of the civil rights problem, led to a second wave of national efforts, beginning with the Civil Rights Act of 1964. The law included a wide variety of provisions, including a prohibition on applying unequal standards in voter registration and denying registration because of minor errors. The act prohibited racial discrimination or segregation in facilities serving or affecting interstate commerce, or when discrimination is supported by state action. The act also provided that discrimination could lead to withholding of national grants. Discrimination could become an expensive proposition.

The Twenty-fourth Amendment, proposed in 1962 and ratified by 1964, banned the use of poll taxes as a requirement for voting in national elections. The poll tax, a relatively low, lump-sum tax, had been used to discourage voting, particularly voting by blacks. It could easily be manipulated by reminding some people to pay and not others, or by refusing to accept payment from some people, or by requiring some people to show proof they had paid—the possibilities were endless. The amendment was extended by the Supreme Court in the case of *Harper v. Virginia Board of Electors* (1966) to cover all elections based on the equal protection clause of the Fourteenth Amendment (see Peltason 1991: 368–69).

Evidence of continued resistance to permitting minority voting in some parts of the South led to passage of the Voting Rights Act of 1965. The law provided that in any state or county using a literacy test or some other special qualifying device for voting, if less than half the residents of voting age were registered or voting in the 1964 presidential election, the Attorney General of the United States could abolish the literacy test and send in national voting registrars to register voters under simplified voting procedures. The law sought to overcome the implementation problems that had plagued earlier efforts to enable blacks to vote by establishing greater national control over the implementation stage.

The second wave of national efforts overcame some of the implementation problems that had undercut the first wave. Progress in school integration followed the passage of the 1964 Civil Rights Act. In fact, southern schools are now generally more integrated than schools outside the South. Black voter registration in the South rose from 36 percent of the voting age population in 1964 to 66 percent in 1970. By 1976, the difference in the percentage of voting age blacks and whites registered to vote was only 5 percent, a far cry from the 37 percent gap that existed in 1964 (Patterson, Davidson and Ripley 1982: 129).

The civil rights issue is far from dead, as continuing controversies over affirmative action, segregation, and various minority issues indicate. In 1992 the U.S. Supreme Court ruled that public colleges and universities in Mississippi were still illegally segregated. The ruling is likely to affect state university systems in nineteen states across the country ("High Court Ruling . . ." 1992: A16–A19). Also, several states including Oregon, Idaho, and Utah have dealt with citizen initiatives to restrict the rights of homosexuals. The issue of abortion often centers on concern over women's right to choose, and the abortion debate still rages in many parts of the country as both voters and legislators struggle with policy. Human rights issues stir intense feelings in people and often result in violence, as evidenced by abortion clinic bombings, attacks on homosexuals, and riots in cities throughout the country.

Civil Rights and the Federal System: A Summary

This brief overview of the civil rights issue clearly indicates the influence of the scope of conflict. When the scope of conflict was restricted to the state level as it was prior to 1861 and later after the Compromise of 1877, the rights of black Americans eroded considerably. As the scope of conflict expanded to the national level from 1866 to 1877 and again in the late 1930s, blacks were generally treated as citizens. There has been, overall, a clear relationship between the scope of conflict of the civil rights issue and the policy which has resulted.

The history of the civil rights issue also reveals a troubling fact. One of the traditional justifications for federalism is its ability to protect citizens' rights. The American federal system clearly did not do a very effective job of protecting the rights of black Americans. Indeed, the existence of relatively autonomous state governments served to delay and obstruct implementation of national policies to protect black rights for nearly a century (see Riker 1964). While few human inventions are infallible, the performance of the federal system on the issue of civil rights should encourage caution regarding the reliability of federalism as a protector of liberty. Another troubling aspect is that throughout history we see that when government fails to act to address inequities, citizens often use very public and violent ways of challenging an existing social order.

National-State Cooperation

While conflicts between the national government and the states attract a great deal of attention, both from political scientists and the news media, a great deal of cooperative activity also takes place. Much of the cooperation attracts little attention, but it is an important feature of the federal system.[10] The variety of cooperative activities is so diverse as to defy a comprehensive summary, but several of the more important ones deserve mention.

Much cooperation occurs through *informal contacts* of many types. National and state officials may exchange letters, discuss a matter of mutual concern by telephone, or meet face-to-face. Attendance at conferences and media appearances also permits exchange of information, ideas, and points of view. Officials may solicit each other's opinions on a proposed policy or inform each other of upcoming actions in order to prevent unpleasant surprises.

Informal contacts have the advantage of considerable flexibility as they can be carried out quickly and without elaborate preparation or organization. Informal meetings may enable officials to be more candid with each other on sensitive matters, particularly if the meetings are conducted without fanfare. Communication can be as continuous as circumstances require.

10. For discussions of national-state cooperation, see Elazar (1984: 75–80), Glendening and Reeves (1984: 113–19), Graves (1964: ch. 23), and Grodzins (1984: Part II).

Informal contacts are not suitable, however, for creating a lasting, official agreement, which is necessary for some problems. Informal negotiations may, however, be a prelude to a more formal arrangement. Unfortunately, more than one official has come away from an informal consultation session with the suspicion that it was held only for appearances and that the other officials had already decided on a course of action, regardless of the results of the session. Finally, an informal agreement between two officials may be disrupted if one leaves office and his or her successor refuses to honor the agreement.

Closely related to informal contacts are efforts to provide *technical assistance* of various types. Officials at one level may have greater experience with a particular program or technique and may offer guidance to officials at the other level. In some cases the assistance involves one level giving the other an answer to a specific question ("Did a particular technique work when you tried it?"), but in other cases the level of government providing assistance helps the other level develop greater capacity to act on its own. Training programs, reference materials, and other methods may be used to increase a government agency's capabilities. While the latter approach is generally more time-consuming and expensive in the short run, it gives the aided government greater flexibility in meeting its responsibilities in the future without further assistance.

The availability of technical assistance does not assure that it will be used. Officials may feel perfectly competent to handle a problem without seeking assistance from another level of government. Even if they feel a need for assistance, ego considerations may make them reluctant to ask for help. In addition, the price of technical assistance may be the revelation of sensitive information or compliance with conditions imposed by the level of government providing assistance (on the latter point, see Glendening and Reeves 1984: 115). In either case the price may appear too high in some instances.

Grants are another mechanism of national-state cooperation. National grants support state programs in fields ranging from education and conservation to transportation and welfare. As noted in chapter 3, grants can and do provoke conflicts of many kinds, but much of the grant system involves cooperative behavior. One level of government contributes resources in exchange for gaining (usually) some influence over a policy. The other level relinquishes some policy discretion, or appears to, in order to gain resources. The need for cooperation at some level is indicated by the desire of officials at the granting level to direct resources to a particular activity (such as highway building), and the desire of the officials at the recipient level to have the resources to spend. Because both sides want to keep the system going, each side has incentives to keep the system at least minimally acceptable to the other side.

Many observers emphasize the coercive nature of the grant system: the granting level (in this case, usually the national level) dangles funds in front of the recipient level (in this case, usually the states), which is powerless to resist whatever requirements are attached to the funds (see Reeves 1992: 401–405). The states are sometimes compared to heroin addicts willing to shoot down old women in the streets in order to receive another "fix" of federal aid. The reality is considerably more complex than that. The states have demonstrated ample ability to weaken, undercut, or ignore aid requirements when the inclination arises, and the national government has not always proven a vigorous enforcer of its own guidelines. For example, all of the states adopted an official 55 miles per hour speed limit in response to a requirement attached to federal highway grant funds, but a number of states did not appear to regard minor violations of the limit (in some cases up to 65 miles per hour) as worthy of much concern. Subsequent maneuvering led to changes in national policy to permit higher speeds on interstate highways outside of metropolitan areas.

National-state cooperation also takes the form of *shared operation* of programs. The national government operates an extensive array of national parks, and the states have many parks of their own. The national government engages in a variety of activities to encourage conservation and environmental protection, and so do the states. Both levels engage in regulatory activities to protect consumers and promote health and safety, and both levels work to control crime. The list of joint activities is extensive.

These shared activities sometimes provoke complaints that the national government and the states are duplicating one another's efforts. These complaints are valid in some instances, but in many cases the efforts are complementary rather than redundant. Each level's activities can reinforce the other's. Crime control and environmental protection, for example, are large, multifaceted problems requiring a variety of approaches and responses. Many policy problems are clearly large enough to permit both levels to be active without exhausting the range of useful contributions.

Emergency assistance is another significant form of cooperation. National disaster relief assists victims of natural disasters, which also trigger state responses. National law enforcement and military forces can be used to supplement state and local efforts to control civil disorders. National assistance saves individual states from the burden of continuously maintaining the capacity to deal with emergencies that may occur only once every twenty or forty years.

Providing assistance to victims of natural disasters is rarely controversial, but coping with civil disorders sometimes presents awkward situa-

tions. State officials may be reluctant to request national assistance because they hesitate to admit being unable to deal with a problem. National
officials may be reluctant to become involved if the use of force may
be required (Glendening and Reeves 1984: 114). Injuries and even deaths
caused by national forces risk adverse publicity, although doing nothing
in the face of serious disorders may provoke as much or more criticism.

Cooperation between national and state governments takes place
through *supporting legislation,* in which one level enacts laws to reinforce
policies adopted by the other level. For many years the national government has outlawed movement of a variety of things through the mails
or across state lines in order to support state laws regarding stolen cars,
prostitution, and gambling. More recently, national legislation has been
adopted to improve compliance with state child support decisions.

Supporting legislation is particularly valuable to the states because
of the permeability of their borders. Outlawing a commodity will have
limited impact if it is permitted to flow into the state from surrounding
states. National legislation can help to shield a state from penetration
by criminal activity from outside and help the state enforce its laws more
effectively. Supporting legislation is limited somewhat by variations in
state laws; beyond some point, national legislation may be unable to
accommodate differences in state policies. However, some diversity can
be accommodated. Transportation of commodities across state lines into
states outlawing them can be banned while transportation into states
allowing them can be permitted.

Joint use of facilities is another important type of national-state
cooperation. A reservoir constructed by the national government for
flood control or irrigation may also be the site for a state park. State
universities are the sites of many national research projects. Personnel,
equipment, and locations may be jointly utilized.

Joint use of facilities can produce significant cost savings by reducing the number of facilities and personnel needed. In addition, joint use
permits a facility to serve more than one purpose at a time, as when a
reservoir built for flood control is also used for recreation. Joint utilization
may also produce a more stable workload for a facility. Fluctuations in
state and national tasks may offset one another somewhat. Although this
effect does not always result, when it does, a facility is less likely to stand
idle for lack of work to do.

National-state cooperation is widespread in the American federal
system. Cooperative activities enable both levels of government to pursue their objectives simultaneously and, in many cases, more efficiently
and effectively than either level could on its own. While cooperation is
not as exciting as open conflict between levels, and makes for fewer
headlines, cooperative efforts are quite common.

Cooperation does not occur automatically, of course. Disagreements may arise over which level should receive credit for shared efforts, how costs should be allocated, or which goals should receive top priority. Cooperation may be preceded by negotiation, bluffing, and outright conflict. As in interpersonal relations, state-national cooperation results from deliberate, conscious efforts.

Cooperation is encouraged by shared goals in many cases. When flooding leaves many families homeless, wrecks businesses, and contaminates water treatment facilities, officials at all levels recognize a need for action. When a murderer travels from state to state and leaves a trail of corpses behind, a consensus on the need for capturing the perpetrator develops quickly.

Shared political needs also stimulate cooperation. A state official may recognize that an improved highway system will please many people, but if the state is poor and sparsely populated, it may not be able to afford the improvements. National officials may also recognize the political rewards that a grateful electorate would bestow and therefore decide to provide grants to help finance highway improvements. Sharing responsibilities can permit both levels to reap political rewards.

Shared program operations can also enable officials to share the blame for controversial or unpopular programs. If one level operates a program alone, officials at that level must bear the full brunt of complaints regarding the program's operation. Sharing a task spreads the political heat and may make it more tolerable. The Reagan administration neglected this consideration when it proposed giving states full responsibility for Aid to Families with Dependent Children (AFDC), one of the most controversial of all major government programs. Although a number of considerations were involved, many state officials opposed the proposal because they did not want to be the only ones to bear responsibility for the program.

Cooperation in some instances is fostered by cost considerations. A reservoir that is constructed for flood control or irrigation can also be adapted for recreational and wildlife habitat uses at a modest additional cost. A research facility constructed for large-scale research projects can, within limits, expand its operations to include additional projects at a relatively low cost.

Where and when the benefits of cooperation outweigh the costs (or are believed to), it is likely to take place. While that situation is far from universal in national-state relations, it is relatively common.

Summary

From the beginning, the American federal system has experienced disagreements regarding the powers and responsibilities of the national government and the states. While the Constitution provides relatively clear guidance in resolving some of these disagreements, a number of important constitutional provisions are very vague and have themselves been sources of disagreement. The Supreme Court has often tried to resolve disputes, sometimes successfully, but critics charge that the Court may be biased because it is part of the national government.

From time to time various states have also tried to be the ultimate arbiters in national-state disagreements. Critics of these efforts contend that they are based on an inaccurate theory of the American federal system. Moreover, state officials can hardly be more objective regarding controversies in which they are involved than can the Supreme Court.

The public also becomes involved in disputes regarding national and state prerogatives. Public involvement is consistent with democratic principles but raises concerns over the sometimes unstable and contradictory nature of public attitudes.

State governments have been criticized for many years because state parties have often failed to be competitive, and legislatures have had too little time or expertise to cope with modern demands. Governors have often lacked the resources to be chief executives in fact as well as name. However, these problems are much less serious than they once were, and in many respects, most governments are now better equipped to deal with policy problems than ever before.

No issue has generated more intense conflict in national-state relations than the issue of civil rights. The historical record indicates the importance of the scope of conflict: when the issue was left to the states, groups that are now protected often had very few rights. Escalation of the scope of conflict to the national level led to greater protection of individual rights. The historical record also provides abundant evidence of the difficulties that the national government faces in changing the behavior of state and local officials. Problems still exist.

While national-state conflict has been an important feature of American federalism, cooperation has also been significant. Cooperation between national and state levels has helped to build much of the nation's highway system, fight crime, combat poverty, educate millions of people, and improve the nation's health. Cooperation is not automatic, however, and often requires negotiation, compromise, persuasion, and/or the use of inducements, as in the case of national-state grants.

CHAPTER 5

Interstate Relations

Officials in the state of Alabama discovered that residents of their state could receive, via satellite transmission, movies that were considered obscene by Alabama standards. The governor of Alabama asked the governor of New York to hand over four executives of the company involved in the movie transmissions for trial in Alabama. In a typical year, the governor of New York approves approximately four hundred extradition requests (Zimmerman 1992: 153). However, in this case the governor of New York refused (Peltason 1991: 147). The executives had apparently never been to Alabama, and the movies involved did not strike many New Yorkers as obscene.

While the study of federalism traditionally emphasized vertical relationships, particularly between national and state levels, scholars have come to recognize the importance of horizontal relationships, such as those between the states. While much work remains to be done, considerable advances in the study of interstate relations have taken place since the 1950s.

This chapter will examine the constitutional framework of interstate relations as well as the various ways in which states cooperate with one another. Some of the major causes of interstate conflict and the techniques for coping with that conflict will be explored. Interstate relations include the diffusion of policy innovations from one state to another. In addition, regional organizations have been used to attack problems which extend beyond individual states.

The Constitutional Framework

The U.S. Constitution provides some guidelines for the conduct of interstate relations, although the provisions are far from clear in several key

121

respects.[1] Not surprisingly, a number of major conflicts have resulted, and not all of them have been resolved effectively.

Privileges and Immunities

Article IV, Section 2 of the Constitution states: "The citizens of each state shall be entitled to all privileges and immunities of citizens in the several states." What does that mean? What are the privileges and immunities? How do we tell who is a citizen of which state? Are you entitled to the privileges and immunities when you are in your home state, visiting another state, or both? These questions have been sources of controversy for many years.

The federal courts have interpreted the privileges and immunities clause to mean that a state may not discriminate against nonresidents regarding fundamental rights. These rights evidently include access to the state for the purpose of making a living, access to the courts, and freedom from discriminatory taxation, as in the case of a tax that must be paid only by nonresidents.

The states may, however, treat nonresidents differently in a number of respects. Nonresident college students may have to pay higher tuition to attend state universities. Hunting and fishing licenses may be more expensive for nonresidents. These differences are often defended on the grounds that residents pay taxes to support these programs, and nonresidents, who have not paid these taxes, should have to pay special fees for certain services. In addition, a state may require a professional who is licensed to practice in another state to obtain a new license issued by his or her new state of residence.

Full Faith and Credit

Article IV, Section 1 of the Constitution provides that "Full Faith and Credit shall be given in each state in the public acts, records, and judicial proceedings of every other state." According to this provision, a legal proceeding that is conclusive in one state must be recognized by other states. If, for example, one man sues another in state court and is awarded damages, the defendant might move to another state and refuse to pay. The plaintiff may take the court decree that was originally issued to the new state where the defendant now resides. The court in the second state would examine the court decree from the first state and, if the decree were found to be authentic, a new enforcement decree

---

1. This section relies heavily on Peltason (1991: 142–48) and Pritchett (1977: 70–79).

would be issued. The plaintiff would not, therefore, have to argue the entire case all over again.

The Full Faith and Credit Clause has not always functioned effectively, particularly in the area of family law. Consider, for example, a divorce case in which the husband and wife lived in different states. If the case was heard in the husband's state without the wife being present, should the wife's state of residence grant full faith and credit to the divorce decree?

The Supreme Court faced this issue in the case of *Haddock v. Haddock* (1906) and responded with what must rank as one of the most peculiar decisions in the Court's history. The Court ruled that because Mrs. Haddock had not been notified of the suit nor represented at the proceeding, the divorce was not binding in her home state of New York. However, the court also ruled that states have the power to regulate their residents' marital status. Therefore, Mr. Haddock's divorce was valid in his state of residence, Connecticut. To quote Pritchett (1977: 74):

> The result of this holding was that the Haddocks, when both were in Connecticut, were divorced; when both were in New York, were married; and when the husband was in Connecticut and the wife in New York, he was legally single and she was still married (to him).

In short, the Haddocks could not determine their marital status without a road map. Moreover, other states were put in a position where they could not simultaneously grant full faith and credit to New York's position (that the Haddocks were still married) and Connecticut's position (that the Haddocks were divorced).

While the Haddock decision could have produced extraordinary confusion, its impact was limited by the tendency for states to recognize one another's divorce decrees voluntarily. However, under the doctrine of the *divisible divorce,* a state may recognize the part of the divorce decree that terminates the marriage without recognizing portions of the decree that deal with property settlements, child custody, alimony, and child support. Consequently, states have often been reluctant to enforce one another's decisions in these areas. Later in this chapter we will discuss efforts to remedy this situation.

Interstate Rendition

Although the Full Faith and Credit provision does not apply to criminal laws, the Constitution provides that fugitives from justice who flee from one state to another shall be returned to the state that has jurisdiction over the crime. This process is rendition—although it is sometimes called extradition. While the provision is clear enough, and was reinforced by an act of Congress in 1793, neither the rendition clause nor the legislation contains any enforcement mechanism. As a result, for many years the Supreme Court held that governors had a constitutional duty to hand over fugitives from other states, but the federal courts had no authority to enforce that obligation. Governors occasionally declined to return fugitives to other states, as in the case of the pornographic satellite transmissions. In 1987 the Supreme Court revised its position and held that the federal courts do have authority to require gubernatorial compliance. Several factors strongly limit the inclinations of governors to refuse very often, however.

No governor wants to give his or her state the reputation of being a haven for criminals. The result could be a massive influx of lawbreakers. In addition, a governor who refuses to return a fugitive today may be seeking the return of a local criminal tomorrow; by refusing, he or she risks losing the cooperation of officials in other states (on both points, see Glendening and Reeves 1984: 298). Also, governors want lawbreakers brought to justice regardless of where the offense occurred. Finally, few governors want to develop a reputation for being soft on crime, a reputation that would provide ammunition for political opponents. On balance, the incentives strongly favor returning fugitives in all but the most exceptional circumstances.

The rendition clause was supplemented in 1934 by congressional legislation that made crossing a state line to avoid prosecution or confinement a federal crime. The law provides that fugitives apprehended should be tried in the federal court district in which the original crime was committed, a practice that makes them readily available to the state officials concerned about the original offense. In most cases the law is a clear example of cooperative federalism: a national policy that helps state officials enforce state laws.

Interstate Travel

While the Constitution does not explicitly mention a right to travel, the courts have held that it can be inferred from a variety of provisions in the Constitution. The ability of the national government to fill offices and raise an army, the conduct of interstate commerce, and citizens' right to petition government all imply a right to travel. Policies that limit citizens' ability to travel could seriously hamper any of those activities.

Based on the principle of the right to travel, the Supreme Court struck down state laws that required a year of residence before an individual became eligible for welfare (*Shapiro v. Thompson,* 1969), eligible to vote (*Dunn v. Blumstein,* 1972), or eligible for free medical care for the poor (*Memorial Hospital v. Maricopa County*, 1974). Collectively these decisions make it easier for mobile citizens to participate in the selection of public officials and reduce the risk of people being left outside the social "safety net" simply because they move to another state.

Interstate Compacts

The Constitution provides for compacts, or agreements, between or among states, although the provision is a somewhat backhanded one. Article I, Section 10 provides that "No state shall, without the consent of Congress . . . enter into any agreement or compact with another state. . . ." The provision, while emphasizing the restriction on states, provides the basis for states to enter into legally binding agreements with one another. We will examine the use of compacts in detail in the next section.

The requirement for congressional consent is not very precise, and the courts have been called upon to interpret it on a number of occasions. Congressional approval may be given in advance or after the compact has been approved by the states. In addition, explicit congressional approval is apparently required only for compacts that would increase state power relative to the national government. For other compacts, a lack of objection from Congress is generally regarded as consent.

Cooperation and Conflict among the States

Interstate Cooperation

One facet of cooperative federalism is the interrelations of the states. While cooperation is far from universal, state officials often find themselves working with their counterparts in other states. Cooperation can take a great many forms and is encouraged (or discouraged) by a number of forces.

Much interstate cooperation is informal, as in the case of a state official who calls a colleague in a neighboring state for advice on how to deal with a policy problem. A state administrator might also consult a published source, such as the *Book of the States*, to determine how his or her state compares with other states in policy areas like education or consumer protection. Neighboring states often serve as a reference group, providing guidance as to what constitutes a reasonable or adequate response to a problem or issue (Sharkansky 1970; Walker 1969).

Informal cooperation also takes place when state officials exchange information regarding future activities that might affect each other's states. A major highway repair program in one state may alter traffic flows in other states, and prior consultation will enable them to prepare.

A governor from a farm state may visit several foreign countries in hopes of finding new markets for the state's products, and other governors may find the information gained to be useful in planning similar efforts in the future.

One other important type of informal cooperation occurs when state officials band together to exert leverage on the national government. A single state, acting alone, has only limited prospects for pushing a major policy change through to enactment by the national government. A great many states, acting together, can exert considerably more influence.

Informal cooperation has its limitations, however. Without a formal agreement, conflict may erupt over the exact nature of the agreement. Misunderstandings may occur, with each side feeling misled or betrayed. An informal agreement may be terminated when a governor leaves office or a department head is replaced. Moreover, no binding commitment is created. A change of heart by one of the participants may terminate the agreement. For many situations, then, a more formal agreement is desirable. Two of the more important types of formal cooperation are interstate compacts and uniform state laws.

Interstate Compacts: Changing Patterns

As noted earlier, the Constitution provides for the states to enter into legally binding compacts with each other. For much of our nation's history—prior to 1920, at least—compacts were not heavily used and were largely confined to resolving boundary disputes between pairs of states (*Interstate Compacts, 1783–1977* 1977: vii). Because of this limited focus, compacts were enacted on an average of about one every four years. Since that time, however, some major changes in the use of compacts have occurred.

First, compacts have been adopted to cover a much broader range of policy issues, including conservation, law enforcement, health, education, parks, and water (*Interstate Compacts, 1783–1977* 1977: vii; Nice 1987b). The Interstate Compact on Placement of Children, for example, established mechanisms to regulate placement of children across state lines. A number of regional compacts have been established to help prevent and combat forest fires. The Compact on Mental Health was established to provide care for the mentally retarded and to develop a framework for other agreements in the mental health field. Compacts are now used to resolve disputes, study problems, coordinate regulatory policies, and provide services to the public (Zimmerman 1992: 142–45). There are few areas of state responsibility that have not been touched, at least in a limited way, by the compact.

A second major change in the use of compacts, reflecting in part the broader range of subjects covered, has been an increase in the adoption of compacts (*Interstate Compacts, 1783–1977* 1977: vii; Welch and Clarke 1973: 478). Enactment of compacts peaked in the late 1950s and 1960s when they were being adopted at a rate of over four each year, although the pace of adoption slowed to about two per year in the 1970s (Glendening and Reeves 1984: 281; Welch and Clark 1973: 478). Even that decline left the rate of adoption higher than during the pre-1940 era.

A third change in the use of compacts, particularly since World War II, is the increasing use of multi-state compacts. Recall that the early compacts typically involved only two states, a circumstance related to the early emphasis on boundary disputes. With the increasing range of subjects covered by compacts, more of them address issues of regional or even nationwide concern. As a result, many compacts now invite the states in a region, states with some common interest, or even all fifty states to participate (*Interstate Compacts, 1783–1977* 1977; Welch and Clarke 1973). This broader range of participation in turn increases the range of subjects that compacts may address.

A fourth change in the use of compacts in recent years is the limited number of compacts that the national government is invited to join (*Interstate Compacts, 1783–1977* 1977). National/state compacts can create some special problems, particularly involving national and state sensitivities regarding each level's powers. However, the combination of national and state participation has promise for both coordinating the activities of the two levels and improving communication.

Interstate compacts can provide a clear, legally binding agreement that can endure despite turnover in office and changes of mind. Should later disputes arise over the nature of the agreement, an official document can provide clarification, and the courts can give a definitive answer if necessary.

Uniform State Laws

One of the virtues of federalism is its ability to provide different policies to accommodate the different needs or preferences of various parts of the country. Unfortunately, the variations in state laws create substantial headaches for the legal profession, which must cope with a variety of conflicting precedents and rulings in different states (Fite 1932: 124). Businesses that operate in several states are similarly burdened by the variations in state laws. Keeping track of what practices are forbidden, allowed, or required, and in which states, can be a difficult task.

In response to these problems, the National Conference of Commissioners on Uniform State Laws was founded in 1892. The conference, which is closely linked to the legal profession (*Handbook of the National*

Conference 1979: 252), draws up model legislation on selected subjects for which greater uniformity would be beneficial. Recognizing that its proposed legislation must be acceptable to a great variety of states—rich, poor, liberal and conservative—the conference seeks to avoid subjects that are too controversial (*Handbook of the National Conference* 1979: 288; Macmahon 1972: 147). To do otherwise would risk division in the conference and widespread rejection of its recommendations. Many of its proposed laws have been widely adopted.

Influences on Cooperation

Interstate cooperation is influenced by a variety of factors, not all of which have been extensively studied. The growth of interstate cooperation during this century is associated with the emergence of cooperative federalism as a model of federalism, although determining which one caused the other is difficult at best. Certainly cooperative federalism, with its emphasis on governments working together to solve problems, is consistent with interstate cooperation.

Interstate cooperation has been stimulated by the emergence of problems that do not correspond to existing state boundaries (Glendening and Reeves 1984: 274). Problems like pollution, crime, and economic forces cross jurisdictional lines. When problems go beyond an individual state, cooperative action may be needed to deal with them. The tendency for states that trade with one another to join compacts together is consistent with this argument, as is the tendency for states whose major cities or capitals are close to their counterparts in other states to join compacts (Nice 1987b; Welch and Clarke 1973: 482). Shared concerns can stimulate cooperative action.

Interstate cooperation can also reflect general orientations toward government action. Research on state adoption of uniform state laws and participation in interstate compacts involving all fifty states revealed that cooperative states tend to have liberal political parties, more capable legislatures, more professionalized legal systems, and higher state-local taxes relative to state income (Nice 1984a). Cooperative states, in other words, have parties that support government action, have government institutions that are capable of tackling problems, and make substantial efforts to raise revenue adequate to address problems. Ideology is particularly important in shaping state decisions regarding compacts for social programs such as health care (Nice 1987b).

These findings indicate a basic problem facing individuals who believe interstate cooperation can be an alternative to national government involvement (Barton 1967: 165–66; Graves 1934: 289; Leach and Sugg 1969: 60). The states that are most opposed to national government action (that is, the states with conservative parties) and least suited to handling major problems on their own (those with weak state institutions and low revenue effort) are also least likely to participate in cooperative actions with all the other states! The pattern is consistent with Schattschneider's (1960) concept of the scope of conflict: those states are opposed to government action at any level, whether state, interstate, or national.

Cooperative activity by one state is also encouraged by the presence of cooperative neighbors (Nice 1984a). In part this reflects the fact that state officials often look to neighboring states for guidance in dealing with issues. In addition, trying to negotiate with uncooperative or adversarial neighbors is likely to discourage further attempts at cooperation.

Interstate cooperation is discouraged in some instances by fears that a state may lose its independence and become hamstrung by a host of commitments to other states (Leach and Sugg 1969: 213; Ridgeway 1971: 298–99). Once commitments are made, they are not easily ended. People who benefit from the cooperative arrangement are likely to react strongly if a state tries to withdraw.

Interstate cooperation is also discouraged by fears that it may create new centers of power that are relatively isolated from public control (Ridgeway 1971: 299–300). Some interstate compacts create new agencies with powers to plan, advise, or even carry out programs. The agencies are often run by people appointed by the various state governments belonging to the compact. The public has, therefore, only indirect and often poorly defined influence over the decision makers in the compact agency.

Cooperation is not, consequently, an automatic process. A variety of factors may encourage state officials to cooperate with officials in other states, but other considerations may, at times, discourage cooperation. When officials believe that the benefits of cooperation will probably outweigh the costs, cooperation is likely to occur. The historical record indicates that cooperation has not always been the case.

Interstate Competition and Conflict

Relationships among the states are not always particularly cordial. In fact, research reveals a substantial amount of competition and conflict among states, although the extent and intensity vary considerably. The sources of tension among states are about as diverse as the sources of political conflict generally, but several major sources should be noted.[2]

Competition for jobs, investment, and industry is a perennial source

2. This section relies heavily on Berkeley and Fox (1978: 27–29); Glendening and Reeves (1984: 269–71); and Hamilton et. al (1937: 37–38).

of conflict among states. Economic growth provides more revenue to support state and local government services, and the governor who succeeds in attracting a large industrial or commercial facility to the state may gain favorable publicity. State officials may find themselves involved in bidding wars with one another, the winner offering the most attractive inducements to a particular firm.

Economic differences can sometimes cause tensions among states. Rising energy prices are a boon to the economies of energy-producing states but a drain on the economies of energy-importing states. States with slowly growing or stagnant economies may regard prosperous states with more than a little envy. A state with higher welfare benefits may attract people from neighboring states that provide lower benefits (Peterson and Rom 1989). States that tax products like minerals or manufactured goods, which are exported to other states, may anger importing states.

Inadequate communication is sometimes a source of interstate conflict, although its overall importance is difficult to assess. Officials in one state may make a decision that affects other states as well as their own. Consultation with officials in those other states could enable them to prepare for the effects or produce program modifications to reduce the effects. Inadequate communications may leave states caught unprepared, reducing the likelihood of their making program modifications before problems develop.

Assessing the significance of inadequate communication as a source of interstate conflict is difficult because state officials may not communicate with officials in other states precisely because a negative response is likely. If officials in South Dakota are trying to persuade a large firm to leave Nebraska, consulting with Nebraska officials would enable them to prepare a counteroffer encouraging the firm to stay. Acting before consulting gives the opposition less opportunity to mobilize.

Spillover effects are another common source of interstate conflict. A state that permits the dumping of pollutants into rivers may draw the wrath of states downstream. A state which allows pollutants to be released into the air will anger states located downwind. A state may be reluctant to sacrifice resources to remedy a situation when the negative effects are largely felt by other states. The affected states are often unwilling or unable to contribute resources to help solve a problem that originated in another state's jurisdiction.

Interstate conflicts may arise because states are affected by a policy in different ways. Abolition of slavery obviously had a different effect in slave states than it did in free states. More recently, national public lands policies have sparked tensions between western states (the tier of states from Montana to New Mexico and those farther west), where national landholdings are extensive, and eastern states, where relatively little land is nationally owned. The western states are much more directly affected by national land policies and have expressed resentment over policies made by "easterners." Interstate disputes of this type often involve the national government as well.

Another source of interstate conflict is drawn from local political considerations. A governor may embark on a highly-publicized "feud" with the governor of a neighboring state as a method for gaining publicity and the image of a staunch defender of state interests. When the governors of North Dakota and Minnesota battled over issues of attracting jobs and state pride, they both received substantial news coverage, much of it favorable (at least within each governor's home state). The feud may also be a way to divert public attention from internal state problems.[3] Unfortunately, what begins as a public relations device may escalate into a genuine conflict, with positive communications being cut off and opportunities for reaching agreement lost.

A final major source of interstate conflict, primarily of historical interest but still occasionally important, is boundary disputes. Early in American history, conflicting and ambiguous land grants, combined with primitive surveying techniques, created a number of controversies over which states had title to various parcels of ground. Other disputes arose, and continue to arise, because of boundaries based on natural features, particularly rivers, which were later altered by natural or artificial means. If the boundary between two states is a river, and the river changes course to a channel a mile east of the old channel, to which states does the land between the old and new channels belong? If the land is valuable, each state will probably have a different answer to this question.

The consequences of interstate conflict are about as diverse as the causes, but several significant effects deserve mention. First, conflict among states reduces their ability to deal with policy problems on their own. Competition for jobs and industry made the states reluctant to move strongly to reduce pollution (Jones 1976: 400–402), since each state's officials feared that strict antipollution laws in their state would cause jobs and industry to flow to more lenient states. In a similar manner, state antipoverty programs are limited by the fear that efforts to redistribute income will drive away affluent citizens—a fear that appears well-founded (Althaus and Schachter 1983). If the states are unable to deal

---

3. Cross-national research indicates that nations that have internal turmoil are more likely to become involved in international conflicts, which suggests that national policymakers use international conflicts to divert attention from internal problems. See Vincent (1981).

with a problem, people who want something done about it are likely to turn to some other level for a solution (Schattschneider 1960).

A second effect of interstate conflict is a reduction of the state's influence in intergovernmental lobbying. When states are busy fighting among themselves, they will be unable to present a united front before either Congress or the president. Either the states will choose to remain on the sidelines or they will publicly display their inability to agree on a common position.

Bear in mind that conflict is not necessarily a bad thing. When genuine differences of opinion exist, a public airing of them can be healthy.[4] The validity of each side's case can be examined, and different viewpoints can be compared. Clearing the air can sometimes help produce a solution to the conflict.

Coping with Interstate Conflict

A number of methods are used to deal with interstate conflict.[5] The advantages and disadvantages of each approach depend somewhat on the nature of the dispute and the inclinations of the parties to the dispute. A common method is some version of diplomacy. In its less formal versions, state officials may exchange letters or phone calls or meet face-to-face in order to resolve their differences. In personal discussions, officials can exchange information, clarify misunderstandings, and better understand one another's points of view. However, informal diplomacy does not produce a binding agreement, and subsequent conflicts may erupt over precisely what was agreed to in informal meetings. When those officials leave office, the informal agreement may be moot.

More formal diplomacy takes the form of interstate compacts, which are analogous to treaties in the international arena. Compacts produce a binding agreement that can endure beyond the current group of officials. As noted earlier, agreement is not always easily achieved, a circumstance that greatly limits the utility of compacts for controversial policy issues. Also, if agreements are not kept, the matter often goes to court, resulting in heightened tensions and further decay in cooperation.

If states are unable to resolve a dispute on their own, either formally or informally, they may turn to an outside source for assistance. People

---

4. Much of the early work examining the positive aspects of conflict is attributed to Mary Parker Follett (1924) in *Creative Experience*. She suggests a variety of approaches to handling conflict. Many contemporary theorists have since elaborated. See Cozer (1964); Fisher and Ury ([1981] 1983); Schaller (1966); and Thomas (1979).

5. See Glendening and Reeves (1984: 271–73); Pritchett (1977: 79–81); and Zimmerman (1992: 136–39).

affected by the problem may seek action by another level or branch of government. Congress may be able to enact legislation to help reduce or resolve interstate conflicts or address issues with which states cannot cope on their own. For example, the states' inability to deal with pollution control ultimately led to congressional action (Jones 1976).

Controversies among states may also be resolved in court. Disputes between states are part of the original jurisdiction of the Supreme Court. The Court has sometimes declined to hear cases deemed insufficiently important and has sometimes encouraged states to resolve their differences by diplomacy rather than litigation. The Court has held that the dispute must be between states and not simply between one state and a limited number of citizens in another state.

If the Supreme Court accepts a case involving an interstate dispute, what laws can be used to produce a decision? Relatively little legislation regarding interstate relations has been adopted. Consequently, the Court may consider relevant international, national, or state laws, as well as precedents established by decisions reached in previous interstate cases.

If the Supreme Court renders a decision on an interstate dispute, a final problem may arise: a state may decide to ignore or disobey the ruling. As Hamilton et al. (1937: 504) noted, the Court, having neither the sword nor the purse, is particularly vulnerable to this problem. When a state refuses to abide by a Supreme Court decision, three possible courses of action are available. First, Congress may enact legislation to encourage compliance or defuse the issue. Second, further litigation may follow. Probably the all-time recordholder in this regard is the dispute between Virginia and West Virginia over debts incurred before the two states were separated. The wrangling began in 1865, and after protracted negotiations, the issues were repeatedly taken to the Supreme Court, with West Virginia repeatedly refusing to abide by the Court's rulings. The dispute was not resolved until 1919, when West Virginia finally agreed to pay its share of the debt. Third, state resistance to a Court ruling may open the way to further negotiations, with state officials seeking to come to a settlement acceptable to all sides.

While turning to Congress or the Supreme Court can produce a relatively binding settlement even when states cannot agree on a solution among themselves, these strategies carry an element of risk. The states may lose control of the decision-making process, with the result that the final settlement may not please any of the states involved in the dispute. A variety of proposals have been adopted to address interstate conflict. In the first of the two case studies in this chapter, national action was eventually sought by states to address conflict over inheritance taxes. In the next case study, national action to address the collection of interstate child support is not yet in place beyond the creation of the Office

Table 5.1: Effect of National Tax Credit

	State A: State Has Inheritance Tax	State B: State Has No Inheritance Tax
Gross National Tax	$100	$100
State Tax	80	0
Net National Tax (a − b)	20	100
Total Tax Paid (b + c)	$100	$100

of Child Support Enforcement. Advocates of increased national involvement in child support collection call for remedies through the Internal Revenue Service; however, the states are working jointly to address the situation without further national involvement.

Case Study: Interstate Conflict over Inheritance Taxes

In 1924, all but three of the states had adopted some form of inheritance or estate tax.[6] Yield from the tax was modest but far from trivial (about 8 percent of state tax revenue). In the fall of 1924, Florida adopted a constitutional amendment banning inheritance taxes as well as income taxes. Florida officials hoped that this maneuver would encourage wealthy people to leave other states and come to Florida.

Officials in other states feared that their wealthy residents would leave, with the result that their tax bases would wither as Florida's grew. Other states began to consider the need to imitate Florida's action in order to prevent the exodus of prosperous citizens, and Nevada actually passed a similar amendment. State officials were therefore put in the awkward position of believing that inheritance taxes were reasonable and desirable in principle, but unworkable in practice because of the behavior of other states.

Because the states were unable to resolve the inheritance tax dispute among themselves, state officials turned to the national government for assistance. The national government in turn adopted a national inheritance tax credit for any state inheritance taxes paid, up to a maximum of 80 percent of the national inheritance tax. That is, for every dollar paid in state inheritance tax, the taxpayer's national tax liability would be reduced by one dollar up to the limit of 80 percent of the national tax (table 5.1). The effect of the national tax credit was to guarantee that a citizen in any state would have to pay inheritance tax on a sufficiently

---

6. This discussion relies heavily on Maxwell and Aronson (1977: 128–31).

large inheritance. In a state with no inheritance tax of its own, the entire tax would go to the national government. If a state did have an inheritance tax, any state inheritance tax paid would reduce the taxpayer's national tax bill by the same amount (up to the 80 percent limit). Wealthy citizens could no longer avoid the inheritance tax by moving to Florida or Nevada. As a result of the national tax credit, panic in the state capitals subsided, and the budding movements to repeal inheritance taxes in other states faded.

The case of state inheritance taxes reveals the conflict which can erupt when states compete for scarce, desirable commodities, such as wealthy citizens. There are not enough wealthy citizens to give all the states abundant tax bases; consequently, some states occasionally try to benefit themselves at the expense of others. The conflicts that result are not easy for the states to resolve among themselves.

This case also reveals that national government involvement does not always occur at the expense of the states. In this instance, national intervention served to protect programs found in almost all the states. The states could not, by themselves, safely do what state officials generally wanted to do. They were able to act as they thought most appropriate only with the assistance of the national government.

The Diffusion of Innovations

One of the major advantages of federalism, as noted in chapter 1, is its ability to provide a variety of arenas in which different policies can be tested on a limited scale.[7] As a result, federalism encourages policy innovation, a tendency that is reinforced in some cases by competition among states. Once a state develops a good program, officials in other states may feel compelled to copy it rather than face complaints from citizens who are angry because they do not receive some benefit enjoyed by residents of other states. Research on policy innovation in the states naturally focuses on two questions: (1) what kinds of states are likely to try new programs first, rather than waiting until most other states have tried them? and (2) how do new ideas spread from one state to another?

In groundbreaking analysis of policy innovation, Jack Walker (1969; 1971) studied the speed with which states adopted eighty-eight different programs in a variety of policy areas ranging from welfare and conservation to highways and taxation. Walker found that some states were usually among the first to try new things, while others tended to proceed more slowly and cautiously (table 5.2). New York, Massachusetts, and Califor-

---

7. Much of the material in this section is from Walker (1969; 1971); Savage (1978); and Nice (1994).

Table 5.2: Innovation Scores for the American States

New York	.66	Kansas	.43
Massachusetts	.63	Nebraska	.42
California	.60	Kentucky	.42
New Jersey	.58	Vermont	.41
Michigan	.58	Iowa	.41
Connecticut	.57	Alabama	.41
Pennsylvania	.56	Florida	.40
Oregon	.54	Arkansas	.39
Colorado	.54	Idaho	.39
Wisconsin	.53	Tennessee	.39
Ohio	.53	West Virginia	.39
Minnesota	.52	Arizona	.38
Illinois	.52	Georgia	.38
Washington	.51	Montana	.38
Rhode Island	.50	Missouri	.38
Maryland	.48	Delaware	.38
New Hampshire	.48	New Mexico	.38
Indiana	.46	Oklahoma	.37
Louisiana	.46	South Dakota	.36
Maine	.46	Texas	.36
Virginia	.45	South Carolina	.35
Utah	.45	Wyoming	.35
North Dakota	.44	Nevada	.32
North Carolina	.43	Mississippi	.30

Source: Walker, Jack. 1969. "The Diffusion of Innovations Among the American States." *American Political Science Review* 63: 883. High score indicates state is quick to adopt new programs.

nia were typically quick to adopt new programs, but Wyoming, Nevada, and Mississippi were usually slow. Why should that be the case?

First of all, innovative states tend to be relatively wealthy. Officials in a state that is hard-pressed to pay for current programs may be reluctant to tackle additional responsibilities. New programs may require new, highly trained personnel, as well as additional equipment, all of which can be quite expensive. Trying something new also involves an element of risk. Substantial resources may be committed to a project that is ultimately unsuccessful. Policymakers in poor states may hesitate to devote scarce resources to a program until it has been tried in quite a few states. At that point the risks may seem less formidable and the usual problems with implementing new programs will have been resolved.

Second, innovative states tend to have large populations. With large populations come a wide variety of demands, which may stimulate officials to develop new programs. At the same time, larger populations can support larger state bureaucracies, which permit greater specialization and expertise. Consequently, they are more likely to have information on new programs and the skills needed to implement them.

Walker's analysis also revealed that urbanized and industrialized states are generally quicker to adopt new programs. Urbanization and industrialization both bring about interdependence. Neighbors living close together affect one another's lives. Industrial society brings conflict between labor and management, seller and buyer, producer and consumer. Government is pressed to provide solutions in this environment. In a related vein, Walker found that states with legislatures that gave urban areas fair representation were quick to adopt new programs. If urban areas are a source of demands for change, legislatures that give them fair representation should be more responsive to those demands.

Bear in mind that Walker's analysis deals with state responses to new programs *on the average*. Individual states may not behave as expected on every program (Gray 1973). Mississippi, which is generally slow to adopt new programs, was the first state to adopt a general sales tax (Walker 1969: 883). When a state faces a major crisis, it may adopt a new program in order to cope with the crisis, regardless of whether the state is usually a pioneer in developing new policies. In other cases a new program may gain quick adoption because it is politically popular, even if the state is usually slow to enact new policies (Nice 1994). The general pattern, then, is subject to these occasional exceptions.

Once a new program has been tried, how does it spread to other states? Walker's analysis found that a group of national pioneers tends to share new ideas. The pioneering states, which are scattered across the country, look to one another for guidance. Other states, the non-pioneers, tend to look to the most innovative state or states in their respective regions for new ideas. Until the pioneer for a particular region adopts a new program, the regional followers are unlikely to adopt it.

Three noteworthy changes in the diffusion of innovations have occurred in this century. First, the length of time that innovations take to spread across the country has declined noticeably (see table 5.3). In the late 1800s, an innovation took an average of fifty-two years from the time it was first adopted until the last state enacted it. By the mid-1900s, the time period had fallen to only twenty-six years. The big change appears to be among states that are generally less innovative. While the time needed for the first twenty adoptions has declined somewhat, this decline is much less dramatic than the time needed for the remaining adoptions.

A second change in the diffusion of innovations involves shifts in the ranks of the national leaders and followers. Some states that tended to be pioneers early in this century have grown more cautious in recent years, and some states that were slow to make changes in years gone by have recently become more innovative (Savage 1978). The shifts reflect a variety of factors. In some cases an era of innovation leads to an accumulation of commitments and expenses that make further innovation diffi-

Table 5.3: Average Time for Diffusion of Innovations (in years)

Time Period	All Adoptions	First 20 Adoptions
1870–1899	52	23
1900–1929	40	20
1930–1966	26	18

Source: Walker, Jack. 1969. "The Diffusion of Innovations Among the American States." *American Political Science Review* 63: 895.

cult. Conversely, a state that is slow to do new things for a number of years may gradually accumulate so much pressure for change that a burst of creativity follows. In other cases changes in the nature of public problems, shifts in the state economy, or changes in the skill levels of state officials may increase or decrease a state's inclination to try new programs.

A third change in the diffusion of innovations involves a blurring (but not elimination) of regional patterns. While regional clusterings do persist, they have grown less distinctive in recent years, a finding that suggests that state officials are somewhat more likely to look beyond their respective regions for solutions to problems. A primary reason for this is the increasing professionalization of state officials.

The increasing speed with which innovations spread across the country and the blurring of regional patterns are both the result of two developments in the federal system. The first development is the increasing professionalization of state employees, a trend that increases their ability to discover and implement new programs and reduces their dependence on neighboring states for ideas. For example, there were only five national associations of state officials prior to 1900; by 1986, there were one hundred associations of state and/or local officials (Walker 1969: 894–95; Penne and Verduin 1986). Among other activities, these associations spread information on methods for dealing with policy problems. Professional meetings, newsletters, and journals all serve as sources of ideas for state administrators. Higher levels of education among state administrators and the increasing mobility of administrators from state to state also indicate increasing professionalization (Wright 1982: 246, 342). The more professionalized administrator is likely to learn of new programs more quickly and is less dependent on regional leaders for information about these new programs.

Second, the federal grant system has often served to stimulate innovation, not only by subsidizing activities but also by requiring actions as a condition for receiving grant money (Welch and Thompson 1980). Some communities that already tend to innovate may view the grants as a way to provide routine services, freeing funds for innovation in other areas. Grants may not stimulate innovation as much as subsidize localities that already tend to innovate and are looking for creative resources.[8]

Research on innovation in state politics confirms that the states are indeed sources of new ideas and provide arenas where programs can be tried on a limited scale and with limited cost. In this respect federalism is beneficial. At the same time the research indicates that new ideas can take a considerable amount of time to spread from state to state. Notice that even with the acceleration in the diffusion process since the 1800s, the average innovation during the mid-1900s still took about a quarter of a century to be adopted by all states. To someone who is seriously concerned about a major problem, twenty-five years can be a long time to wait for a solution.

Case Study: Enforcing Child Support across State Lines

Between 1949 and 1984 the proportion of households headed by women more than doubled. Most families headed by women have below-average incomes.[9] Many of these households fall below the poverty line. A particularly alarming result is that the number of children in these households (and therefore exposed to poverty) has increased dramatically.

Several factors have contributed to this situation. Divorce rates have risen and children are usually placed with their mother. Divorced mothers find that their career opportunities are limited in some cases by child care duties, job discrimination, and a lack of either job skills or work experience. Both parents in many two-parent families must work

8. Jondrow and Levy (1984: 174–78) and Zampelli (1986: 33–40) applied Martin McGuire's perceptions on fungibility (1978: 25–44) to local government. Jondrow and Levy found that grants may replace local funding on a short term and on a permanent basis and in fact the government units they studied reduced local spending by as much as two-thirds. Zampelli discovered that local governments found a variety of creative ways to attain the grants and to reduce local funding of the project subsidized by the grant. Obviously, policies established by the Reagan and Bush administrations to curtail the grant programs would have had some effect on these actions, but local government innovation also appears to extend to budget and funding techniques.

9. Data on gender and income distribution is available through the U.S. Bureau of the Census, *Historical Statistics of the United States* and *Current Population Reports* as used in *Dollars and Dreams: The Changing American Income Distribution* by Frank Levy (1988). Statistics and conclusions relating to child support enforcement are available from a variety of sources. The bulk of the data for this section is available from the United States General Accounting Office and a series of reports on interstate child support from 1989 to 1992.

to make ends meet and the mother who must try to provide for her children without help faces a daunting task.

To reduce the danger that divorce will throw children into poverty, most states have laws requiring nonresident parents to provide for their offspring. The legal system often enforces these laws by requiring the nonresident parent (usually the father) to provide financial support to the household in which the children reside. States try to monitor and enforce compliance through a variety of mechanisms but efforts have often been unsuccessful when the divorced parents live in different states. In 1975, Congress created the Office of Child Support Enforcement (OCSE) to administer the Child Support Enforcement Program. The program was developed to assist state efforts to ensure compliance with support orders. Efforts to insure compliance usually involve cooperation between local enforcement agencies, courts, and state-level agencies.

The growing proportion of interstate child support cases compounds the already complicated mesh of regulation and cooperative programs. According to the OCSE ". . . up to 30 percent of all child support cases involve a custodial parent and child living in a different state than the absent parent" (*Interstate Child Support: Need for Absent Parent Information* 1990: 2). With interstate cases, compliance enforcement also requires state-to-state cooperation between agencies in addition to the varying agency levels within each state. Concerns raised about the difficulty of obtaining regular child support when the absent parent is out of state prompted more legislation designed to facilitate cooperation between states.

A number of issues hinder interstate support enforcement. First, obtaining information about the nonresident parent is often difficult. Officials may need to search through a variety of records in different locations, an effort that may be hampered by a lack of computerization and by laws governing access to certain types of records. The process becomes even more complicated when two or more states are involved, each with different procedures and regulations. Second, even if accurate information is eventually obtained, one of the most effective enforcement mechanisms, interstate withholding of wages, is fraught with obstacles. Wage withholding within a state is fairly uncomplicated, but because states have many different withholding procedures, the interstate process is slow (*Interstate Child Support: Wage Withholding Not Fulfilling Expectation* 1992: 3). Enforcing withholding is also complicated by differing state laws, court interpretations and local employment practices.

Although federal law theoretically governs the interstate enforcement procedures, the process for acquiring information and enforcing decrees is neither uniform nor efficient and as a result is not effective. The proportion of child support awards is approximately the same for intrastate and interstate cases. Unfortunately, families receive substantially less support when the case is interstate (*Interstate Child Support: Mothers Receiving Less Support,* January 1992: 15).

Interstate child support enforcement illustrates several challenges to an intergovernmental relations model of government. Although the federal government may develop a national policy, states have a great deal of individual flexibility to implement their own policy objectives. Because states develop programs to fulfill the needs of the residents within their states, administrators may have little incentive to mesh programs with those of other states. However, very positive examples of cooperation and innovation do exist—some states have developed joint approaches to enforcement and collection of support orders. Interstate enforcement of some court decrees like child support, though governed by Article IV, are also difficult given the differences between state laws. Finally, legislation that attempts to enforce parental responsibility is always challenging because of the diversity of human values and behaviors at issue. Structures of belief will vary between localities and states, and the objectives and priorities of legislation like the Child Support Enforcement Program are subject to a multitude of interpretations by states and local officials.

Regional Organizations

Most state boundaries were established prior to 1900, and social, economic, and technological changes since then have produced a variety of problems that cover two or more states. The existence of problems extending beyond individual states that are not nationwide in scope has led to pressures to create regional organizations that are large enough to cover the area affected by the problem, but not so large as to involve unaffected groups.[10] A regional organization may be able to cover the affected area without producing the excessive centralization that a completely national program might entail.

Many different regional organizations have been created over the years, with widely varying results. Many of the organizations have given the states a direct role, and others have been subject to indirect state influence. A brief overview of some examples will indicate the variety of approaches used and the problems that often face regional organizations.

The Tennessee Valley Authority

Probably the most important regional organization is the Tennessee Valley Authority, which was created by the national government during

10. A valuable overview of regional organizations is found in Derthick and Bombardier (1974).

the Great Depression (Selznick 1949; Derthick and Bombardier 1974: ch. 2). The TVA is a public corporation with responsibility for water projects, such as flood control and navigation improvements; power generation; and fertilizer manufacturing. Its proponents believed it would foster economic growth in the Tennessee River Valley, improve agricultural production and land use, and harness the sometimes unruly Tennessee River.

The TVA did not provide the states in the region with any official role in its operations, but in practice the states do influence TVA decisions in many cases. In part this occurs because the TVA was deliberately designed to be somewhat insulated from national government control. With its directors appointed to staggered, nine-year terms, its own personnel system, and its ability to keep and spend revenues from its projects, such as the sale of electricity, the TVA has considerable independence from the national government. In addition, from the beginning the TVA emphasized the "Grass Root Doctrine" (Selznick 1949), which involved consulting with state and local governments, private citizens, and interest groups in the Tennessee Valley. The doctrine was adopted largely because the TVA was so controversial when it was created. TVA officials believed that consulting state officials would reduce the risk of antagonizing them and might make them more supportive of the TVA and its programs. The combination of insulation from national control and the Grass Roots Doctrine made the TVA relatively sensitive to state and local concerns.

While many of the changes in the Tennessee Valley would have occurred without the TVA, the pace of change probably would have been slower (Derthick and Bombardier 1974: 41–42). By coordinating a variety of programs on a regional scale, the TVA fosters economic growth, flood control, and rural electrification. It is a record of accomplishment that few other regional organizations can match.

The Delaware River Basin Commission

The Delaware River Basin Commission is a very different type of regional organization (Derthick and Bombardier 1974: ch. 3; Lord and Kenney 1993). The commission is a compact of four states (Delaware, New Jersey, New York, and Pennsylvania) and the national government. It was created because of interstate conflicts over the use of water from the river and problems of flooding. Proponents believed that the commission could help resolve the conflicts and provide a coordinated program to develop and protect the river's water resources.

The commission has not accomplished as much as its advocates had hoped, in part because as a compact, it cannot proceed unless its members agree on a course of action. Moreover, the commission has no independent sources of revenue, which limits its ability to act decisively. Finally, national government agencies have often ignored the commission and proceeded with their activities without regard for commission recommendations. In recent years, the commission has included New York City in some of its negotiations, a development that raised some observers' hopes of greater progress in the future (Lord and Kenney 1993: 20–22).

Regional Commissions for Economic Development

Various regional commissions have been created to stimulate economic growth in different parts of the country (Derthick and Bombardier 1974: chs. 4 and 5). When John Kennedy sought the Democratic presidential nomination in 1960, many politicians felt that a Catholic could not win in predominantly Protestant states. To allay those fears, Kennedy campaigned heavily in West Virginia and won its presidential primary (Polsby and Wildavsky 1980: 85). While campaigning there, Kennedy was struck by the poverty of the Appalachian Region. With continued urging by governors in the area, Kennedy took a series of steps that resulted in the creation of the Appalachian Regional Commission in 1965.

The commission, which consists of a federal co-chair and state representatives, who elect a co-chair from their ranks, gained substantial control over federal aid to the Appalachian region. The commission has devoted considerable effort to lobbying for more federal benefits for Appalachia. The commission's activities have been directed toward bringing prosperity to a region that seems to remain poor regardless of the performance of the national economy.

One of the predictable features of federalism is that whenever some states receive a benefit, other states begin clamoring for it. The creation of the Appalachian Regional Commission to foster economic growth led to demands from other states for similar programs. The Title V Commissions were a response to those demands. While they resembled the Appalachian Regional Commission in some respects, there were some noteworthy differences (Derthick and Bombardier 1974: ch. 5). Like the Appalachian Regional Commission, each commission included a national co-chair and state representatives, one of whom would be selected to be the state co-chairperson. The Title V Commissions also developed plans to foster economic growth in their respective regions.

Unlike the ARC, however, the Title V Commissions did not gain much control over the federal grants to their areas. A very limited amount of federal funding was channeled through them, but the vast majority was not. Moreover, national agencies have paid little attention to the commissions' plans, and presidential support has been lukewarm at best. Because the commissions have little money to distribute to the states, state officials have had little interest as well.

Reflections on Regional Organizations

A major obstacle to the formation of regional organizations that are powerful enough to obtain satisfactory results is the suspicion of national officials. Presidents and members of Congress fear that the regional organizations will become lobbying groups for state and local governments, who will use these organizations to extract more resources from the national treasury. National departments and agencies, as well as presidents and Congress, fear that powerful regional organizations will reduce national control over whatever programs and activities are operated by the regional organizations (Derthick and Bombardier 1974). Both of these considerations may have spurred the Reagan administration's decision to end national participation in a number of regional organizations, including the Title V Commissions. While ending national participation was expected to be fatal for many regional organizations, a number have survived national withdrawal, albeit sometimes in a new form (McDowell 1983). Whether that survival will continue over the long term remains to be seen.

State officials are also wary of regional organizations. Some officials fear that the regional organizations will be instruments for increasing national control over the states or will subject one state to undue influence by the other participating states (Derthick and Bombardier 1974). State agencies may fear regional organizations that operate programs independently of similar state programs.

Marion Ridgeway's (1971) concerns regarding interstate compact agencies and accountability are also pertinent. If a regional organization is powerful enough to accomplish anything significant, how is that power to be made accountable to the public? A number of regional organizations are made up of representatives appointed by governors. The TVA's governing board has long overlapping terms and is appointed by the president. Popular control is, at best, indirect. The creation of a multiplicity of regional organizations gives the public even more units of government to monitor, a task that is already overwhelming for many people.

Summary

Relationships among states are an important aspect of intergovernmental relations. While the Constitution provides a partial framework for interstate relations, the limited number of constitutional provisions and the vagueness of those provisions give the states considerable latitude in dealing with one another.

Interstate cooperation, which is relatively common, takes many forms, ranging from informal discussions to interstate compacts and uniform state laws. Cooperation is enhanced by shared problems, positive orientations toward using government powers, and cooperative neighbors. However, concerns over excessive entanglement in interstate agreements, fears of creating uncontrollable centers of power, and the difficulty of reaching consensus often limit cooperation.

Disagreements among states arise from many sources. A state may take actions that adversely affect people in other states. States compete for new industries and investment, and actions that enhance the economic well-being of one state may have the opposite effect on other states. Conflicts may be resolved through negotiations, litigation, or national legislation, although some conflicts persist for long periods.

One of the traditional justifications for federalism is its ability to stimulate innovation. Many new programs have been developed by America's state governments, but the states vary considerably in the speed with which they adopt new programs. Innovative states generally tend to be wealthy, urbanized, industrialized, and large in terms of population, but even states that are usually slow to adopt new programs may become innovators at times, particularly in the face of a serious problem.

Because some policy problems have an impact on more than one state but are not nationwide, a number of regional organizations have been formed over the years in order to deal with these problems. Most regional organizations have a relatively limited record of accomplishment, in part because neither national officials nor state officials have had sufficient confidence in the regional organizations to trust them with substantial power, whether legal or financial.

CHAPTER 6

State-Local Relations

Most of the early discussions of federalism, such as *The Federalist* (Hamilton et al. 1937), paid little or no attention to local governments. Dual federalism recognized only the national and state levels of government. The U.S. Constitution does not even mention local governments, which were regarded as creatures of the states. Local governments are generally under the legal control of the states. However, municipalities, counties and special districts are still able to maintain a significant degree of autonomy and to play a major role in the federal system. Local officials often exert substantial political influence on the states; and state officials are not always willing to exercise their legal powers over local governments.

This chapter will examine the legal environment of local governments, an environment that is largely shaped by state decisions. Changes in the state and local shares of funding and personnel will be assessed. The causes of tensions between states and localities will be explored. Two key cases of state-local relations will be analyzed.

The Constitutional and Legal Setting

The legal context of state-local relations is complex and has many important implications for relations between the two levels. While provisions vary from state to state, some general themes exist.

Dillon's Rule

Because the U.S. Constitution makes no reference to local governments, and because state constitutions generally assume that local governments receive their authority from the state government rather than directly from the people, the legal framework of state-local relations is based largely on state policies. A general framework is provided by Dillon's Rule, a legal doctrine named for Justice John Dillon, one of its leading exponents.[1] Dillon's Rule limits local governments' authority to:

1. Powers that are explicitly granted to them;
2. Powers that are clearly implied by the explicitly granted powers; and
3. Powers that are essential to meeting the declared objectives and responsibilities of the local government.

If there is any significant doubt regarding whether a local government has authority to do something, then it does not have that authority.

One consequence of Dillon's Rule is that local governments may become embroiled in legal wrangling over whether they have authority to enact a policy (Adrian and Fine 1991: 82–83), a prospect that may discourage them from addressing a problem. Unless the local government has a clear grant of authority, there may be uncertainty over whether a particular program is permitted. While state and national governments also face legal challenges to their authority from time to time, Dillon's Rule makes challenges particularly effective at the local level.

Dillon's Rule also enhances the role of state government in local policy-making. If local officials do not have sufficient legal authority to deal with a problem, they may have to go to the governor and legislature for a grant of authority. That prospect is often very irksome to local officials, who resent having to ask the legislature's "permission." This situation may have political advantages for local officials, who may respond to conflicting demands of citizens by pointing out that the local government lacks the authority to make a decision. The difficult task of resolving the conflict is then transferred to the state government.

A final consequence of Dillon's Rule is the potential expansion of national and state power. If local officials cannot enact the policies that people want because the local government lacks authority, citizens may turn to state or national officials. The long-term result will be expansion of national and state power.

Charters

Municipal authority is drawn from a charter, a document that is analogous to a constitution at the national or state level. The fundamental

---

1. For discussions of Dillon's Rule, see Adrian and Fine (1991: 82–83); Marks and Cooper (1988: 193–98); and Zimmerman (1992: 166–69).

law of a city is its charter. The charter specifies the structure of city government, including what officials it will have, how they will be chosen, and what powers they will possess. The charter also indicates what programs a city may operate, and specifies city boundaries, along with a variety of other provisions. The states have used a variety of techniques for providing city charters.[2]

The *special act charter* approach, a relatively old-fashioned system of chartering, requires the state legislature to draft an individualized charter for each city. The special act approach provides a certain degree of flexibility: not all cities have the same needs or goals, which implies that a charter suitable for one city might not be suitable for another. A city charter can be drawn up to fit a community's particular needs.

The shortcomings of the special act charter, at least in the eyes of many local officials, stem from the fact that it is drafted and adopted by the legislature, not the city. As a result, a city that is out of favor with the state government may be saddled with a very restrictive charter permitting very little local decision making. Another city, on better terms with the state government, may receive much more favorable treatment. If changes such as grants of additional authority are needed at a later date, the city must go to the legislature and request revisions, which may or may not be forthcoming.[3] The special act approach maximizes state control over local government. Note, however, that in a state with many cities, the special act approach can also generate a large amount of work for the state legislature, which would face a continuous barrage of requests for charter revisions. This in turn risks embroiling state officials in many local controversies, leaving them less time for handling other state issues.

Partly as a reaction to problems with special act charters, some states began to use the *general act charter*. Under this system, one charter applies to all of the cities in the state. The state government is freed from some of the burdens of drafting individual charters. The problem of unequal treatment is reduced, since restrictions applied to one city apply to all.

Unfortunately, the general act charter provides little flexibility to accommodate the differing needs or preferences of individual cities.

2. See Adrian and Fine (1991: 84–97); Grant and Nixon (1982: 355–57); and Zimmerman (1992: 170–73).

3. Special legislation, which explicitly singles out a particular city, is now forbidden or restricted in many states, at least officially. However, many states continue to use techniques which resemble special legislation in practice (Marks and Cooper 1988: 111–22; Zimmerman 1992: 167). For example, a state may adopt a law applying to all cities with a million or more people; if the state has only one city of that size, the effect is very similar to special legislation.

Some may be saddled with responsibilities they do not need or cannot handle, while other cities may lack authority to deal with their special problems. All cities are forced into the same mold. The apparent even-handedness of the general act charter may be misleading. If the state's only charter is exactly what people in one city want, and very different from what people in another city want, then the result is hardly equally satisfying for the two communities.

The *classified charter* system seeks to combine the flexibility of the special act charter and the fairness of the general act charter. The cities of a state are divided into classes, usually by population, and a charter is drafted for each class of cities. For example, all cities with a million or more residents would have a Class A charter; all cities with 100,000 to 999,999 residents would have a Class B charter; and so forth. The classified approach includes some recognition that different cities may have different needs and also somewhat limits the possibilities for favoritism.

The benefits of the classified system are limited by the fact that cities with similar populations may still have different needs or preferences. The classified system lumps all cities with a similar population size in a class together. The apparent fairness of the classified approach may also be undercut if, as sometimes happens, the state legislature develops classes that include only one city each. If a state has only one Class A city, for example, that city will have the equivalent of a special act charter. Relatively little ingenuity is required to create single-city classes if a state has few cities or if one city is much larger than others. The single-city classes permit as much favoritism as the special act charter. The classified approach may also produce unwanted and conceivably disruptive changes in city charters when city populations shift above or below the classification limits.

The special act, general act, and classified charter systems are all enacted by the state, not the city. Cities may try to influence state decisions and request changes when needed or desired, but the decision rests in the hands of state officials. A city that has friendly relations with the state government may receive a sympathetic response, but other cities may not.

Efforts to give cities more control over their own charters have produced two other chartering systems. Under the *optional charter* plan, the state prepared a number of different charters. Cities are free to choose from the charters offered by the state. As a result, no city can be singled out for special privileges or restrictions that do not apply to other cities, as with the special act charter approach. Cities that are the same size but have different preferences or needs can select different charters.

The optional charter system recognizes the need for some adaptability to local needs, but the choices are limited to whatever options the state provides. Localities are also restricted by their inability to amend the charters; any alterations must be adopted by the state.

Home Rule

The chartering system that maximizes local flexibility and minimizes the potential for state favoritism is home rule, which has been advocated by municipal reformers for decades.[4] Under home rule, a city writes its own charter and adopts it, generally subject to voter approval. A city need not fear the restrictions or inflexibility of a state-imposed charter, and revisions do not usually require city officials to go to the legislature for approval. A city's charter can be drafted to meet the city's particular needs, and updated when necessary. Authority for a city or county to have home rule is still granted by the state through either statute or the constitution.

Many reformers believed that home rule would greatly increase local government control over local affairs, but that hope has generally not been fulfilled. Home rule does increase local autonomy and flexibility to some degree. State officials are relieved of some of the burden of local legislation, a considerable benefit for them as cities have proliferated and as state governments grow and demand more attention themselves. In several respects, however, home rule has had less impact than reformers hoped.

Probably the most important limitation on the effects of home rule is the superiority of state laws over local policy, even with home rule, whenever a state interest can be shown. This is usually not difficult for state officials to do. Some states restrict home rule to cities above a certain population, and cities may be required to receive authorization from the state legislature in order to exercise home rule powers, as in the case of Pennsylvania. That authorization may not be easy to obtain, especially for cities that have poor relationships with the state government. In addition, while forty-eight states had some sort of home rule for cities by 1990, only twenty-eight states had home rule that granted cities broad functional authority (*State Laws Governing Local Government* 1993: 21). The remaining states granted only limited functional authority or, in a few cases, effectively none at all (Hill 1978: 43). A city in that case could change its form of government from, for example, a

---

4. Useful overviews of home rule are found in Adrian and Fine (1991: 86–87); Dye (1981: 230–32); Marks and Cooper (1988: 203–207); McCarthy (1983); and Zimmerman (1992: 172–73).

commission plan to a city manager plan, but could not give itself authority to regulate peanut vendors at baseball games.

Other critics of home rule express concern about its success. Home rule, and the expectation of local autonomy that accompanies it, may at times undercut needed state involvement in local affairs. In addition, home rule may encourage individual localities to pursue their individual interests without regard for other localities, with the result that conflict and even deadlock over interlocal concerns increases. Finally, in politically active communities, home rule may produce an endless stream of proposals to change the city charter at nearly every local election, a process that may exhaust the voters and jeopardize local government stability (Zimmerman 1992: 172–73).

Approximately half the states have adopted some form of *devolution of authority* for at least some of their local governments. Devolution, with or without home rule, grants local governments the authority to utilize all powers that have not been forbidden to them (*State and Local Roles in the Federal System* 1982: 156). It gives local officials greater ability to respond to demands than if they had to obtain individual grants of authority from the state before acting. Once again, however, the apparently broad grant of authority may be significantly narrowed by a long list of "forbiddens" from the state capital.

While the failure of home rule to provide fully independent cities is a source of frustration for some observers, the failure should not be too surprising. As Elazar (1984: 205–206) notes, can a federal system that cannot establish rigid separation between national and state levels be expected to establish rigid separation between state and cities? In a highly mobile and interdependent society, decisions made by one city may affect many people outside the city. In that event, completely independent cities would subject those people to decisions over which they would have no control. Too much urban independence could create as many problems as too little independence (Grodzins 1984: 363). In addition, as the principle of the scope of conflict indicates, people who are unhappy with local government decisions are likely to press for state intervention.

The county as a form of local government exists in every state except Connecticut and Rhode Island. Although states have different names for this structure, the origins of the county system in the United States are drawn from Virginia in 1634 (Grant and Omdahl 1993: 317). The role of county government varies regionally from the South and rural America, where counties play a foundational role, to the Northeast and urban areas, where they are secondary to municipalities.

Unlike municipalities, counties are considered to be formal ". . . extensions of state governments," (Grant and Omdahl, 1993: 320). Counties are creatures of their environment, often expected to perform different functions depending upon whether they are located in rural or urban areas. In rural areas they may provide services like water, sewage, and fire protection, which, in urban areas, would be provided by municipalities.

The many criticisms of county government are drawn from their ambiguous role. Many counties lack population and therefore a tax base to support basic services. Governments in the county may lack coherence and authority in addressing local needs. The problems have been compounded by shifting population bases and the emergence of large concentrated urban areas. The duplication in services sought from counties and municipalities has prompted reformers to call for consolidation and mergers to improve efficiency. A major reason for the increase in special districts over the years is the need to offer services that counties and municipalities cannot provide with existing laws and resources. Finally, some suggestions for improving county government focus on calls for home rule as in city government. In theory, county home rule would offer the same advantages it does to cities, increasing discretion and flexibility.

By 1990, thirty-seven states had granted home rules to at least some of their counties, compared to only twenty-eight in 1978 (*State Laws Governing Local Government* 1993: 21). County home rule is subject to the same limitations as is home rule for cities.

In addition to counties and municipalities, special districts are an important and growing type of local government structure. The Census Bureau defines special districts as units with autonomy from other local governments and a defined function or purpose (see also Bollens 1957).

Special districts are a nebulous category because states define them very differently, and because they perform a wide variety of functions. Although a common special district is a school district, special districts in the United States handle many other functions as well. Responsibilities for special districts range from general natural resource administration to fire and civil protection, health, transportation, and even recreation. Special districts are created by state laws and constitutions and, though often autonomous, interact in a variety of ways with other local governments. Unlike counties and cities, many special districts do not raise revenue through property taxes but through user fees (Grant and Omdahl 1993: 370). The expansion of special districts in the United States is due to several factors. Because of the legal and political constraints on local government, these districts have often been created because they are a more flexible method of providing services to the public. The districts can transcend municipal or county boundaries and pool regional resources to provide services.

Incorporation, Annexation, and Consolidation

The states shape the development and operation of local governments in a variety of ways beyond establishing charter systems. Among the more important state influences are the determination of local government boundaries and the formation of new local governments. The three major activities involved are incorporation, annexation, and consolidation.

Incorporation is the creation of a new, legally recognized city government. Annexation is the expansion of city government boundaries to include new, unincorporated territory. Consolidation is the merger of two or more established local governments; for example, two cities might merge to become one city, or three school districts might be combined to form one larger district. State policies regulate these activities and, in the process, shape the system of local governments.

While state policies regarding incorporation, annexation, and consolidation vary from state to state, a general pattern is clear. For most of this century, incorporation has been relatively easy and annexation has been relatively difficult in most states (Bollens and Schmandt 1982: 98). Consolidation is extremely difficult for city and for county governments. As a result, urban growth has produced a multiplicity of local governments—the typical metropolitan area has approximately one hundred local governments. This phenomenon will be examined in chapter 8.

School Consolidation as a Deviant Case in State-Local Relations

While the states have substantial legal, financial, and administrative powers over local governments, a host of factors often limit the willingness of state officials to use these powers. As noted earlier, traditions of local autonomy, fear of adverse reactions by the public and local officials, and concern that state action may produce adverse results all serve to restrain state intervention in many instances. As a result, local government structures often develop in an unplanned, haphazard fashion and are difficult to improve in any comprehensive way. For example, despite repeated complaints that many of the nation's counties are too small to provide economical services or afford professional personnel, efforts to consolidate county governments have been essentially fruitless (Grant and Nixon 1982: 342–43, 438).

A major exception to this pattern is the massive consolidation of school districts across the country. In 1932, the United States had nearly 130,000 school districts. Many of them were created in the nineteenth century or earlier, and their sizes reflected the capabilities of the transportation system of that era. In sparsely populated areas, geographically small districts contained relatively few pupils; as a result, the nation's school system included over 140,000 one-room schools in 1932 (Grant and Nixon 1982: 470).

Critics of the small districts complained that they could not afford modern laboratory equipment, specialized curricula, and other services needed for modern education (Harrigan 1984: 373). While these problems may not have generated much concern in the 1800s, when few people aspired to a higher education, increasing educational ambitions in the twentieth century made the shortcomings more glaring and important. Students who wanted to go to college found their prospects limited by the lack of foreign language, science, or advanced mathematics classes in the one-room school. Specialized vocational education programs that are available in larger school systems were generally unavailable in small districts. Merging small districts into larger ones makes specialized programs for the college-bound, vocation-oriented, or slow learner available everywhere.

Small districts, combined with a heavy reliance on local finance, also produced great variation in the financial resources available for local schools. Some districts were unable to afford even basic services, while others had money for virtually any programs either parents or students desired. A desperately poor district might be adjacent to an enormously wealthy one; merging them produces a larger district with resources sufficient to meet educational needs.

Proposals to consolidate school districts on a massive scale provoked a storm of controversy in many states. Residents of small districts feared that merger with large districts would reduce their children's prospects for receiving individual attention and recognition. Small communities also feared loss of control of their school systems after merger with a much larger one. Residents of wealthy districts feared that their taxes would increase to help improve education in poorer areas after consolidation. The new, larger school buildings needed for consolidation added to concerns about costs. Small towns feared that closing their schools would take away an important community symbol and, consequently, hasten the loss of population and business activity that many small towns have experienced through much of this century. Finally, some parents feared for the safety and comfort of their children, some of whom had to endure long bus rides over rural roads in all manner of weather (Kammeyer 1968; Grant and Nixon 1982: 470).

In spite of the substantial opposition to school consolidation, it succeeded to a degree that is nothing short of astounding to observers familiar with the generally lackluster record of local government reorganization in the United States. The nation's 127,000 school districts shrank to just under 15,000 by 1987, along with roughly 1,500 other school systems operated by counties, cities, or other local governments. No other local government reorganization of even remotely comparable magnitude has ever taken place in this country. How did it happen?

A major factor in the success of the school consolidation movement was the support of the education profession. Educators believed that consolidated schools would provide superior educational performance. Many parents of school-age children felt the same (Bollens and Schmandt 1982: 323; Grant and Nixon 1982: 470). Given that parents and educators, acting together, are a formidable force in education policy-making, their combined support gave a substantial boost to consolidation efforts.

With the backing of educators and many parents, state governments acted to encourage consolidation in several ways. State education aid formulas were revised to reward consolidated districts and penalize unconsolidated ones. Consolidation procedures were revised to make consolidation easier to adopt. Referenda requirements calling for majority approval in each district to be merged were relaxed to the point of simply requiring an overall majority in the area to be merged or, in some states, requirements were eliminated entirely. Some legislatures redrew the district boundaries themselves or adopted other procedures that bypassed established local governments altogether (Bollens and Schmandt 1982: 323). The combination of streamlined consolidation procedures and support by educators and parents facilitated consolidation in state after state, although not without some bitter struggling.

The success in consolidating the number of school districts is dramatic. Currently, there are fewer school districts than there are municipalities, townships, or other types of special districts. However, the average school district has more employees than other types of local government, with the exception of counties (table 6.1). This reflects a major shift from 1952, when the typical municipality had four times as many employees as the typical school district. As the education profession has grown more specialized, the consolidation movement has produced school districts large enough to have specialists in mathematics, foreign languages, and other disciplines.

The history of school consolidation demonstrates the enormous powers that states have to reshape local governments. At the same time, the fact that consolidation of school districts has not been accompanied by comparable treatment of cities or counties alerts us to the limitations on those state powers. Abundant state legal powers over localities are not necessarily accompanied by a willingness to use them, especially when use risks antagonizing voters and local officials.

State Mandates

States also shape the activities of local governments through the use of state mandates. Because states have vast legal powers over local governments, a state may order its local units to do all sorts of things: regulate private activities, provide services, refrain from using some types of taxes,

Table 6.1: Units of Local Government and Employee Concentration

	Counties	Municipalities	School Districts	Towns and Other Special Districts
1952				
Governments	3,052	16,807	67,355	29,542
Employees	573,000	1,341,000	1,234,000	312,000
Average Number of Employees per Unit of Government	188:1	80:1	18:1	11:1
1987				
Governments	3,042	19,200	14,721	46,223
Employees	1,963,000	2,541,000	4,620,000	951,000
Average Number of Employees per Unit of Government	645:1	132:1	314:1	21:1
1991				
Governments	3,042	19,200	14,721	46,223
Employees	2,196,000	2,662,000	5,045,000	1,027,000
Average Number of Employees per Unit of Government	722:1	139:1	343:1	22:1

NOTE: The exact number of 1991 governmental units is not yet available as the census is conducted every five years.
Source: Stanley, Harold W., and Richard G. Niemi. 1994. *Vital Statistics in American Politics*, 4th ed. Washington, DC: Congressional Quarterly Press, pp. 315–16.

limit tax rates, utilize a particular personnel system—the possibilities are endless (Sokolow and Snavely 1983; Zimmerman 1992: 180–83).

The extent of state mandating is a matter of some controversy, but virtually all observers agree that state mandates are widespread. A study by the Advisory Commission on Intergovernmental Relations (*State and Local Roles in the Federal System* 1982: 164–65) found that the typical state had thirty-five different mandates that required spending by local governments. Research by Catherine Lovell and her colleagues, based on a wider variety of types of mandates in five states, found that the state with the fewest mandates (North Carolina) had more than 250 on the books. California had well over 1,400 (*State and Local Roles in the Federal System* 1982: 162–63). Clearly the states are willing to require a variety of activities by local governments, from use of particular accounting techniques and procedures for adopting local ordinances to delivery of various public services.

State mandates are a source of considerable irritation to local officials, partly because local officials resent being told what to do. In addition, compliance with mandates may be very expensive, and the orders from the state capital may not be accompanied by funds to cover the costs. Local officials sometimes feel that state officials are insensitive to the costs of mandates, partly because the problem of covering the costs is a local, not a state, responsibility. Local officials may also dislike individual mandates because they oppose the mandated policy.

Mandates can provide needed policy uniformity, as in the case of state requirements for road and highway signs or educational standards. Mandates can also foster coordination, both among various local governments and between state and local governments involved in the same programs. Although local officials sometimes criticize mandates, most find that at least some mandates promote policies they also support (Sokolow and Snavely 1983: 74). Mandates can also serve as a form of political protection for local officials. When confronted with conflicting or unreasonable demands, officials can use a mandate to justify a course of action (and hope that any disappointment will be aimed at the mandate instead of themselves).

Much of the debate over mandates involves the scope of conflict. If a decision is left entirely to local governments, different policies may result than would be the case with a state mandate. Citizens who are unhappy with a local policy may press the state government to require a change. Individuals and groups opposed to the substance of a state mandate are likely to push for its repeal or modification to allow local governments to adopt other, more agreeable, policies.

Other Mechanisms of State Influence

The states' ability to issue mandates to local governments would mean little without some sort of enforcement machinery. A state could order local governments to do all sorts of things, but the state needs mechanisms to determine whether localities obey, assist them in complying, and when necessary, force obedience. Without these capabilities, states might find their mandates ignored entirely, implemented ineffectively, or executed half-heartedly. The same machinery keeps officials informed of local problems and enables them to provide assistance to local governments when needed.

State mechanisms for monitoring and regulating local government activities are numerous, and vary from state to state, but several of the more important deserve mention (Adrian and Fine 1991: 114–18; Caraley 1977: 62–70; Glendening and Reeves 1984: 151–57). *Consultation*, either formally or informally, may improve state-local communications and provide an arena for negotiation. Officials may confer by telephone or mail, meet in someone's office, or attend a conference together. Unfortunately, consultation is often too sporadic to provide dependable information regarding local activities, and may not be able to resolve disagreement if opinions are strongly held.

States also provide local governments with many forms of *advice and technical assistance* on subjects ranging from accounting techniques to water treatment. Technical aid is particularly useful because many local officials, particularly in small towns and rural areas, have only limited training and expertise (Glendening and Reeves 1984: 153; Grant and Nixon 1982: 343). Issuing state mandates will accomplish little unless local officials know how to carry out the required activities.

States may require their localities to submit *reports* on their activities to enable state officials to monitor local programs, assess the degree of compliance with state guidelines, and detect problems when they occur. Unfortunately, the reports are not always carefully read by state officials, a circumstance that often convinces local officials that the reports deserve little attention at the preparation stage (Glendening and Reeves 1984: 153). Changes in reporting guidelines and standards from year to year can create problems of comparability over time. Moreover, unless state officials have some mechanism for checking the accuracy of the reports, omissions and distortions may go undetected.

Because of the limitations of reports from local officials, states also utilize *inspections and investigations* to gather information on local activities. Inspections are generally a routine matter; state officials visit a locality and check the condition of streets, or perhaps the content of drinking water. Inspections may be announced in advance, leading to concerns that localities engage in temporary window dressing for the duration of the inspection. Surprise inspections may give more accurate information on day-to-day operations but risk antagonizing local officials. Investigations are generally reserved for non-routine matters, such as suspected corruption or a major breakdown in some important service.

Grants and grant guidelines can also be used to shape behavior of local officials. Although the states have broad legal powers to compel local compliance, financial inducements are often more palatable to local officials. At the same time, grants can reduce local complaints regarding the costs of state mandates. As noted in the discussion of fiscal federalism, however, grants require careful monitoring to assure that funds are used according to state guidelines and regulations. Violations risk the cutoff of state funds, although complete cutoffs are likely to be unpleasant to state and local officials alike. Few state education administrators, for example, want to stop state aid to a local school district in any but the most extreme situations.

Some states provide for state *review* of certain types of local decisions or require state *approval* of some local actions before they are carried out. State review is somewhat analogous to judicial review in that both are generally performed after an action has been taken. As Caraley (1977: 67) notes, review after the fact may not be able to change something that has already been done. Once an historic landmark has been bulldozed, it is gone forever. Reviews can bring about reversals of other types of decisions and can also convey approval or disapproval, serving as guides to future decisions. Prior approval can prevent irreparable damage and costly or inconvenient policy reversals.

In more extreme cases, some states have the authority to *remove local officials* and to appoint replacements. Generally the removal power is limited to cases of misconduct, corruption, or incompetence, although other grounds may be used in some instances, including financial problems. Removal is unlikely to be used to curb subtle footdragging or unenthusiastic performance by local officials. Some fairly dramatic problem is usually needed to trigger this power, as in the case of Major James Walker of New York City. In 1932 he was the subject of a hearing conducted by Governor Franklin Roosevelt after evidence of corruption and misconduct in the city government surfaced. The hearing could have led to Walker's removal from office, but he resigned before it was completed.

The most drastic method for state control of local governments is the assumption of *direct state control* over one or more local government programs. When this measure is applied, local officials are essentially shunted aside and the affected programs are run from the state capital. Direct state control is reserved for extraordinary situations, such as widespread corruption, impending financial collapse, or a major disruption in vital services. In 1989, New Jersey officials assumed direct control of Jersey City schools after reports of political influence in hiring decisions, poor student performance on standardized tests, unclean and unsafe school buildings, violations of procedures for bidding on contracts, and failure to provide adequate programs for handicapped students ("New Jersey Seizes . . ." 1989). Once the crisis passes, control is returned to local officials.

The use of direct state control is limited by a number of factors, not the least of which is its conflict with a U.S. tradition of local autonomy and control. Local electorates may resent state intervention unless the need is obvious. Since these voters also help choose governors and state legislators, state officials heed their concerns. Local officials across the state would react with alarm if state officials were to assume direct control of local programs without a compelling justification. State officials may hesitate to become involved in a quagmire of complex local problems; assuming direct control may prove embarrassing if the situation does not improve. However, when a genuine crisis exists, state officials risk considerable criticism if they do not act, and much of that criticism will come from the affected locality.

The various methods that states use to create and influence local governments raise a perennial issue: how can local governments be given sufficient power and discretion to deal with local problems while, at the same time, the states reserve sufficient power to protect concerns that transcend individual localities? The history of state-local relations indicates that the issue cannot be readily resolved.

State Centralization

A major development in state-local relations in this century is the growth of state governments relative to their local units (Stephens 1974). While the states, as noted earlier, have often been described as the "fallen arch" (Campbell and Shalala 1970: 6) of the federal system, in many respects they have shown greater vigor and vitality than local governments. The extent of state growth relative to local growth, and the causes and consequences of growing state centralization, carry important implications for the federal system.

Signs of Centralization

At the turn of the century, local government was the dominant financial partner in the federal system, raising and spending more money than the national and state governments combined (Stephens 1974: 49). The omission of local governments from the models of federalism that were most influential at that time, notably dual federalism, stands in stark contrast to the financial strength of local government. Local government also employed more people than the national and state governments combined (Stephens 1974: 49). Given that human resources are essential for providing many government services, the labor advantage of local governments was considerable.

The financial and labor strengths of local governments at the turn of the century appear even stronger when directly compared with the states (see table 6.2). Local revenues, expenditures, and employment outstripped their state counterparts by a margin of roughly five to one. In addition, local governments raised almost all of their revenues themselves; only approximately 6 percent of local revenues came from grants in 1902, the bulk of it from the states (Maxwell and Aronson 1977: 85; Mosher and Poland 1964: 162). Local governments may have been in a constitutionally weak position, but they displayed considerable financial strength and independence.

The position of local governments relative to the states has changed considerably since the turn of the century. The most dramatic change has occurred in the area of raising revenues, where the local share of state-local revenues has fallen from 83 percent in 1902 to well under

Table 6.2: Changes in State Centralization

	State	Local
Own-Source General Revenues		
1902	17%	83%
1988	57	43
1990	57	43
Direct General Expenditures		
1902	13%	87%
1979–1980	39	61
1988	40	60
1990	40	60
Personnel		
1901	14%	86%
1980	28	72
1989	29	71
1990	30	70

Sources: *Book of the States.* 1992. Lexington, KY: Council of State Governments, p. 479; Mosher, Frederick, and Orville Poland, 1964. *The Costs of American Governments.* New York: Dodd, Mead, p. 156; Stephens, G. Ross. 1974. "State Centralization and the Erosion of Local Autonomy." *Journal of Politics* 36: 62; *Significant Features of Fiscal Federalism,* vol. 2. 1990. Washington DC: Advisory Commission on Intergovernmental Relations, pp. 64, 70. *Significant Features of Fiscal Federalism,* vol. 2. 1992. Washington, DC: Advisory Commission on Intergovernmental Relations, pp. 90, 150; *Book of the States* 1993. Lexington, KY: Council of State Governments, p. 479.

50 percent in recent years. The local share of state-local expenditures declined less substantially, but the states were still able to triple their share by 1990. The fact that the local share of state-local revenues has declined more than the local share of state-local spending alerts us to another important change: local governments have grown heavily dependent on other levels of government, particularly the states, for financial support. While local governments received roughly 6 percent of their revenues from other levels of government in 1902, local dependence on outside aid reached approximately 40 percent by 1979–1980, with state aid alone providing 31 percent of all local revenues. By 1990, local reliance on aid had fallen to 33 percent of all local revenues, with the states providing 30 percent of local revenues (*Significant Features of Fiscal Federalism* 1992: 90).

Less dramatic but still clear is the decline of the local share of state-local employment from 86 percent in 1901 to 71 percent in 1989. With a larger share of the state-local personnel pool, the states have a higher capability to monitor local government activities and provide services directly.

One other sign of growing state centralization, at least at first glance, is the development of state departments of community affairs (Stephens 1974: 72–73). While these organizations were virtually nonexistent prior to 1960, all the states had some form of community affairs agency by 1980. Thirty-five are cabinet departments, but nine are agencies in other departments. The remainder are found in the Office of the Governor (*State and Local Roles in the Federal System* 1982: 153, 192).

Whether state departments of community affairs are actually a sign of centralization is a matter of some controversy. They seem to emphasize assistance and service to local governments rather than exertion of control (*State and Local Roles in the Federal System* 1982: 153). Assistance and service can easily lend themselves to exertion of subtle but important forms of influence, however. A great deal of state control over localities is exerted through functional agencies, with the state education department supervising local schools (Blair 1981: 28). Consequently, the creation of a state department of community affairs may not change things very much.

Causes of Centralization

How do we account for the centralizing tendencies in state-local relations? Undoubtedly one contributing factor is increasing social and economic interdependence. When the United States was primarily rural and agricultural, decisions made in one locality had only limited effects elsewhere. As the nation became more urbanized and industrialized, decisions made in one community often affected people elsewhere, a situation that produced demands for state intervention.

The weaknesses of local governments may have provided additional pressure for state centralization. County governments, with significant exceptions, have lagged behind higher levels of government in developing expert personnel, administrative coherence, and a size sufficient to permit economical, competent performance (Grant and Nixon 1982: 343, 348). America's metropolitan areas are a jungle of overlapping, uncoordinated local governments that are often unable to cope with areawide problems, an issue to which we will return in chapter 8. Local governments' financial powers are also regulated by the states, a situation that obviously puts localities at a disadvantage in competing with the states for revenues.[5] Local inaction may stimulate state action (Graves 1964: 705).

State centralization may have been fostered by the growth of the national grant system (Stephens 1974: 69). Many of the state grants to local governments are financed, directly or indirectly, by national grants

5. For a general overview of weaknesses in local government, see Leach (1970: 133–65).

to states. In addition, national grants to states help support direct state provision of services. According to this view, the national grant system, which is widely regarded as increasing national power relative to the states, has significantly enhanced state power relative to the local level.

Technological changes may in part account for the trend toward greater state centralization. When dirt roads were supplanted by paved highways and multi-lane expressways, local governments had difficulty financing them alone. Modern police crime laboratories, modern schools, and state-of-the-art health care facilities cost more than many localities can afford. If these services are to be provided, state support may be unavoidable (Graves 1964: 705).

Finally, the growth of state centralization in some instances reflects the operation of the scope of conflict. Individuals and groups who are dissatisfied with the policy responses of local governments are likely to turn to the state capital for help. Parents and educators who are unhappy with the lack of uniformity in schools from one district to another, and the low standards in some districts, pressed state governments to be more active in education policy, and their efforts often succeed. Once state government becomes involved in a program, a host of factors make that involvement difficult to terminate. State officials are often reluctant to give up influence over programs, and state administrators want to retain their jobs. Local officials often appreciate state assistance, and program clienteles may fear that state withdrawal will mean a loss of services. The result is a ratchet effect: once a level of state involvement is reached, it may increase but rarely declines.

Effects of State Centralization

The consequences of state centralization are numerous, although the effects may vary from state to state. Growing state involvement has helped to increase levels of services in many instances (Blair 1981: 28). State funding enables localities to provide services they could not afford otherwise, and state supervision and technical aid can help local officials improve service quality.

State involvement can equalize service levels and distribute costs and benefits more equitably (Blair 1981: 28). Poor communities, acting on their own, can rarely afford to match the services provided by their wealthier neighbors. State aid, if targeted to localities with greater needs and fewer resources, or direct state provision of services, can provide a minimum service level everywhere. If residents of one community use services of another community without paying for them, the state may use a combination of tax and grant programs to require beneficiaries to pay for the services they receive.

At a more general level, increasing state centralization produces a shift toward policies based on state-level coalitions rather than local ones. Groups that are powerful in some localities but weak on a statewide basis are likely to lose influence in the process, other things being equal. Of course, other things are not always equal. A locally dominant group in a very poor community may not be able to afford desired programs; state aid, even with restrictions, may still leave them closer to their program goals than they would be without it.

As local officials have often complained, state centralization has increased the range of local decisions that are subject to some manner of state influence, review, or control. Even with home rule, a city that depends on the state for 30 percent of all local revenues can hardly afford to ignore the wishes of state officials. The exposure of local decisions to extensive state influence led Stephens (1974: 74) to ask whether local governments in the United States have become "counterfeit polities." His answer is a troubling one: "Our localities are increasingly dependent upon larger governments for money, for resolution of basic policy issues, for reallocation of resources, and even for the delivery of many public goods and services" (Stephens 1974: 74).

A loss of local autonomy is not necessarily a cause for alarm. Would we want an interstate highway to abruptly terminate at the boundary of a county that decided not to build its share or could not afford the cost? With roughly a fifth of the population moving from one county to another every five years, and over half changing residence in the same period, large variations in local schools from one locality to another would be a serious problem for school-age children. Unlimited local autonomy in a mobile, interdependent society may be as impractical as unlimited personal freedom.

Note, too, that while local autonomy has declined it has not disappeared entirely. The political influence of localities, home rule, traditions of local control, and the reluctance of state officials to become involved in many conflicts preserve some local discretion. Also, the willingness of local governments to innovate, and the risk-taking involved, lead some state governments to maintain a hands-off policy until they know whether a new approach will work.

Local officials in many parts of the country have tried to preserve local autonomy in a variety of ways. They have organized their own intergovernmental lobbies to influence state government decisions. They have made more use of diverse revenue sources, including fees and charges. In some states, local governments have also won legal standing to sue their state governments, a development that helps to equalize the comparative legal vulnerabilities of the two levels (Pagano 1990: 96–101). The sheer volume of local government activity, combined with the many responsibilities of state governments, also guarantees that much local activity cannot be controlled very effectively by the states.

State-Local Tensions: Real or Imagined?

One of the most widely held beliefs in state-local relations is that states and their localities, especially large cities, do not get along. The states, in this view, are unsympathetic to the needs and problems of local governments and, far from being helpful, are a genuine hindrance to local problem-solving—particularly the problems of large cities.[6] Harmon's (1970: 147) survey of the chief administrative officers in over six-hundred cities revealed that 55 percent of the officers in large cities (500,000 or more residents) felt that state officials were only seldom or occasionally sympathetic or helpful. Officials in smaller cities generally had a more favorable view of state officials. The Reagan administration's efforts to reduce contacts between the national government and localities served to heighten the concerns of many local officials regarding relations with their respective state governments, because they would now be more dependent on these state agencies.

Several major sources of tension should be noted. A cultural norm held by many state officials is that the good life lies in a rural or small town existence and that large cities are corrupt, immoral, and unnatural. Consider, for example, how many of the major state universities are located in small towns rather than the largest cities in their respective states. While this viewpoint is undoubtedly less widespread than it once was, cultural prejudices against large cities are still found in many state capitals.

State-local tensions also result from contending groups seeking the scope of conflict that will produce the policy decisions they desire. Groups with supportive allies at the state level will prefer state decisions, a situation likely to provoke conflict with groups that have more local influence. State-local tensions, in other words, often involve conflicts between private groups, some of which are stronger at the state level and some of which are stronger locally. For example, business groups are often stronger locally than environmental groups; however, at the state level, relative powers tend to balance.[7]

Tensions between a state and large cities may be aggravated by political rivalries between governors and big city mayors. If the governor

6. For discussions of state-local conflicts, see Caraley (1977: 61–63, 70–71); Martin (1965: 76–82); and Pagano (1990).
7. McConnell (1966) and Peterson (1981) both provide interesting discussions of the role of local interest groups, primarily business, in local government policy.

and mayor belong to the same party, they may be rivals for control of the state party. If they belong to different parties, partisan quarreling may occur. The mayor may even be a contender for the governor's job. None of these situations is conducive to harmonious relations (Cronin 1977: 244).

State restrictions on local government powers are another point of contention. Many states give local governments only limited grants of authority, leaving local officials unable to act or forcing them to go to the state for help. State limitations on local financial powers, which are found in all but a handful of states, render local governments less able to raise revenues on their own and borrow money when needed. As noted earlier, state mandates also restrict local discretion, and may force additional costs on localities. Local officials often resent the restrictions and costs.

Finally, tension between states and large cities results when state officials try to supervise the activities of local bureaucrats who feel that they have greater expertise than their state superiors. Listening to the advice of a politically appointed state administrator with limited training, or being required to gain that administrator's approval, is likely to be irksome to local officials with superior technical abilities. When that irritation is communicated to state officials, they are likely to reply in kind. The increasing professionalism of state administrators (Wright 1982: 245–46, 343) may be reducing the severity of this problem.

The genuine conflicts between states and localities should not obscure the fact that a great deal of state-local cooperation takes place. The states provide their localities with all sorts of administrative and technical assistance. State grants to localities now provide roughly 30 percent of all local revenue, and although much of the state-local grant money originates with the national government, the states clearly provide substantial financial aid to local governments. Moreover, research reveals that states do a reasonably effective job of targeting state aid to localities that need it the most.[8] In recent years, many states have given localities broader discretion in the types of taxes they may utilize. Relationships between bureaucratic specialists, such as law enforcement officers, are often very cooperative at the state and local levels, as picket and bamboo fence federalism indicate. In addition, relationships between the states and smaller local governments are often relatively cordial, although tensions produced by state mandates and restrictions as well as scope of conflict issues do occur.

While state-local tensions are very real, they should be kept in per-

8. For evidence on this issue, see Dye and Hurley (1978; 1981); Ward (1981); and Pelissero (1984).

spective. The city halls and state capitals are not in a state of constant warfare, although occasional salvos are exchanged. Feuds undoubtedly attract more attention than harmonious relations. As long as states and localities have the ability to make decisions somewhat independently of one another, disagreements will arise from time to time. Nevertheless, a great deal of cooperation takes place between state and local levels, and relations between them may even be improving. One possible reason for the improvement is a major change in the state legislatures, a change to which we now turn.

Case Study: Redistricting and Intergovernmental Relations

Imagine an interlocal conflict that grew into a state-local conflict, and then a national-state-local conflict. This is precisely what happened with the issue of redistricting, the drawing of boundary lines for state legislative districts. Most state constitutions since 1900 require the legislature to redraw the boundaries periodically, usually every ten years, to adjust for population shifts. In many states, however, the requirements were ignored for decades. In addition, some states required the state senate to give equal representation to each county, regardless of its population. The result of this requirement, coupled with a failure to redraw district boundaries periodically, was an enormous variation in the populations of legislative districts in the same state.[9]

Why did the problem occur? Probably the most basic reason was the reluctance of rural areas to give the growing cities more legislative seats, and therefore, more influence over state policy-making (Caraley 1977: 72). The issue of redistricting reflected a conflict between localities that would lose legislative power and localities that would gain if boundaries were redrawn.

Controversies persistently erupted when legislatures tried to redraw boundaries. Redistricting could change the political compositions of legislators' districts, slicing off supporters and adding hostile voters. Some areas might lose one or more legislative seats, which would pit the affected legislators against each other in a battle for survival. One party might try to draw boundaries that would weaken the opposition party, leading to bitter partisan squabbling. In view of the conflicts that redistricting could create, many state legislators preferred to avoid the issue altogether.

---

9. The literature on redistricting is vast. See Butler and Cain (1992) for a recent overview.

The same problem also occurred in U.S. House districts. The national government allocates House seats among the states, but each state has the responsibility for drawing the district boundary lines. The states were little more conscientious in keeping the congressional district boundaries up to date than they were with state legislative districts. As a result, large variations in the populations of congressional districts existed within many states.

Irate citizens, concluding that the state legislatures would not correct the situation, went to court. To their dismay, however, the U.S. Supreme Court ruled in *Colgrove v. Green* (1946) that determining boundaries of U.S. House districts was a "political question" and not subject to judicial remedy (Pritchett 1977: 60–61). The victims of the problem had to persuade the state legislatures responsible for the problem to correct it.

The major problem with the legislative solution lay in the fact that unequal legislative representation was so severe in many states that the areas hurt by it had too little legislative representation to enact changes. Convincing a majority of the legislators to approve redistricting plans was generally not feasible.

After years of fruitless effort, the advocates of redistricting again turned to the courts. The second effort proved to be successful. In the landmark decision of *Baker v. Carr* (1962), the U.S. Supreme Court ruled that districting in state legislatures was within the jurisdiction of the courts. Dozens of lawsuits were filed to force redistricting, and a number of new districting plans were adopted by legislatures.

The *Baker* decision did not clearly establish whether requirements for equal representation applied to both the senate and the house in a state (Jewell 1969: 19). That uncertainty was resolved in the case of *Reynolds v. Sims* (1964). A number of states had given each county a single seat in the state senate, a practice defended as analogous to the U.S. Senate's apportionment of two senators to each state. The U.S. Supreme Court rejected the "federal analogy" on the grounds that while the states, as sovereign political units, had a right to equal representation in the U.S. Senate, counties (and other local governments) were not sovereign political units, existed at the discretion of the states, and, therefore, had no claim to equal representation in state senates (Pritchett 1977: 63). The *Reynolds* decision concluded that state senates, as well as state houses, must have districts with approximately equal populations.

These initial rulings spawned a number of other decisions. One applied to the county-unit system, an ingenious technique for conducting statewide elections used in Georgia and Maryland. Under the county-unit system, a concept similar to the national electoral college, each county was given a specified number of unit votes. The candidate winning the county received its unit votes, and the candidate receiving the most unit votes was declared the winner. As with the national presidential race, a candidate in Georgia or Maryland could win the popular vote in a state and still lose the election based on county unit votes.

The county-unit system was complicated by the allocation of unit votes. In Georgia, the least populated counties controlled a much larger share of the unit votes than their population warranted, and the heavily populated, urban counties had a much smaller share of the unit votes than their populations warranted.

The Supreme Court ruled in the case of *Gray v. Sanders* (1963) that the county-unit system was unconstitutional on the grounds that it created a preferred class of voters, an act that violated the Fourteenth Amendment (Grant and Nixon 1982: 155; Pritchett 1977: 62). While not all scholars regard the *Gray* decision as a redistricting case, strictly speaking, it clearly was part of the effort to equalize political influence within states.

The Supreme Court returned to the issue of U.S. House districts within a state in the case of *Westberry v. Sanders* (1964). The court reversed itself and the earlier *Colgrove* decision and declared that each state must make its U.S. House districts as equal in population as possible. The case is one of the most striking examples of the complexity of intergovernmental politics in our federal system: the state legislatures, having failed to resolve a dispute between urban and rural localities in an equitable manner, were ordered by the U.S. Supreme Court to alter state districting plans for elections to the U.S. House.

The last of the major cases, *Avery v. Midland County* (1968), struck down unequal district populations in county government as well as other local governments, such as cities. What began as a battle for control of state legislatures and the U.S. House had significant impact on local governments as well. Intergovernmental conflict is often contagious.

The Supreme Court rulings, along with related lawsuits, led to a massive wave of redistricting activity, and some observers predicted huge changes in state policy decisions. Controversies continue over the policy effects of changed legislative districts,[10] but the effects seem to be smaller than many people expected. Why is this the case?

Probably the most important limitation on the impact of redistricting was the tendency for the biggest gains in political power to go to the suburbs, not the central cities (David and Eisenberg 1961; Grant and Nixon 1982: 233). In many states, suburbanites are little more sympathetic to central city problems than rural residents. In a related vein, the

10. See Dye (1965); Feig (1978); Firestine (1973); O'Rourke (1980); and Walker (1969).

diversity of opinions and interests in urban areas often makes exertion of united urban influence difficult or impossible, even with fair districting (Dye 1981: 133–34).

Assessing the effects of redistricting is difficult because a host of other developments occurred during the 1960s that also affected state governments. Expanding national grant programs, the civil rights movement, a booming economy, and changing social values all swept through the states. Separating their effects from the results of changing legislative districts is a difficult task.

This is not to say that redistricting is unimportant. It may have improved relations between the states and cities, as tensions between them contributed to the growth of national-local ties in the past (Glendening and Reeves 1984: 96). Redistricting also increased the state legislatures' claims to be representative institutions. Democratic respectability and legitimacy are valuable assets in the intergovernmental struggle for public esteem. Legislatures that give equal representation by population have a greater claim to legitimacy than an unrepresentative predecessor.

The redistricting issue, then, grew out of a struggle among localities over control of the state legislatures. The failure of many legislatures to resolve the problem equitably led to an escalation of the scope of conflict to the U.S. Supreme Court, which led to widespread changes in district boundaries. Ironically, the states, by losing the court battles, ended up with legislatures far better suited for the responsible exercise of power than they were prior to 1962. Had the states won the court battles and retained their unrepresentative legislatures, proposals to enhance the states' role in domestic policy-making would undoubtedly have faced more opposition than they have. In losing the reapportionment battle, the states experienced the opposite of a Pyrrhic victory; losing left them better off than they were before.

While the landmark decisions of the redistricting issue were handed down in the 1960s, the issue is by no means dead. Disputes continue to erupt over gerrymandering, the practice of drawing district boundaries to benefit a particular political party or racial group. Disputes have also arisen over the use of multimember districts, in which a single district elects two or more legislators, and over the use of at-large elections in local governments. These controversies promise to be with us for years to come.

Summary

Historically, one of the most important features of state-local relations has been Dillon's Rule. Local governments have only the powers clearly granted to them, clearly implied by the granted powers, or essential to executing their responsibilities. As a result, local governments have often lacked authority to deal with policy problems. Home rule, and more recently, devolution of broad grants of authority, have given local officials greater ability to act without prior, specific state approval, but local policies generally remain subordinate to state policies.

States shape the structure of city governments by making policies regarding incorporation, annexation, and consolidation. Because incorporation has been relatively easy in most states in this century, and because annexation and especially consolidation have been difficult, most American cities contain numerous separate local governments, many of them special districts. States influence the operation of local governments in many ways, such as providing advice and technical assistance, offering grants, issuing mandates, and, in extreme cases, assuming direct control of local governments.

The state share of state-local revenue raising, spending, and personnel has grown significantly in this century. That development has been stimulated by growing mobility and interdependence, fiscal and political weaknesses of local governments, and grants from the national government. Demands for state intervention in local policy by people who have not been satisfied with the policy responses of local governments are a major source of state power.

While state-local relations are often cordial, disagreements do arise, especially between states and large cities. Some conflicts stem from cultural suspicions regarding large cities, but other tensions reflect the scope of conflict, political rivalries, and state restrictions on local decision making. One of the most noteworthy state-local conflicts, the battle over legislative reapportionment, was not resolved until the U.S. Supreme Court intervened. The long-term result seems to be some improvement in relations between states and large cities, although the changes have not been as dramatic as some observers expected.

The framework of state-local relations is very conducive to the use of scope of conflict tactics. The extensive legal, financial, and administrative relationships between states and local levels of government provide many opportunities for moving disputes from one level to another. The many political ties between levels also provide avenues for altering the scope of conflict. State legislators can hardly afford to ignore the local concerns of their districts, and state party leaders need to be attentive to local party needs.

CHAPTER 7

National-Local Relations

One of the most noteworthy developments in the American federal system in the past half-century has been the proliferation of direct contacts between the national government and local governments. National-local relations are a very old feature of American federalism (Elazar 1984: 98; Martin 1965: 32–40, 109–11); they date back at least as far as the Northwest Ordinance of 1787, which provided land grants to support education. However, national-local relations have undoubtedly become more open, extensive, and important during this century. This chapter will examine the reasons for the growth of national-local ties, the forms these ties may take, and differing perspectives on them. The implementation problems that have beset a number of national-local programs will be examined, along with efforts to improve implementation and coordination of national-local programs. Finally, the results of national-local programs that have tried to involve program beneficiaries in operations will be assessed.

The Development of National-Local Connections

A number of factors have contributed to the growth of relationships between national and local governments in this century.[1] First, the increasing urbanization of American society meant that more people

1. See Elazar (1984: 98–99); Glendening and Reeves (1984: 171); Graves (1964: 657–60); Martin (1965: 37–40, 111, ch. 3); and Sundquist and Davis (1969: 10–11).

were living close together. They were therefore affected by one another's actions, a situation likely to produce demands for government action. In addition, problems such as poor housing became more visible when people were living close together, a circumstance that also produced calls for government action.

Second, the Great Depression, which created demands for government intervention, overwhelmed state and local governments. The magnitude of the Depression could only have been dealt with by the national government, and some of that effort involved national-local contacts. Once these connections were established, they could not easily be eliminated.

National-local connections were also stimulated by the mobilization of local political influence. The growth of the urban population meant the growth of urban voting power in congressional and presidential elections. Organizations of local officials pressed their demands on Washington and often received a sympathetic response. Why did they go to Washington? They were motivated, in part, by another force encouraging the development of national-local ties: the reluctance and/or inability of many state governments to respond to local needs.

As noted in chapter 6, states do not always have harmonious relations with their local governments. In addition, some states have been unable to cope with costly or complex local problems. States' unresponsiveness to local needs encouraged local officials to expand the scope of conflict and take their business elsewhere. Even where state-local relations were relatively cordial, many local officials found the option of going to the national government attractive so that in the event of an occasional disagreement with the state government, they would have somewhere else to go. They could also use the "national option" to encourage greater responsiveness by state governments, analogous to the way customers go to a competitor if a company does not satisfy their requirements.

The growth of cooperative federalism as a model of federalism also fostered national-local connections. Cooperative federalism, with its emphasis on solving problems and achieving social goals rather than drawing boundaries between levels of government, was far more consistent with national-local contacts than were the older, competitive models of federalism. Of course, cooperative federalism was a reflection of the changes as well as a cause, but clearly the two came together. Had dual federalism remained the dominant model of federalism, direct national-local ties would undoubtedly have remained relatively limited.

Finally, national-local contacts were facilitated by the development of the national grant system. The U.S. Constitution makes no mention of local governments, providing little basis for national-local contacts.

The broad spending powers granted to Congress by the general welfare clause do provide a basis for national grants to localities. Those grants mushroomed from only $10 million in direct national-local grants in 1932 to approximately $22 billion in 1981, declined slightly to $18 billion in 1989 and have increased to only slightly over 18 billion in 1990 (*Significant Features of Fiscal Federalism* 1991: 78; *Significant Features of Fiscal Federalism* 1992: 90).

Varieties of National-Local Relations

National-local relations take many forms, not all of which involve direct, official contacts between national and local officials.[2] National-local relations, like human relationships, sometimes take an informal and/or indirect form.

Some national-local relationships emerge from national programs that deal directly with people but indirectly affect local governments. For example, national mortgage assistance programs and income tax deductions for mortgage interest payments and property taxes on homes amount to national government subsidies for home ownership. By one estimate, these programs provided a subsidy of roughly $30 billion annually during the mid-1980s (*Statistical Abstract* 1985: 310). By 1990, this homeowner subsidy had increased to approximately $51 billion. In 1993, the projected homeowner subsidy was even higher at $58 billion (*Statistical Abstract* 1993: 334). The programs decrease the cost of home ownership relative to renting and narrow the price differences between newer and older homes. As a result, they have encouraged relatively affluent people (who benefit the most from the income tax deductions) to move from central cities, where housing is relatively old, to suburban areas, where housing is newer. Central city economies have suffered in the process (Downs 1974: ch. 1–3).[3]

In a similar vein, the Social Security system, which provides a system of direct national payments to retired people, disabled workers, and survivors of deceased workers, has relieved local governments of much of the burden of providing for these people. Also, national contracts with local businesses may have a significant effect on the local economy and eventually upon local government revenues.

National-local relations also take the form of local governments, like special districts or quasi-governments, which are created by national

2. See Glendening and Reeves (1977: 259–71) and Grodzins (1984: 190–97).
3. Bear in mind that a great many other factors have also encouraged the movement to the suburbs. Moreover the national government is not responsible for the fact that the suburbs are legally independent from the central cities.

government actions. Some of these creations are closely linked to state and local governments but others are largely autonomous. Many are associated with the U.S. Department of Agriculture, such as Soil Conservation Districts and farm-loan associations, but a variety of others have been formed over the years. Some have been quite controversial, a matter that will be examined shortly in a case on public land management.

The national government has created new local governments or quasi-governments for a variety of reasons. National officials did not always trust local officials to carry out a particular program according to national goals. Local government boundaries do not always correspond to the boundaries of problems addressed by national programs; a new organization may provide a better fit. Some nationally created organizations have been formed to assure that certain constituencies have considerable influence over particular programs. A new organization can also hire personnel and establish rules and procedures, allowing it more flexibility to try new approaches to problems. The constraints created by tradition, habit, and inertia can be overcome, at least for a time.[4]

National-local relations also take the form of financial assistance through grants and loans. The financial assistance may flow directly from the national government to local governments or may be channeled through the states. The distinction between the two approaches should not be overdrawn; state officials may pay little attention to some national-local grants channeled through the states, and, conversely, states may use their legal powers over localities and state-local grants to exert influence over national-local programs that do not give states a formal role.

National grants to the states may enrich local coffers without any formal indication that any funds must be given to local governments. Many "state" programs are actually state-local programs; local governments operate schools, build and repair roads, administer antipoverty programs, and participate in many other programs with the states. National aid to state governments to support these programs may find its way into local treasuries. In addition, national aid to states may replace state revenues, making them available for state grants to localities.

National-local relations also take the form of advice, consultation, and technical assistance. National agencies may assist local officials in improving their personnel systems, fighting disease, or analyzing evidence of crime. Local officials who have experience in dealing with a problem may share their expertise with national officials. Consultation can permit exchanges of ideas, prevent the actions of one level from hampering the efforts of the other, and improve coordination.

4. Jeffrey Pressman and Aaron Wildavsky (1979) examine the advantages and disadvantages of new organizations and the implementation of programs. See pages 128–30 for specifics.

Advice, consultation, and technical assistance take a wide variety of forms, ranging from very informal meetings and telephone calls to formal conferences and enactment of legislation that facilitates provision of assistance. The Intergovernmental Personnel Act of 1970, for example, was adopted in part to provide national assistance for improvements in local (as well as state) personnel systems (Hays and Reeves 1984: 384).

National-local contacts sometimes take the form of emergency assistance, often provided by the national government for localities but sometimes flowing in the other direction. Local fire departments in Maryland and Virginia helped protect national buildings during the 1968 Washington, D.C., riots (Glendening and Reeves 1977: 261). Natural disasters, civil disorders, and dangerous toxic waste dumps can trigger provision of national emergency aid. The process is far from automatic, as controversies surrounding the national government's toxic waste cleanup program in the early years of the Reagan administration clearly indicate.

Perspectives on National-Local Relations

The growth of direct relationships between the national government and local governments has been a controversial development in American federalism. Evaluations of those relationships seem to vary from one level of government to another and from one political party to the other.

The National Perspective

While national officials do not all agree with one another regarding national-local relations, some views are fairly common (Martin 1965: 137–45). National officials tend to be interested primarily in programs and policies, not abstract issues of federalism and national-local relations. The preoccupation with policies is clearest in national administrative agencies, as picket fence and bamboo fence federalism indicate. However, policy concerns are also very strong in the White House and Congress, although these concerns may be voiced in somewhat misleading language. While positions may sometimes be expressed in terms of theories of federalism, the principle of the scope of conflict reminds us that the rhetoric of abstract theories may conceal intense policy preferences.

The national concern for programs leads to the use of a variety of mechanisms for influencing local officials (Martin, 1965: 138–139). Local officials may be required to submit program plans or project proposals (in the case of project grants) so that national officials can determine whether local intentions correspond to national goals. Requirements for periodic reports enable national officials to monitor program performance as it proceeds. Field inspections and program audits provide additional information to national officials and serve as a check on the accuracy of local reports. Some national programs require local officials to utilize specified techniques and procedures. Federal court decisions may require local officials to revise programs and policies. All of these mechanisms are designed to encourage local actions consistent with national goals.

National concern for the exercise of these controls, reinforced by the carrot of grants, is enhanced when the national government assumes a large share of program costs or when the national government's commitment is open-ended. In either case national officials may fear that local officials will try to milk the program for as much money as possible unless strict controls are used. Some national agencies are more forceful than others in seeking to control local behavior.

National officials face problems in coordinating national-local programs. An example is the attempt to establish consistency among the national policies themselves. When some national policies were trying to revitalize central city economies while other national policies encouraged middle and upper-income families to leave the central cities for the suburbs, the second group of policies seriously undercut the first. Another set of coordination problems arises at the local level: how are the efforts of various national and local (as well as state and private) agencies to be coordinated? Given the structures of local governments in many metropolitan areas (see chapter 8), the many nonlocal agencies, and the wide range of government programs, the coordination problems in the field can be severe. Since we often see innovation in local government it should be no surprise that cities and counties are developing a number of approaches to coordinating programs locally. Nationally mandated coordination programs have serious drawbacks, as illustrated in cases later in this chapter.

National officials are also concerned about striking a balance between national control and local autonomy. If national controls are too lax, some localities may misuse national funds and ignore national goals. If national controls are too restrictive, they may stifle local initiative and flexibility and antagonize local officials, even to the point that these officials decline to participate in a program at all. Moreover, at a certain point compliance with filing reports and showing inspectors around may begin to pull resources away from program operations without adding any useful information.

National officials sometimes resent the pressures placed on them by local officials, who may want to use national aid for purposes not intended by national policymakers. When local officials sought to avoid laying off local government employees during the early 1970s, Washington was pressed to permit localities to use a program designed primarily to help chronically unemployed people to keep regular employees on the payroll instead. The result of that effort will be examined shortly. Local officials may also press national officials to handle difficult, controversial problems to reduce frictions between the local officials and their constituents (Martin 1965: 144). National officials are put in the position of taking the political heat in that case, although they may decline to become involved in some instances.

The Local Perspective

Local officials are generally pleased to receive the resources provided by Washington, and many support the option of dealing with Washington directly.[5] Localities are often reluctant to involve the states in national-local programs. Local officials, especially those from big cities, often believe that the states are unsympathetic and unresponsive, although this phenomenon seems to be less widespread than in the past.

Not all the aspects of national-local relations are pleasing to local officials. Some complain that national rules and procedures are applied too rigidly; compliance with reporting requirements, inspections, and audits provokes further dissatisfaction. Local officials also resent the delays and uncertainty that characterize some national grants. In some cases, local budgets are adopted based on educated guesses regarding when and how much national money will arrive. If those guesses are incorrect, traumatic changes in local revenues or spending may be required. A county may enact a budget based on the assumption that a major grant program will be funded at the same level as last year. If that grant program is cut substantially, county officials will be forced to reduce spending for the affected programs or raise additional revenues. Citizen expectations about service levels become set with the infusion of national funds, and local officials are then pressed to maintain programs even if funding is cut. This dilemma was a constant during Reagan's New Federalism era.

Local generalists, such as mayors, city managers, and county commissioners, also complain that the national emphasis on categorical grants tends to make local bureaucracies more independent of the city or county government, and, therefore, encourages picket fence federalism. When city officials must spend grant funds on a particular function or lose them, the agency in charge of that function can be relatively confident of receiving the money. Finally, local officials in smaller jurisdictions complain that they have great difficulty keeping track of the many na-

---

5. See Martin (1965: 145–62); Hale and Palley (1981: 100–105, 139–51); and Advisory Commission on Intergovernmental Relations (1981: 43–44).

tional-local programs and the requirements for participating in them. They feel at a disadvantage particularly in competing for project grants.

The State Perspective

State officials have somewhat ambivalent attitudes regarding direct national-local relations (Martin 1965: 162–69). Some state officials fear that national-local programs represent an unnecessary and potentially dangerous growth of national government power. Some also believe that direct national-local relations threaten state control over local governments. While the latter fear has some justification, it is often overblown. The states have legal powers over localities far beyond what the national government possesses, and state grants to localities (some of which are supported by the national government) vastly exceed direct national-local grants, especially in recent years. In 1989, direct national-local aid was roughly $18 billion, while state-local aid was $158 billion (*Significant Features of Fiscal Federalism* 1991: 78). State officials who oppose direct national-local action have sometimes pressed for channeling that aid through state governments in order to assure protection of state interests. That call received a sympathetic response during the Reagan administration, which may account for the proportional increase of state-local aid over national-local assistance.

At the same time, many state officials recognize that national-local programs do help to satisfy many demands. If those programs did not exist, state governments would be faced with even louder cries to aid their localities, and state budgets would be further strained. State officials would also find themselves dealing more directly with controversial policy issues, rather than letting national officials bear much of the burden.

Partisan Perspectives

National aid to local governments has been a source of conflict between Democrats and Republicans for many years.[6] Since the early 1930s, Democratic presidents have generally pressed for more aid to urban areas, while Republican presidents have generally tried to limit or reduce national aid, most recently during the Reagan and Bush administrations. Not all the efforts on either side have been successful, but the directions are clear.

In a similar fashion, party differences emerge in Congress when questions of aid to urban areas arise. Analyses of votes on a number of major national-local aid proposals indicate that Democrats in the House

---

6. This section relies heavily on Caraley (1976; 1977: 144–54) and Evans (1986).

and Senate are considerably more likely than Republicans to support national-local aid. Approximately three-fourths of all Democrats in both houses are likely to support national-local aid on any given vote, but little more than one-fourth of the House Republicans, and just over one-third of the Senate Republicans, are likely to support it.

Northern and southern Democrats display noticeably different levels of support for national-local aid, however. Northern Democrats are considerably more likely to vote for aid than their southern counterparts. Southern Democrats are, in turn, clearly more supportive than Republicans of urban aid. In a related vein, liberal members of Congress are more supportive than conservatives of national aid to cities. Not surprisingly, then, direct national-local aid declined from 7.8 percent of all local revenues in 1981, the first year of the Reagan administration, to 3.3 percent in 1989, Reagan's last year (*Significant Features of Fiscal Federalism* 1991: 78). In 1991, national-local aid declined slightly more to 3.2 percent (*Significant Features of Fiscal Federalism* 1992:90).

The low levels of Republican support for national aid to urban areas should not be interpreted to mean that Republicans are anti-local government. Rather, that low support reflects a general reluctance to use national government power in domestic policy-making. In addition, a number of the national-urban aid programs are particularly important to hard-pressed central cities, which tend to vote Democratic (Axelrod 1972). Because Republicans receive less support from these areas, they may feel less obligation to provide aid in return. Republican members of Congress from urban areas do tend to be more supportive than rural Republicans of urban aid.

Bear in mind that these descriptions of national, local, state, and partisan perspectives are only broad generalizations. There is considerable diversity of opinion within each grouping, and opinions do shift at times. Different tendencies are discernible from one group to another, nonetheless.

Implementation Problems in National-Local Programs

Programs that are conceived and adopted in Washington but implemented by local agencies do not always perform as expected. The priorities of the president and Congress may be very different from the priorities of local officials. The incentives facing local officials may be very different from those in Washington. The diversity of local political systems may pull national-local programs in different directions from one locality to the next, a situation that may produce unexpected results. Moreover, the existence of thousands of local governments (not all of which necessarily participate in any particular national-local program) makes close monitoring of local behavior difficult (see table 6.2). As Murphy (1973: 194–95) notes, the law that creates a program may be relatively vague, which makes implementers uncertain regarding what is expected of them, and enables them to read their own interpretations into the law. Murphy also notes that a shared professional identity among administrators makes higher level officials reluctant to embarrass or second-guess their counterparts at lower levels. Public health officials at one level are likely to trust the judgement of similar officials at another level rather than closely monitor their every move. Note, too, that national officials may not agree among themselves regarding a program's objectives and may therefore give mixed signals to local officials, as in the case of education funding.

Title I of the Elementary and Secondary Education Act

One example of the implementation problems that can emerge in national-local programs concerns Title I of the Elementary and Secondary Education Act of 1965.[7] Title I was designed to target aid to educationally deprived children in poor areas. Most educators, however, had wanted a system of general national aid to education, not a program just for poor children, and the U.S. Office of Education was not accustomed to policing state and local educators. Local school systems were given considerable discretion in the program.

Problems did not take long to emerge. Audits conducted between 1965 and 1969 revealed that numerous districts distributed funds without regard to whether children were educationally disadvantaged; some districts simply used Title I funds to replace state or local funds, and some spent the money for dubious or even illegal purposes. Investigators concluded that over 15 percent of the Title I funds had been misused. The U.S. Office of Education had also called for creation of local advisory committees to assist local schools in allocating the funds, but by 1969, roughly three-fifths of all districts did not have them.

In spite of evidence of numerous problems, the Office of Education did little. It was not accustomed to regulating local schools, and its officials feared creating conflict with local educators—conflict might have provoked unfavorable reactions in Congress and jeopardized the programs. Some officials in the Office of Education believed that the law should have created a system of general aid to education and were not, therefore, very upset that some school districts used the funds in that way. Moreover, when the office tried to control local use of funds, it was rebuffed by state and local educators and Congress.

Some changes appeared likely when publicity regarding the pro-

7. See Murphy (1974).

gram led to demands for changes. A diverse coalition of groups ranging from the League of Women Voters to the National Welfare Rights Organization and a number of other antipoverty groups pressed for stronger enforcement of national guidelines in 1969. The U.S. Office of Education was reorganized the following year in order to improve enforcement, and some initial efforts to do just that followed. However, the coalition fell apart in 1972, and the Office of Education began to lose enthusiasm for the crackdown. Enforcement efforts subsided. The New Federalism of the Nixon administration was not very supportive of national efforts to control the behavior of local authorities, and the educators constituted a more durable, better organized, and more highly motivated lobby than the coalition that tried to support enforcement of national guidelines. More recent evidence indicates that implementation of national education policies at the local level continues to be problematic, although efforts to improve it are underway (*Education Grants Management* 1991; *Within School Discrimination* 1991).

CETA

Implementation problems emerged in the Comprehensive Employment and Training Act (CETA) of 1973. The CETA program, which included grants to states as well as localities, was intended to provide unemployed and underemployed people with temporary jobs that would simultaneously give them work experience and provide necessary public services where unemployment was high. Job training, along with the work experience, would enable those people to move on to permanent employment—much of it, presumably, in the private sector (Peterson 1976: 88–89).

The CETA program was a victim of bad timing. Shortly after it was enacted, a recession struck. Coping with rising unemployment began to seem more important than providing job training, and local officials saw CETA as a way to avoid laying off local employees while reducing pressure on locally raised revenues. Congress adopted amendments that eliminated the original requirement that CETA workers be used to provide new or previously inadequate services. Administration regulations requiring CETA to prepare workers for permanent employment were transformed into goals.

As a result of these combined forces, the CETA program was transformed from a program to help unemployed people gain job skills and experience, which would enable them to attain permanent employment, into a program resembling revenue sharing. Much of the money was used to replace local revenues, and many of the jobs "created" by CETA actually existed before the CETA program; what changed was who paid the salaries. The emphasis on giving the unemployed marketable job skills was lost (Peterson 1976: 90–92).

The experience of the CETA program should hardly be surprising. State and local officials, pressed by a recession and anxious to maintain services without raising taxes, were joined by public employees anxious to retain their jobs. National officials concerned with controlling the recession were receptive to their demands. On the other side were the more or less chronically unemployed, who were unorganized and had few political resources to support their claims. Their defeat was predictable.

More recent experience with job programs indicates continuing difficulty. The Job Partnership Training Act, which was adopted to provide training to economically disadvantaged young people, has been criticized for its failure to help those most in need, abuse of on-the-job training (for example, "training" people for jobs they were already doing), and other management and operational problems (*Job Partnership Training Act* 1990; *Job Partnership Training Act* 1992). The temptation to use the funds in ways not consistent with the original program goals is as strong now as in the 1970s.

Urban Renewal

A third example of the implementation problems that can arise in national-local programs is urban renewal.[8] The urban renewal program began as an effort to combat urban deterioration, particularly in housing. The national government offered to pay two-thirds of the costs of the program. Local urban renewal authorities were created to condemn and purchase deteriorated properties, demolish the decaying buildings, and sell the cleared parcels of land to private developers. The original emphasis, to a large degree, was on improved housing.

The incentives facing local officials and private developers produced some changes in the program. In many cases, local officials wanted to minimize their costs and maximize the return to the city treasury through both the sale of land parcels and the taxes generated by the property when developed. The developers wanted to maximize their profits by acquiring relatively attractive locations and constructing profitable housing. From these incentives flowed a number of unexpected results.

First, because developers wanted marketable locations and local

8. The literature on urban renewal is vast. See Anderson (1964); Lineberry and Sharkansky (1978: 376–82); Harrigan (1981: 351–53); Orfield (1974–75); Palley and Palley (1981: 203–205); Stedman (1975: ch. 11); and studies they cite.

authorities wanted to be able to sell the land to developers, urban renewal authorities often avoided the worst slums and instead focused on marginal slums. Few cities wanted to emulate the city of Newark, which devoted considerable time and expense to clearing a site that no one would buy (Lineberry and Sharkansky 1978: 379). As a result, many urban renewal projects destroyed marginal slums and pushed their residents into worse slums.

Second, because developers wanted to build profitable buildings and city officials wanted to strengthen the local tax base, neither group was very enthusiastic about using urban renewal sites for low-income housing. Business and commercial properties and middle-to-upper income housing were more profitable for developers and added more to the local tax base. Consequently, urban renewal substantially reduced the supply of low-income housing in many cities.

Third, urban renewal authorities were expected to help poor families displaced by urban renewal programs to find new housing. That activity, while not producing revenue for the city treasury, involved considerable expense. Many cities provided only token relocation assistance. Although the urban renewal authorities were required to verify that suitable housing was available for displaced families, that requirement was often ignored. As Lineberry and Sharkansky (1978: 381) note, if adequate housing had been available at prices those families could afford, why would they have been living in slums?

Finally, urban renewal projects in a number of cities promoted residential segregation (Orfield 1974–75). Integrated slums were torn down, and a variety of public and private actions (some will be discussed in chapter 8) separated people along racial and ethnic lines. This result was not intended by the national officials who enacted the urban renewal programs.

The record of these and other national-local programs indicates that implementation problems are not unusual. The local officials implementing a program may have different priorities from the national officials who adopted the program, and the incentives facing local officials may be very different from the incentives facing national officials. As Pressman and Wildavsky (1979: 133–42) note, the multiplicity of national and local agencies and officials also creates problems of coordination for many programs. Inducing everyone to cooperate is difficult in many cases and impossible in some. Finally, many programs are designed with relatively little regard to how easy or difficult they will be to implement; subsequent problems are often surprises, but in many cases they could have been anticipated (Pressman and Wildavsky 1979: 143–46).

Efforts to Improve Coordination of National-Local Programs

The implementation problems that have occurred in a number of national-local programs, as well as the many national, state, local, and private actors that influence local conditions, have led to a variety of efforts to improve the coordination of national-local programs.[9] Demands for improved coordination in national programs generally have been described by Seidman (1975: 190) as "the search for the philosopher's stone":

> In ancient times alchemists believed implicitly in the existence of a philosopher's stone which would provide the key to the universe and, in effect, solve all of the problems of mankind. The quest for coordination is in many respects the twentieth-century equivalent of the medieval search for the philosopher's stone. If only we can find the right formula for coordination, we can reconcile the irreconcilable, harmonize competing and wholly divergent interests, overcome irrationalities in our government structures, and make hard policy choices to which no one will dissent (Seidman 1975: 190).

The task of achieving coordinated action among many different agencies, public and private, is indeed formidable, as Seidman indicates. When participants face widely different incentives or have very different policy goals, not to mention when they are less interested in coordination than in other activities, coordination is likely to be very difficult. In addition, as the federal system was created to help accommodate differing goals and values, and so have many units of government, each with some degree of autonomy, coordination will often be problematic.

Community Action Agencies

The Community Action Agencies, created as part of the War on Poverty, were expected to help coordinate the activities of national, state, and local antipoverty agencies, as well as private agencies of various kinds (Sundquist and Davis 1969: ch. 2). The CAAs encountered numerous problems in trying to improve coordination.

The speed with which the CAAs went into action provided little time for advance planning, which might have enabled program participants to work out some of their differences before programs began operating. The controversies that soon enveloped many CAAs also made

9. For an insightful discussion of a number of these efforts, see Sundquist and Davis (1969).

coordination difficult. Agencies racked by infighting could hardly make decisions for themselves, much less exert influence over other program participants.

The CAAs began with numerous opponents, none particularly anxious to see them succeed. Established antipoverty agencies' personnel took offense at the creation of the CAAs; their creation implied that established approaches were faulty. Republicans were skeptical or even hostile to what they regarded as a Democratic program, and some southerners believed the Office of Economic Opportunity, which sponsored the CAAs, was too integrationist. The CAAs were also regarded by many established antipoverty professionals as amateurish, a perception that did not enhance their respect for CAA recommendations. Because the CAAs did not have the authority to command other actors to obey or the money to induce cooperation, the lack of acceptance was a serious problem.

The CAAs also encountered administrative problems, in part because of the emphasis on innovation, a central feature of creative federalism. Because the CAAs were new agencies established to develop new approaches, few reliable guidelines existed to guide program development and operation, shape personnel selection, or encourage consistency in decisions. As a result, numerous scandals and charges of mismanagement, as well as inconsistent decisions, further undercut the abilities of CAAs to serve as coordinators.

Model Cities

The limited success of the CAAs as coordinators led to other efforts to improve program coordination. The Model Cities program, first proposed by President Lyndon Johnson in 1966, was expected to combine national, state, local, and private efforts to attack the problems of urban decay (Sundquist and Davis 1969: ch. 3). A City Demonstration Agency (CDA), which could be an existing local government or a new organization, would be in charge of the program. Regardless of their form, the CDAs were to work directly and closely with established local governments, in part to avoid the conflict that occurred in the Community Action Program.

The Model Cities programs began with a much stronger emphasis on advance planning than the Community Action Program. Consequently, more opportunities for anticipating coordination problems were available. Some of the opportunities were used effectively, but not others.

The Model Cities program encountered conflicts over control of the CDAs, although the conflicts did not generally seem as severe as those in the Community Action Program. Coordination efforts were also limited by the fact that the CDAs often did not cover entire cities but were limited to deteriorating neighborhoods. Any activities outside the areas covered by CDAs were difficult for them to influence. Finally, national government agencies were not always inclined to cooperate with the CDAs. The Model Cities program was merged with a number of other programs in 1974, and its coordination role ended.

A-95

A very different approach to coordination is reflected in Circular A-95, which was issued in the late 1960s by what is now the national government's Office of Management and Budget (Hale and Palley 1981: 87–88). The circular required area-wide review of local grant applications to the national government in order to improve coordination from one functional program to another, from one local government to another, and from one level of government to another. The area-wide review could be provided by a council or representatives of local governments in the area, or a regional planning agency.

The A-95 approach had little value for programs not funded by national grants, and national agencies were not always inclined to cooperate with the effort. Representatives of local governments were reluctant to deny one another's grant requests for fear of retaliation. The clearinghouses established to review grant applications often had too many applications to consider and too little time for thorough reviews. Consequently, the A-95 process had relatively little impact. National government requirements for the review process were terminated during the Reagan administration.

Urban Enterprise Zones

A final strategy for improving national-local coordination is the urban enterprise zone, which was endorsed by the Reagan administration. An urban enterprise zone is an area where businesses are given tax reductions and more lenient regulation in order to stimulate economic growth and provide employment opportunities. According to supporters of the approach, by locating the zones in or near economically depressed areas, government can combat poverty, unemployment, and urban decay just as the Community Action Agencies and Model Cities Program sought to do.

Urban enterprise zones could reduce coordination problems in two ways. First, by maintaining relatively few national policies, in contrast to the Community Action Program's "shotgun" approach, urban enterprise zones should reduce coordination problems. Second, by placing greater emphasis on market decisions, urban enterprise zones shift much of the coordination activity to the private sector, where, in theory, private agreements can resolve many conflicts.

Unfortunately, urban enterprise zones have several of the same limitations as some previous coordination efforts. A zone that covers only a portion of a city will have little ability to coordinate activities taking place outside the zone. In addition, established government agencies are unlikely to be much more inclined to cooperate with the activities in urban enterprise zones than with those of Community Action Agencies or Model Cities programs. A zone with incentives limited to tax reductions and fewer regulations will be in much the same situation as Community Action Agencies in trying to induce state and local governments to cooperate. Moreover, if local governments in nonzone areas adopt new tax breaks and relax business regulations in order to avoid losing jobs and business activity to zone areas, the program will do little to stimulate the economies of the zones (*Enterprise Zones* 1988). Finally, conflicts in the private sector are often settled in court, which would further complicate coordination attempts.

Coordination: The Philosopher's Stone?

The quest for improved coordination of national-local programs has been a frustrating one. A number of lessons learned from these and other efforts (Sundquist and Davis 1969) indicate that the obstacles to improvement are formidable indeed.

First, as long as the basic policies of each level of government are inconsistent with one another, improved coordination will remain elusive. When some national policies were trying to revitalize central city economies while others were subsidizing the flight of affluent residents, business, and industry to the suburbs, how could coordination be achieved? When some local governments tried to improve the plight of the poor while other local governments acted to exclude poor people from areas of economic vitality (an issue to be examined in the next chapter), how can those actions be "coordinated"?

Second, given that the typical metropolitan area includes one hundred different units of local government, how can local coordination be achieved? If all the relevant local governments agree on a course of action, coordination is possible, but that agreement is difficult to achieve because each government has differing goals, objectives, and constituencies.

Third, excluding the states from national-local programs may increase coordination problems, especially for programs dealing with small towns and rural areas (Sundquist and Davis 1969: 261–70). The states can help to monitor conditions and activities in local areas, and a variety of state-local programs also affect local conditions. Excluding the states allows little opportunity to coordinate their programs with national and local efforts. Including the states raises fears among some local officials, particularly in large cities, that state participation will result in less concern for local needs. Also, some states are poorly equipped to contribute significantly to national-local programs. Sundquist and Davis (1969: 270–72) propose that state participation could vary, depending on each state's ability to make useful contributions to the programs. The proposal has considerable appeal, although excluding some states because they are judged to be unreliable while allowing other states to participate could provoke controversy and result in political manipulation.

Finally, at the heart of the issue of coordination is the question of power. As McConnell (1966: 214–15) notes, proposals to improve administrative organization and coordination are often proposals to change who will exert control over policies and who will benefit from programs. Given that our political system is generally not very successful at producing agreement on goals, coordination will always be difficult to achieve (Seidman 1975: 216–17).[10] Unless voluntary agreement can be reached, coordination requires that some individual or organization possess the ability to induce others to obey. That capability is difficult to establish in a federal system. Not surprisingly, then, the prospects for effective coordinated implementation of national-local programs can be heavily influenced by the local political climate. Where the climate is hostile to a particular program, that program may be weakened noticeably (Scholz et al. 1991: 829–50).

Some Rays of Hope

Although much of the early research on national-local program implementation presented a rather discouraging prospect, more recent work offers hope that national-local programs can work effectively, at least some of the time.[11] Programs are likely to go through an initial shakedown period that is relatively difficult. People struggle with new and unfamiliar procedures, and agencies that have never worked

10. Recall that one of the advantages of federalism is its ability to accommodate varying goals and preferences. Nations that need federalism to cope with varying goals must accept something less than ideal coordination with the existing dispute resolution processes.

11. See Bullock and Lamb (1984) and Peterson et al. (1986).

together before take time to develop a working relationship. Initial expectations may be unrealistic, and strategies may not be entirely appropriate. Program goals may be unclear, and they may not have dependable support from the president, Congress, or the agencies involved in the program.

With time and effort, however, these problems may be overcome. People become more familiar with procedures and may revise them to improve performance. Working relationships gradually develop and help agencies and people work together more effectively. A clearer set of goals and priorities may emerge, and the program may develop a base of support. None of this happens automatically, of course, and it may not happen at all for some programs.

As the previous cases indicate, part of the difficulty in coordination is due to the diversity of policy actors. National, state, and local governmental agencies join with nonprofit and business groups to address some societal and local concerns. Partnerships between public and private organizations are increasingly important avenues for service delivery, as we see with the privatization movement. To facilitate problem solving in this environment, some public administrators call for a renewed emphasis on management. According to Deil Wright (1990: 168–76), Intergovernmental Management (IGM) provides a different focus to policy implementation. IGM emphasizes problem-solving—professional management is thus accorded a greater formal role in policy development. IGM recognizes that implementation requires an interlocal and interlevel as well as a public and private sector mix, rather than traditional national-state, national-local, and interstate relationships. Finally, in further contrast to the traditional federalism models, conflict resolution for IGM approaches emphasizes collaborative decision making and dispute settlement rather than the traditional win/lose judicial or elective systems. The keys to IGM also appear to be crucial to successful program coordination. A problem-solving focus centers on results and moves toward interdependent rather than competitive policy-making. IGM appears to combine the best of the interdependent models of federalism (cooperative and creative federalism) with the functional models (fence federalism).

This all may sound very nice, but the crucial question is: does it work? Stephen Forman (1989: 23) says that cooperation is not possible without "... complex bargaining and negotiation processes." Thus, many communities and organizations are turning away from the traditional dispute resolution system—the courts—to collaborative negotiation approaches to community decision making (Brock and Cormick 1989; Stephenson and Pops 1989; Syme and Eaton 1989). These nonad-

versarial approaches are drawn from a wealth of cultural and organizational research.[12]

The evidence indicates that implementation of national-local programs is not always doomed to failure. The evidence also suggests that
decision makers need to pay attention to the implementation process
when deciding whether to adopt a new policy.

Case Study: The Battery Bridge Controversy

National-local conflicts arise on all sorts of issues and are sometimes
resolved in unexpected ways. Even such a seemingly routine matter as
building a bridge can produce complex interactions among a variety of
national and local actors, as well as state officials. The controversy over
the Battery Bridge in New York reveals the intricacies of decision making
in a federal system.[13]

New York City, trying to cope with burgeoning traffic, was considering construction of a tunnel to connect Brooklyn with the southern end
of Manhattan, where Battery Park was located, to enable traffic to cross
the East River. The city was short of funds in the depths of the Great
Depression of the 1930s, and the national government declined to finance the project. Mayor LaGuardia approached Robert Moses, head
of the Triborough Bridge Authority, for assistance. The authority had
been created by the state of New York to build and operate bridges in
the New York City area. As with most special districts, the authority was
legally independent of the city and had independent sources of revenue.

Moses agreed to build the tunnel if the Triborough Bridge Authority could be given control of the New York Tunnel Authority, a requirement that was met. He decided, however, to make "a slight modification"
in the plan: the tunnel became a bridge (Caro 1974: 641). The modification provoked a storm of controversy. Critics charged that a bridge, with
its massive elevated approaches, would block out light and ventilation
for many commercial buildings in Lower Manhattan, a situation that
would reduce property values and, therefore, property tax revenues—
the latter, according to one estimate, by approximately $29 million (Caro
1974: 647).

Other critics complained that the massive bridge and elevated approach ramps would cover much of Battery Park, one of the few major

12. In organization theory, Mary Parker Follett (1924) first identified a collaborative approach to addressing healthy conflicts. Since then many practitioners and aca-
demics have developed variations on her approach to solving problems and maintaining relationships (Fisher and Ury [1981, 1983] and Thomas [1979]).

13. This section relies heavily on Caro (1974: ch. 29).

open areas in Lower Manhattan, and would obstruct the view from what was left of the park. In rural, sparsely populated areas, the loss of a limited area to a huge bridge might seem trivial, but Lower Manhattan had very few such places to spare. A tunnel, as it is underground and does not need elevated approach ramps, would have done less damage to property values, Battery Park, and the view from the park.

Critics of the bridge appealed to Moses, as head of the Triborough Bridge Authority, but he ignored them. The critics then turned to the New York City Planning Commission, which had the power to approve or disapprove the project. Although the Planning Commission was sympathetic to the critics, it faced a basic problem: the Triborough Bridge Authority could finance a bridge but would not build a tunnel, and no one else had funding for a tunnel in 1939. Traffic demanded some type of thoroughfare. The bridge was approved.

Critics then turned to the city council and mayor of New York. If the bridge could not be converted to a tunnel, critics hoped to delay the decision and conduct further studies of the issue. The mayor and council sympathized with opponents of the bridge but faced the same problem as the Planning Commission: Moses and the Triborough Bridge Authority had the funds; no one else was willing to provide funding. The city council approved the bridge project, and the state legislature and governor soon followed.

The only step left before the bridge could be built was gaining the approval of the U.S. War Department, since the bridge would cross a navigable waterway with naval installations upstream. Approval seemed assured. However, opponents of the bridge contacted First Lady Eleanor Roosevelt and President Franklin Roosevelt, who were natives of New York.

After a delay of several months, the War Department announced that the bridge was *not* approved because it would, if knocked down, block the Brooklyn Navy Yard's access to the sea. Given the tense international situation in 1939, that concern seemed plausible. However, there were already two bridges over the navy yard's route to the sea, a situation that suggested some other factor may have been the basis for the decision. Local opposition to the bridge seemed a likely possibility.

Further evidence that something more than military necessity was at work was provided when the Reconstruction Finance Corporation, a national agency created to fight the Depression, reversed itself and decided to loan the city's Tunnel Authority enough money to finance the tunnel. Opponents of the bridge finally won.

The controversy over the Battery Bridge is eloquent testimony to the complexity of policy-making in the American federal system. The Triborough Bridge Authority, the Tunnel Authority, the mayor and city council of New York City, the New York City Planning Commission, the governor and state legislature, the Army Corps of Engineers, the War Department, the president of the United States, his Cabinet, and the Reconstruction Finance Corporation all participated in the decision in one fashion or another, as did a variety of private individuals and groups—all for a decision about a bridge! More complex issues can produce even more complex patterns of involvement.

The controversy also illustrates the scope of conflict in operation. Opponents of the bridge went from one decision-making arena to another until they found a sympathetic response. Had the scope of conflict remained at the local or state level, the Battery Bridge would have been built. Escalating the scope of conflict to the White House changed the outcome.

Finally, the controversy indicates that governmental responsiveness is not necessarily greatest at the local level, particularly when decisions are made by local authorities whose officials do not answer directly to the voters or other locally elected officials (as in the case of special districts like the Triborough Bridge Authority), or when local officials lack the resources to respond to citizen demands. Certainly the opponents of the bridge were unable to find any local government with both the inclination and the ability to respond to their demands. How common is that situation? Although this is difficult to determine, the nation has many local governments, particularly special districts, whose leaders do not answer directly to the voters, and it has many local governments lacking the resources—authority, monetary, and other—to satisfy public demands. Citizens facing this situation are not likely to be content with local decisions, and may take their unsatisfied demands to the state or national level or to the judicial branch.

National-Local Programs: Decentralization is not always Local Control

Over the years the national government has been involved in a number of programs that have tried to involve program clienteles, those people served by the program, in decision making and delivery of services. Some of those efforts fall under the heading of national-local relations, broadly defined, but local governments have not always played a formal role in the programs' operations. Moreover, clientele participation has sometimes produced unexpected results.

The Community Action Programs

One of the most controversial efforts of this type began with the passage of the 1964 Economic Opportunity Act. The law created the

Office of Economic Opportunity, which was to support development of innovative methods for combatting poverty. A major component of the law was the creation of the Community Action Programs (CAPs) which were to be carried out locally, with national aid, by public or private nonprofit organizations. Communities were encouraged to create Community Action Agencies with representatives of government agencies, the private sector, and the poor. As noted earlier, some observers hoped that the Community Action Agencies would improve coordination of national-local programs. The law provided that programs were to be developed and conducted with the "maximum feasible participation" of people served by the program—the poor.[14]

While that struck some people as a radical idea, it was consistent with a number of beliefs and practices established long before 1964. First, by involving local residents, the law reflected a belief in the value of grass roots decision making rather than programs dictated from a distant national capital. Second, many government agencies at all levels of government have had advisory committees or boards made up largely of people served or regulated by the agency, or selling goods or services to the agency. Many states have boards to regulate various professions that are composed substantially or even entirely of members of the professions they regulate. Third, government has often acted to strengthen groups that are relatively weak in order to enable them to defend themselves in economic or political affairs. Alexander Hamilton's economic policies under President Washington helped to strengthen American industry. Legislation adopted in the 1930s did the same for organized labor. Some of the officials involved in the Community Action Programs believed that organizing the poor and involving them in the political arena would protect their interests (Moynihan 1970: 96–98, 131–32).

The CAPs were underway in roughly one thousand counties by early 1966, but they quickly became embroiled in controversy. As noted earlier, part of the controversy resulted from the fact that the CAPs' emphasis on developing new solutions to the problem of poverty implied that older programs were ineffective, an implication that offended established antipoverty agencies. Indeed, the very creation of CAPs implied that older antipoverty agencies were somehow deficient (Sundquist and Davis 1969: 47–61). In addition, some CAPs included programs similar to those run by older, established agencies, which generally did not welcome new competition.

Further controversy erupted when many CAPs were racked by

---

14. For a valuable overview of the Community Action Agencies, see Moynihan (1970) and Sundquist and Davis (1969: ch. 2). This discussion relies heavily on their analyses.

infighting over who would control them. Some conflicts occurred along ideological lines, while others followed racial, ethnic, or class lines. In some agencies the conflicts followed several lines at once. The internal squabbling damaged the images of many CAAs, as did the low turnout in a number of CAP board elections (less than 6 percent in several large cities) and the highly publicized administrative problems in some CAAs (Moynihan 1970: 137–38; Sundquist and Davis 1969: 66–72). Such problems were understandable: poor and uneducated people generally have low rates of political participation (Verba and Nie 1972: ch. 8), and new agencies created without established guidelines for operation are vulnerable to administrative problems.

Probably the most serious controversies erupted when the CAAs came into conflict with established local governments, as well as some state and even national agencies. In some cases the conflicts did not directly involve the CAAs but did involve groups identified with them. City and county agencies were the targets of picketing, sit-ins, and other demonstrations. Local officials complained to Washington about the situation, and their complaints received a sympathetic hearing in Congress, which passed amendments in 1967 to increase local government control over the CAAs.

The CAAs grew even weaker when their parent body, the Office of Economic Opportunity, lost most of its programs and then was abolished altogether. Deprived of national support, many of the CAAs closed down; some were supported by city governments, but those CAAs came to be an arm of city hall rather than an independent base of power (Harrigan 1981: 180–81).

The fate of the CAAs indicates, first of all, the ability of local officials to influence national-local programs—in this case to remove a significant irritant. The CAAs also reveal the vulnerability that may come with financial dependence. The CAAs could function only by maintaining the support of Congress and the president, their sources of funding. When the activities of the CAAs caused that support to erode, they had little ability to protect themselves. Finally, as suggested earlier, without a mechanism to handle conflict and maintain relationships, cooperation is difficult.

While the fate of the Community Action Agencies might be explained as the natural result of a collision between newly created government agencies lacking constitutional protection and long-established governments with constitutional protection,[15] other collisions have produced different results. One of the most noteworthy examples resulted

---

15. In state constitutions.

from conflicts over public lands owned by the national government (McConnell 1966: ch. 7).

Control of Grazing Lands

By the latter part of the nineteenth century, the practice of using public lands as if they were private property was well established. In a number of western states, ranchers fenced off large tracts of land owned by the national government, grazed livestock on the land, and excluded other users—sometimes at gunpoint. Moreover, the ranchers often paid nothing for the use of government property, and the free use of land they did not own sometimes encouraged overgrazing, which in turn produced erosion. A number of efforts to establish regulations to control the situation were successfully resisted.

The situation changed with the enactment of the Taylor Grazing Act in 1934. The law created a system of grazing districts, the use of which required a permit issued under the authority of the Secretary of the Interior. Ranchers receiving the grazing permits were required to pay a fee for the privilege. Finally, the law required the secretary to administer the program "in cooperation with local associations of stockmen." If this did not make the point clearly enough, an amendment two years later required that program administrators be residents of western states, where public land holding is substantial, and selected with an eye to "practical experience" (McConnell 1966: 203). In effect the law required administration with "maximum feasible participation" of the ranchers.

As implementation of the act began, the director of the Grazing Service called for elections of district advisors—elections in which only ranchers could participate. Officially the district advisors could only comment and recommend, but in practice their recommendations carried a great deal of weight. During the first fourteen months, the advisor's recommendations regarding grazing permits were followed in more than 98 percent of all cases (McConnell 1966: 204–205).

Things proceeded fairly smoothly for a time, but near the end of World War II a new director of the Grazing Service proposed some changes in the system. A new program to improve rangelands and an increase in grazing fees to reflect the value of the feed obtained from the land were recommended. While the proposals do not strike the outside observer of today as particularly outrageous—the ranchers were asked to pay what they would have had to pay to rent equivalent private land, in return for which the Grazing Service would work to improve the land—ranchers who had become accustomed to using public lands for free prior to 1934, and for very low prices thereafter, reacted with outrage.

The Grazing Service collided head-on with the advisory committees of ranchers, much as local governments collided with the Community Action Agencies years later.

In this case, however, the battle between a legally established government body and a group of quasi-governmental bodies representing program clienteles had a decidedly different outcome: the Director of the Grazing Service was replaced, the Grazing Service lost nearly 80 percent of its personnel, and what was left of the service was merged with the General Land Office to form the Bureau of Land Management. The message was clear: the ranchers did not want the national government encroaching on what they felt were their rights, and, unlike the clienteles of the Community Action Agencies, the ranchers had the resources and organization to defend their position.

Indeed, the organization of ranchers raised serious questions regarding whether the Taylor Grazing Act actually created decentralization or local control. For one thing, by 1940 the district advisory boards formed a National Advisory Board Council and then a system of state boards. In addition, the "local control" of the act was largely restricted to ranchers. Other local residents might have been affected by the decisions, but that did not enable them to participate in the decision-making process. The act in operation appeared to be less a form of decentralization and more a matter of handing control of a national program to an interest group (McConnell 1966: 206–207), one organized on a national basis by 1940. The appearance of decentralization, in the form of local advisory boards, masked the reality of centralization in the hands of an interest group.

More recent evidence points to continuing, substantial influence by ranchers over public lands policies. Conservation programs on public rangelands have been plagued by fears that rancher opposition undercuts management support for the programs. Agency staff in a number of grazing districts believe that ranchers can block initiatives they oppose, and easily get rid of agency personnel who are not sufficiently compliant by having them transferred, demoted, or even fired (*Public Rangelands* 1988: 4, 46–49). One of the Clinton administration's early appointments, former Arizona governor Bruce Babbitt, has a long history of active involvement and conflict with ranchers over public lands policies. Increased activism by Clinton's administration, with its emphasis on innovation and partnership with private enterprise, may result in a shift in the influence of local ranchers on policy.

Decentralization or Interest Group Control?

Decentralization usually means that control of a program is assigned to a local organization to which all segments of the local community have roughly equal access.[16] The history of the Community Action Program, the Taylor Grazing Act, and a number of other programs (McConnell 1966: 232–45) indicates that much of what passes for decentralization is nothing of the sort. In particular, whenever a program is designed to operate "in cooperation with," "with maximum feasible participation by," or some other euphemistic language to the effect that program clienteles will run the program, under the guise of "local control," "decentralization," or "grass roots democracy," one of two outcomes is likely:

1. The clientele group will have the political resources to essentially assume control of the program, to the exclusion of other local interests that may also be affected. In this case the effect will be the transfer of control of the program to an interest group, which may be national in scope.[17]
2. The clientele group, though lacking the necessary political resources, will try to assume control of the program. The resulting backlash will lead to the destruction of the program or elimination of requirements for cooperation, participation, and the like.

Neither of these outcomes resembles decentralization.

This is not to say that participation by program clienteles is invariably negative: it may enhance the efficiency of a program and provide officials with valuable feedback on program operations. It may also be the only genuine alternative to having no program at all. Whether it is a good or bad alternative varies from program to program and may depend on one's individual values. However, it runs the risk of turning a program over to well-organized groups with abundant political resources, groups that will probably run the program to benefit themselves, to the neglect of other interests. Such an arrangement cannot appropriately be labeled decentralization. Once a group becomes accustomed to a particular set of arrangements that enable the group to control an agency or program, making changes to improve management efficiency or pursue new goals is likely to be very difficult (U.S. Department of Agriculture 1991).

Summary

National-local relations, which were relatively limited during much of America's early years, have grown to be very extensive in this century.

16. Leaving aside complications produced by people who are eligible to become involved but choose not to.
17. For a thorough review of interest group power and program capture, see Theodore Lowi (1979: 294–97).

National-local contacts have been stimulated by many factors, including greater population mobility and interdependence, the Depression, mobilization of local political influence, greater acceptance of cooperative federalism, and the national grant system. National-local relations take many forms, including informal contacts, emergency assistance, grants, and national programs that do not formally include local governments but have localized effects.

National-local programs are perceived differently by different actors. National officials tend to be interested primarily in achieving policy goals and, therefore, often seek to shape or regulate the behavior of local officials and administrators. Local officials typically appreciate receiving national resources but often dislike the accompanying restrictions, regulations, and paperwork. State officials are sometimes suspicious of national-local contacts, but many state officials also recognize that an end to national-local aid would produce greater demands on the state governments. Finally, Democrats at the national level are generally more supportive than Republicans of national-local programs, although differences of opinion are found in both parties.

A number of national-local programs have encountered problems at the implementation stage. Problems have arisen from many sources, including disagreements over goals and priorities, differing incentives, the complexity of local government structures, and the number and complexity of many government programs. Although a number of efforts to improve coordination and implementation have been made in recent years, the fundamental causes of the problems are deeply rooted in the American political system and cannot readily be eliminated. The more promising avenues for improvement may involve paying more attention to the incentives facing local officials and offering alternative conflict resolution processes, but implementation will generally remain a difficult process.

Many national-local programs have given program clienteles major roles in program operations. While this practice is often portrayed as a version of grass roots democracy, the result is often closer to interest group control—most conspicuously when the clientele group is organized on a nationwide basis.

CHAPTER 8

Interlocal Relations

Americans have created one of the most complex systems of government in the world, and this complexity is perhaps most evident at the local level. The typical metropolitan area in the United States has roughly a hundred local governments, including numerous municipalities, school districts, and other special districts. Many rural areas are covered with a variety of general-purpose and special-purpose governments with geographical jurisdictions that often bear little resemblance to one another. The multiplicity of local governments has been the subject of many studies, which have reached a number of different conclusions.

This chapter examines several perspectives on interlocal relations. Proposals that seek to reduce the number of local governments or reduce the problems caused by having numerous local governments will be assessed. Finally, proposals to increase the number of local governments and make local governments more responsive to neighborhood concerns and problems will be examined.

Perspectives on Interlocal Relations

Over the years many analysts have questioned whether the United States has too many local governments, and examined the consequences of having over 80,000 local governments. A number of divergent perspectives on these questions have emerged. Each perspective contains important insights into relationships among localities. While the bulk of the literature in this area emphasizes urban government, many of the issues are equally pertinent in rural and small town settings.

The Classical Administrative Perspective

The classical administrative perspective contends that the United States has too many local governments.[1] According to this view, many local governments are too small to achieve economies of scale through such techniques as using specialized equipment and hiring highly trained personnel. For example, Arthur County, in rural Nebraska, has fewer than six hundred residents. A multiplicity of small local governments produces unequal needs and resources. Some jurisdictions face enormous problems with a limited tax base and other jurisdictions are blessed with wealth and few significant problems. Mounting a coordinated attack on areawide problems is very difficult with many independent local governments, because the task of getting them to agree on a plan of action is formidable and, at times, impossible.

Further problems arise because the existence of many small local governments produces a neglect of spillover effects. If people in one city within a metropolitan area permit a factory to pollute the air, people in other jurisdictions will be affected, but will have no voice in the decision. A community may adopt traffic control measures that discourage people from traveling through it, an action that may increase traffic problems in surrounding communities.

A final problem created by multiple, overlapping local governments, according to the classical administrative view, results when citizens try to hold local government accountable. Someone who lives in one local jurisdiction, works in another, and shops and seeks recreation in others, may be affected by several dozen local governments. Very few people are willing to devote the time and energy needed to determine which officials in each of those governments are responsible for local policies. Even a single city block may be served by a county, a municipality, a school district, and several other special districts. If the public cannot keep track of which officials are doing what, accountability suffers (Lyons and Lowery 1989).

The Public Choice Perspective

A very different view of interlocal relations is reflected in the public choice perspective, which holds that having many, small local governments is beneficial.[2] According to this perspective, a local political system

---

1. See Bish and Ostrom (1973: 7–10); Grant and Nixon (1982: 383–87); and Gulick (1961).
2. See Tiebout (1956); Bish and Ostrom (1973); and Ostrom (1972).

is similar to a market. Different local governments offer different packages of services, and citizens shop around for the combination of services they want. For example, one community might have schools that emphasize strict discipline, highly structured classes, and the basics of reading, writing and arithmetic, while another community might offer schools that permit students to pursue their individual interests at whatever pace is comfortable for them. Families could pick the community providing the kind of education they prefer. As a result, the existence of many small governments enables more people to have the policies they desire than would be the case with a single area-wide government, which could only provide one package of programs. Competition among local governments encourages efficiency and responsiveness. A municipality that fails to satisfy citizen demands at a reasonable cost will lose taxpayers to communities that do a better job.

Adherents of the public choice perspective note that larger jurisdictions are not necessarily more efficient. In fact, city governments of over 250,000 in population may experience diseconomies of scale (Bish and Ostrom 1973), with greater size bringing greater cost per unit of service, in part because of the greater problems of controlling larger organizations. The most efficient size for providing one type of service may not be the most efficient for other services. If one service is most efficiently provided by small jurisdictions while another service is most efficiently provided by a large organization, an area with many overlapping governments may be more efficient than it appears. A jurisdiction that is too small to provide a service itself in an economical fashion could purchase the service from another government or a private vendor.

According to the public choice view, small local governments may produce other benefits as well. Smaller jurisdictions may be less threatening to individual citizens, who find themselves dealing with huge, impersonal bureaucracies in big cities. A smaller jurisdiction is less likely to shuffle someone from office to office, and can give a personal touch to government. A small local government, being more accessible, may encourage citizen participation. However, some evidence indicates that contrary to the public choice perspective, fragmentation and smaller suburban communities do not encourage political participation, in part because those communities lack a clear identity, and in part due to confusion as to which governments handle particular programs (Lyons and Lowery 1989; Verba and Nie 1972: 235–47).

In the view of public choice theorists, small local governments should not be eliminated but, rather, preserved. Problems created by the existence of numerous small governments are more than offset by the benefits.

The Class Conflict Perspective

A third view of interlocal relations is the class conflict perspective,[3] which is related in some respects to the classical administrative view. In the class conflict perspective, the benefits of allowing people to shop among different local governments for a desirable package of government services are severely limited by the fact that some people are not permitted to "shop" in some communities.

Zoning regulations and building codes can be used to require large lots, large single-family houses, and expensive building techniques. As a result, people who cannot afford to buy an expensive home can be excluded from a municipality. In a similar fashion, tract development, in which a construction firm builds a large group of homes—perhaps an entire community—may fail to provide any inexpensive housing and therefore excludes people of modest means. Using these mechanisms, a community can exclude poor people with high service needs and little ability to pay for them, creating a haven where prosperous people enjoy low taxes and whatever services they desire. What happens to the poor? They are forced to live elsewhere. In short, the concept of shopping for local services applies fairly well to people who can afford to live anywhere, but leaves others who are not so affluent with few options.

In addition to promoting segregation by class (Hill, 1974: 1559–66), fragmentation—or having many different local governments in one area—may encourage segregation by race. For many years, the titles of many houses contained restrictive covenants that did not permit current or future owners to sell the houses to non-whites. As a result, racial minorities were excluded from communities even if they could afford to buy. Those covenants are no longer legally binding, but the effects of the past linger on, and a variety of informal mechanisms continue to steer minorities away from some communities.

In a similar fashion, limitations on the availability of credit, particularly when black families tried to move into white areas, fostered residential segregation. While that practice has been largely eliminated, at least officially, the effects remain. Also, realtors may steer customers to particular communities and away from others, further increasing segregation.

The practice of excluding people with high service needs and little ability to pay for them produces communities with great wealth and few serious problems, and communities with little wealth and enormous problems. The prosperous jurisdictions can finance their programs with relatively low tax rates, thus encouraging affluent citizens and businesses to move there. In the process, the less affluent jurisdictions grow even

3. See Downs (1973); Hill (1974); and Newton (1975).

poorer, and their poor residents cannot relocate to the affluent communities. The poor remain crowded in localities that are hard-pressed to finance basic services.

Because fragmentation tends to concentrate the poor together, it often compounds their problems. The cost of meeting their needs tends to drive jobs and affluent citizens to other jurisdictions that exclude the poor, leaving them isolated from opportunities for economic advancement. The isolation and lack of economic opportunities increase feelings of alienation and frustration, which in turn create problems of social control. In the class conflict perspective, then, the existence of many small local governments creates a governmental system that greatly compounds the problems of poor people and racial minorities.

A key driving force in this process is competition among local governments. To the degree that people and businesses shop around for the package of services they prefer, local officials do not necessarily regard all customers as equally attractive. Wealthy residents and businesses that can contribute substantially to a locality's tax base but demand relatively few services are a net gain for the treasury. Poor people contribute little to the tax base but need many services; they are a net drain on the treasury. While local officials may anxiously court the favor of affluent citizens and businesses, even to the point of bidding against one another to attract new firms (Feiock 1991; Schneider 1987), the poor are rarely the objects of such treatment. Competition among local governments leads to greater sensitivity to the affluent and relatively less interest in the needy.

The Intergovernmental Perspective

A final perspective on interlocal relations is the intergovernmental perspective (Nice 1983c), which is primarily concerned with two questions. First, how did metropolitan areas become so fragmented? Second, what implications does fragmentation have for intergovernmental relations?

Fragmentation resulted from many factors, including differing lifestyle values, and the desire of many citizens to escape central city problems and relocate in smaller, more personal communities. However, a major cause of fragmentation lies with state policies on annexation, consolidation, and incorporation. Prior to 1900, annexation was comparatively easy. As people and businesses moved away from the city, its boundaries were moved outward to include them. Annexation activity slowed greatly in the 1920s and 1930s (Griffith 1974: 289), partly due to changes in state laws that made annexation and consolidation more difficult (Bollens and Schmandt 1975: 239–41; Harrigan 1976: 218). City boundaries could not keep pace with population growth, new suburbs were incorporated, and the fragmented metropolis began to form.

Why would state officials do such a thing? Political scientists have long recognized that states have often had strained relationships with their large cities. Malapportionment in state legislatures served to limit the influence of large cities. State restrictions on local financial powers and legal authority reflect, in part, state mistrust of local governments. Bear in mind that the 1920 Census was the first to show that a majority of Americans lived in cities. Since state officials were wary of the political power of the cities, they supported making annexation and consolidation more difficult, as this would encourage the cities to fragment, limiting the likelihood of urban unity.

Recent research provides some support for the argument that urban fragmentation results in part from tensions between states and their metropolitan areas (Nice 1983c). In states where there is conflict between metropolitan and non-metropolitan areas, large scale annexation by big cities is less common and fragmentation is greater. In a related vein, where local governments carry a larger financial role in state-local government, large-scale annexations are less likely and fragmentation is greater. Both patterns fit the intergovernmental perspective, for conflict between metropolitan and non-metropolitan areas heightens concern over the power of large cities. In a similar fashion, where local governments play a larger financial role, fears about big city influence are likely to be greater than in states where local governments are fiscally weak.

Research on the proliferation of special district governments, which constitute about one third of all metropolitan-area governments, also supports the intergovernmental perspective. Where state governments have imposed more restrictions on local governments' financial powers (hardly a sign of cordial state-local relations), the number of special district governments has grown more rapidly (MacManus 1981). If a city or county government is financially unable to meet a public demand, creating a new special district can overcome that problem. As a result, however, fragmentation increases.

Metropolitan fragmentation has a number of important implications for intergovernmental relations. Fragmentation, along with zoning regulations, building codes, and other mechanisms, encourages residential segregation by race and class. Residential segregation by class is associated with greater class conflict in voting (Almy 1973). Communities that are noticeably different in terms of social class are less likely to join together in interjurisdictional agreements or participate in joint authorities to deal with a common problem (Dye et al. 1963). In short, fragmentation tends to aggravate internal disagreements in metropolitan areas. Disagreements will occur whenever large numbers of people live close

together, but fragmentation tends to encourage disagreements and provides no local arena for resolving them. The prospects for united metropolitan action are correspondingly reduced.

At the same time, fragmentation often separates needs from resources, leaving some cities too poor to cope with their problems. Even
if resources are evenly distributed, the task of getting several dozen local
governments to agree on a plan of attack for area-wide problems is difficult if not impossible. People who want action on those area-wide problems will be inclined to turn to state or national officials for help, because
the local governments will often be unable to cope.

From an intergovernmental standpoint, fragmentation makes local
resolution of problems very difficult and, therefore, encourages intervention by higher levels of government. By encouraging disagreements
within metropolitan areas, fragmentation reduces the ability of these
areas to exert influence on higher levels of government. The resulting
combination is not very encouraging to people who believe in grass
roots government.

Too Many Local Governments? Some Strategies

Critics who believe that the United States has too many local governments have developed a number of solutions, which, with varying effectiveness, seek to eliminate or minimize problems created by the multiplicity of local governments.[4] The continued existence of numerous localities
indicates that major obstacles stand in the way of at least some of the
proposed remedies.

Informal Cooperation

Probably the least drastic method for coping with the existence of
numerous local governments is informal cooperation and consultation
among local officials. For example, if a county planning to make major
repairs on a road that carries heavy traffic informs neighboring counties,
the neighboring counties are able to prepare for different traffic flows.
Police departments can exchange information on law enforcement problems and coordinate use of radio frequencies to avoid interfering with
one another's communications. Misunderstandings can be avoided, and
unintentional inconveniences prevented.

Unfortunately, the value of informal cooperation is seriously limited by the all-too-frequent absence of a spirit of cooperation. Officials

4. For overviews of these proposals, see Bollens and Schmandt (1982: chs. 10–
12); Leach (1970: 152–58); and Schneider (1980: 269–301).

in one jurisdiction may prefer to do as they please, regardless of the problems that may result in other jurisdictions. Voluntary agreement is particularly hard to reach on controversial policy issues. Informal cooperation does not address inequalities in needs and resources or create economies of scale, nor does it provide a binding agreement to which all parties must abide. An informal agreement may collapse when a mayor leaves office or a new city council is elected.

Service Contracts

A somewhat more effective and widely used solution to some of the problems created by fragmentation is the service contract. A local government purchases a service, such as water, trash collection, or fire protection, from a contractor, who may be another local government or a private firm.[5] One of the national leaders in this technique is Los Angeles County, which sells a wide variety of services to other local governments in the Los Angeles area. Using service contracts, a local government that is too small to provide economical sewage treatment or a modern police crime laboratory can have access to these services at a reasonable cost. A service contract also provides a binding agreement that can be enforced in court, should the need arise. Approximately half of all cities and counties in the United States are now involved in service contracts (Hamilton and Wells 1990: 155).

The contract approach has limitations, however. One of the most fundamental problems is that all relevant parties must agree to the contract. Controversial policy areas, therefore, are generally not suitable for handling using the contract approach. A suburb that has gone to great lengths to exclude low-income people is highly unlikely to approve a contract with the central city to enable low-income people to move into the suburb. Service contracts also do not equalize needs and resources. Communities that cannot pay the going rates for services cannot participate.[6]

Councils of Governments

An apparently more drastic solution to problems arising from the existence of numerous local governments (although appearances may be deceiving) is the Council of Governments. The Council of Governments,

5. On the concept of privatization, see Savas (1982).
6. If, as Savas (1982) contends, private contractors are more efficient than government agencies at providing services, then using private contractors could help poor communities get more services from their limited budgets.

consisting of representatives of local governments, provides an arena where information can be exchanged and disputes can be resolved. Strategies for attacking areawide problems can be formulated, and the actions of individual governments can be coordinated. The capabilities of Councils of Governments were enhanced for a time by their responsibility for reviewing federal grant applications emerging from their respective areas.

In a variety of respects, Councils of Governments have not proven to be as effective as some observers had hoped (Bollens and Schmandt 1982: 372-73; Harrigan 1981: 332-33). The councils are limited by the problem of reaching agreement among the participants. As in the United Nations, representatives of individual governments do not easily reach agreement, particularly on controversial issues.[7] As a result, councils often tend to limit their efforts to relatively minor matters. They also have very little ability to bind the various local governments to commitments made in the council. Even the grant review process was handled gingerly, in part because individual participants feared retaliation from local officials whose grant proposals were disapproved. Councils do not equalize needs and resources, and they cannot provide economies of scale in service delivery.

Special Districts

A widely used device for coping with numerous small local governments is the special district, which is discussed in chapter 6. This governing body is created to handle one or more responsibilities, such as education, transportation, or sewage treatment. The special district raises money through taxation, the sale of bonds, and/or user fees, and uses the revenue to provide a service. Because a special district may cover a number of jurisdictions, it can provide a coordinated, areawide approach to dealing with a policy issue. An areawide special district can tap pockets of wealth and target funds where they are most needed. Moreover, it can make binding policy decisions.

The advantages of special districts are offset by several disadvantages. The use of special districts, while helping to overcome fragmentation by area, creates functional fragmentation, with one special district handling parks, another dealing with transportation, still another providing waste treatment, and so forth. New coordination problems may result. The proliferation of special districts gives the public many additional units of government to keep track of, a task that is difficult and confusing

---

7. The comparison between the United Nations and Councils of Governments was first made by Joseph Zimmerman (1972). For a more positive assessment, see Wikstrom (1977).

(on both of these points, see Leach 1970: 156). Public interest in the activities of many single-purpose special districts appears rather low, a situation that is hardly conducive to democratic accountability. Not all special districts are headed by elected officials; some special districts are governed by appointed leaders, in which case public control becomes problematic. Many special districts are much less than areawide in coverage—the typical metropolitan area has nearly as many school districts as municipalities. In that event, the ability to produce economies of scale, areawide coordination, and equalization of needs and resources will be very limited.

Annexation and Consolidation

A more drastic approach to the problem of excessive local governments lies in the twin processes of annexation and consolidation (see chapter 6). A city could expand its boundaries outward to include or "annex" an entire metropolitan area. Several small, rural counties could consolidate into one large county. These techniques, if carried far enough, could create an area under a single local government, producing economies of scale, areawide coordination, and equalization of needs and resources. In addition, the final result would be a government far more visible than a collection of areawide special districts and, therefore, more easily held accountable to the public.

Some cities have practiced annexation on a massive scale. Between 1950 and 1978, Atlanta, Georgia, expanded from a land area of 37 square miles to over 131 square miles. In the same time period the area encompassed by Dallas, Texas, roughly tripled. Other cities expanded even more rapidly; Oklahoma City's area grew more than tenfold, and Phoenix, Arizona, covered more than fifteen times as much territory in 1978 and it did in 1950 (Bollens and Schmandt 1982: 306–307).

The primary limitation of annexation and consolidation is feasibility. Annexation and consolidation are often bitterly and successfully resisted by jurisdictions whose residents do not want their cities or counties merged with one another. Central city residents may fear the dilution of their voting power by the addition of outsiders to the central city electorate. Local politicians may fear the loss of their jobs due to consolidation; a metropolitan area with twenty municipalities can have twenty mayors, but a consolidated area with one municipality can have only one mayor. Many of the nation's older central cities, such as Milwaukee, are completely surrounded by suburbs, a situation that rules out the use of annexation (Bollens and Schmandt 1982: 304, 308). Annexation appears to be particularly difficult when a relatively poor central city is surrounded by relatively prosperous outlying areas (Dye 1964). In that case, wealthy suburbanites generally resist the prospect of paying higher taxes to address downtown problems.

County-Based Solutions

Given the difficulty of adjusting city boundaries, some reformers see a solution in county government. The urban county approach involves transferring some city government programs to the county government. Instead of having twenty separate city police forces, an area would have a single county police force. The transfer may involve a single program, as in the case of Minnesota's shifting of welfare from city governments to counties, or may involve a number of programs, such as the transfer of sewers, mass transit, and health programs from Cleveland's city government to the county (Bollens and Schmandt 1982: 358–59).

A more drastic county-based approach is city-county consolidation, in which a county and the cities within it merge into a single political unit. This has been done in Indianapolis, Jacksonville, and Philadelphia. The county-based approaches can provide economies of scale and equalization of needs and resources, as well as improved coordination, particularly with city-county consolidation. Because counties are probably more visible than special districts, the former are easier to hold accountable than the latter.

The primary limitation of county-based approaches is the difficulty in getting them enacted, particularly when city-county consolidation is proposed. Another limitation arises from the fact that many metropolitan areas cover two or more counties. Even in that case, however, two counties would provide greater coordination than twenty municipalities. Also, many rural counties are too small to improve matters very much, and consolidating them is extremely difficult. Some observers question whether counties are structurally suitable for increased responsibilities. Although structural reforms have enhanced the capabilities of some county governments, mainly those in urban areas, many counties still lack coherent executive leadership and personnel systems emphasizing competence (Grant and Nixon 1982: 348–52). Since counties and cities define their legal authority differently, some cities may have more policy latitude than the corresponding county.

Federated Metropolitan Government

The most elaborate response to the multiplicity of local governments is the federated metropolitan government, which is essentially a miniature federal system. One level of government handles areawide responsibilities and covers the entire metropolitan area. A second level of smaller governments handles more localized responsibilities. The most notable example of this technique in North America is Toronto, Canada. The federated system provides coordination, economies of scale, and equalization of needs and resources. At the same time, it provides some flexibility to accommodate differing needs and preferences from one part of the metropolitan area to another. The visibility and simplicity of the system enhance public accountability. While most of the literature on federated local governments focuses on metropolitan areas, the same approach could be used in rural areas as well.

The fundamental shortcoming of the federated metropolitan government approach is the great difficulty in getting it adopted. The rarity of federated metropolitan governments in the United States is eloquent testimony to the odds against enactment. Other problems arise because of disagreement over which level should handle a given problem or responsibility. The Miami-Dade County metropolitan government, which gives the county government responsibility for areawide matters and assigns local functions to city governments within the county, has faced numerous conflicts over the powers and responsibilities of each level in the system (Bollens and Schmandt 1982: 324–32; Grant and Nixon 1982: 397–98). As the earlier discussion of national-state government disputes indicated, these conflicts are not easy to resolve.

As a general rule, the most effective approaches to the problem of numerous small local governments are least likely to be adopted (Advisory Commission on Intergovernmental Relations 1976: 361, 364; Glendening and Reeves 1977: 299). In part, this tendency reflects the principle of the scope of conflict—people who benefit from the existence of multiple, independent local governments do not want to lose those benefits. As a result, informal cooperation, service contracts, councils of government, and special districts are common but not always effective. By contrast, the use of annexation and consolidation on a broad scale and the adoption of federated local governments are effective solutions theoretically, but are extremely difficult to put into practice.

Non-Local Solutions

If effective local solutions to the multiplicity of local governments are generally not politically feasible, what are people who are concerned about the problem to do? Previous material on intergovernmental politics suggests one possibility: if local solutions are not feasible, try state or national solutions. Two non-local solutions present themselves.[8]

8. In this case, non-local solutions are solutions that require the continued involvement of national and state governments. A number of the more drastic local solutions, such as the federated metropolitan government, would require state approval but would not entail continued state involvement.

First, grants in aid may provide help in dealing with some of the problems created by the multiplicity of small localities. Through grants, national or state revenue systems can redistribute wealth from affluent jurisdictions to poorer ones, a process that helps equalize needs and resources. Grants can also include requirements for areawide coordination and review to create some consistency across an area, and can compensate for spillover effects.

Second, a higher level of government can take a direct role in a program in order to provide uniformity, coordination, and economies of scale. In Hawaii, for example, education is in the hands of state government, a system that can create a more consistent quality of program than one that places much of the responsibility on small, local school districts. Also, a state police crime laboratory can provide technical assistance to local police forces.

The growth of national and state grants, and national and state roles in the domestic policy arena, indicate that the non-local solutions have some degree of feasibility as well as effectiveness. Unfortunately they also have a problem that is reflected in the old adage: "You can shoot a horse with a broken leg, but that won't fix the broken leg." The non-local solutions do not reduce the number of small local governments, but only ameliorate the problems they create. However, given the extreme difficulty of reducing the number of localities, policymakers may have little choice.

Case Study: Metropolitan Reform in Nashville

Although the more drastic local government reorganization proposals have generally not proven to be politically feasible, exceptions do exist. One exception involves the city of Nashville, Tennessee, which consolidated with Davidson County in 1962.[9] Several conditions helped this consolidation pass. These conditions indicate that abstract arguments in favor of reforms are not sufficient to convince voters to approve them.

A key factor that helped generate support for the consolidation was public dissatisfaction with suburban services. Poorly maintained septic tanks had begun to pollute the groundwater, threatening wells used for drinking water. Private systems of fire protection gave uneven coverage, resulting in higher insurance rates.

Consolidation also benefitted from suburban anger at the mayor of Nashville. After a similar consolidation proposal failed in 1958, the city embarked on a major annexation effort—one that did not require

9. The material in this section is drawn from Bollens and Schmandt (1982: 315); Harrigan (1981: 292–94); and Hawkins (1966).

voter approval in the area being annexed. The city also passed a law requiring suburbanites to purchase green stickers to display on their windshields to pay for the privilege of using Nashville's streets. The 1962 consolidation proposal attracted support from residents in outlying areas who saw it as a way to exact revenge on the mayor, who publicly opposed the proposal.

Finally, city-county consolidation was less traumatic because there were only six incorporated suburbs, and these were relatively small. It is likely that larger and more numerous suburbs could have provided a more formidable base for opposition. Even in Nashville's case, the suburbs were allowed to remain in existence, in part to avoid antagonizing their residents.

The conditions that contributed to the Nashville-Davidson County consolidation's approval are notably absent in many other areas. Service problems are not usually perceived as crises, although citizens grumble about services almost everywhere. Suburbanites rarely see reform as a means of getting rid of a politician who has angered them, and many of our central cities are surrounded by a considerable number of large, well established suburbs. Not surprisingly, therefore, the usual result of major local government reorganization efforts is defeat.

The Limits of Reform

Assuming that some of the more effective solutions to the problem of an excessive number of small, local governments could be adopted on an extensive scale (bearing in mind that the historical record indicates otherwise), could the long-term decline of local government noted earlier be reversed? A definitive answer is not possible, but an educated guess would be: "Not completely." Local governments that cover large areas and populations, either through annexation/consolidation or the formation of federated local governments, would certainly be in a better position to attack areawide problems coherently and tap pockets of wealth regardless of their location in the metropolitan area. Achieving economies of scale and making binding decisions would enhance their ability to find policy solutions. In these respects, reorganization would make local governments better able to compete with national and state governments.

In other regards, however, local governments would remain in a disadvantaged position. First, in a highly mobile, interdependent society, few problems have purely local effects. Transportation flows, economic changes, pollution, and many other problems have statewide, nationwide, and even international consequences. Local governments, acting alone, are unlikely to resolve these problems effectively.

Second, technological changes in many policy areas have escalated costs to the point that local governments have difficulty amassing enough resources to deal with them. A mass transit system can cost hundreds of millions or even billions of dollars, a sum that gives pause to almost all local officials. No longer can a horse-drawn trolley down the middle of the street suffice.

Third, because local governments are generally smaller than state governments or the national government, interjurisdictional competition is most influential locally. Even if local officials have the resources to tackle a problem, they may, for fear of driving away jobs, investment, and the like, do nothing.

The prospects of restoring local governments to the position they occupied at the turn of the century appear, therefore, bleak. Local governments are likely to remain heavily dependent on other levels for much of their revenue and subject to considerable influence by other levels. Structural reforms could enhance local government vitality somewhat, but the social and technological changes that have occurred in this century will not disappear.

Community Control

While one group of reformers has pressed for the creation of larger, all-encompassing local governments and the reduction of the number of local governments, another group has pressed for the creation of smaller local governments, typically at the neighborhood level. This second group advocates community control—that is, formation of new governmental structures at the neighborhood level.[10]

The Case for Community Control

Community control draws support from a number of sources. Some advocates note that particularly in large cities, there are likely to be considerable differences in needs, values, and priorities from one area to another. Neighborhood governments permit policies to be tailored to the specific needs and desires of individual neighborhoods. Note that this argument is similar to one of the traditional justifications for federalism: it can accommodate variations in needs or opinions.

Advocates of community control charge that in very large local governments, most individual neighborhoods are too small to exert much influence over elected officials or the large and powerful local bureaucra-

10. The literature on community control is extensive. See Fainstein and Fainstein (1976); Yates (1973); Yin and Yates (1975); and Zimmerman (1972).

cies. Moreover, people may be discouraged from even trying to influence a large, impersonal, and, in some cases, physically distant local government. Feelings of powerlessness and alienation discourage citizen involvement, thus producing even greater feelings of powerlessness. Neighborhood governments, by virtue of their small size and accessibility, may foster greater feelings of confidence and, therefore, more involvement.

Advocates of community control also contend that, in many localities, even if groups have access to elected officials, many large bureaucracies are considerably independent of both the elected officials and the nominal heads of individual departments.[11] If the mayor has only limited control over the department head, and the department head has only limited control over the police officer on patrol or the teacher in the classroom, neighborhoods may be better off establishing direct control over neighborhood services.

Finally, community control draws support from groups who feel that they cannot get a sympathetic or respectful hearing from existing local officials because of class, racial, or ethnic antagonisms. These groups believe that contracting the scope of conflict to the neighborhood level, where their point of view may be dominant, will assure them of a more sympathetic hearing.

Types of Community Control

Community control can take many forms. As we might expect, the form used can make a great deal of difference in the results. The most modest version of community control is some type of *community* or *neighborhood advisory board.* As the name indicates, this board has no formal authority to make policy decisions. It may, however, air complaints about local services, study problems, recommend changes in existing programs, or make suggestions regarding program operations.

The influence of advisory boards is limited by several factors. First, the fact that they may only advise means that agencies may ignore the advice, unless the people on the board and the views they recommend have substantial political support behind them. Second, even if local bureaucrats in a particular neighborhood want to follow the recommendations of a neighborhood board, rigid city, county, state or national regulations and policies may not provide sufficient flexibility. Finally, if advisory board members serve only part-time and have little staff assistance, both common conditions, board members may have great diffi-

11. On the power and independence of urban bureaucracies, especially at lower levels, see Lipsky (1980) and Lowi (1968).

culty in merely keeping informed of agency procedures and programs, not to mention competing with the expertise of agency professionals.

A second approach to limited community control is *little city halls*, which are now found in dozens of cities, including Boston. Little city halls are typically branches of the mayor's office. They serve as forums where citizens can register complaints regarding city services and policies, often provide citizens with information regarding city programs and regulations, and may provide some routine services, such as voter registration. They do not, however, make policy decisions, nor do they have discretion to tailor programs to the needs of particular neighborhoods.

Critics of little city halls charge that they create the appearance of neighborhood control without the reality of it, a charge that has considerable merit. Little city halls may, however, increase city officials' awareness of the needs of particular neighborhoods. Other critics have expressed the fear that little city halls may be operated for the political benefit of the mayor. A citywide network of organizations financed by the taxpayers, staffed with people loyal to the mayor, and designed to help citizens cope with the complexities of urban life sounds vaguely like a political machine.

The more drastic forms of community control involve the creation of neighborhood organizations with some degree of control over services and programs. These organizations may be limited to a single program, such as health or neighborhood schools, or may be involved in a variety of programs. They may have fairly broad discretion in decision making, or may be required to operate within fairly narrow limits. Yates (1973) found that neighborhood organizations with a broader range of responsibilities typically had only limited discretion, while organizations limited to a single program had broader discretion.

Community Control in Practice: New York City Schools

Previous experiments with community control have sometimes sparked controversy. One example is the New York City school system.[12] During the 1960s, many blacks complained that schools in predominantly black neighborhoods were typically the oldest and in the poorest condition of any in the city, had the poorest facilities and least experienced teachers, and that the city's educational bureaucracy did not seem very concerned about the problems.

In 1967 an experiment was begun: three neighborhood school districts in poor neighborhoods were created within the larger New York

12. See Gittel (1971) for a discussion of the New York experiment.

City school system. Each district had its own board elected by neighborhood residents, as do most school districts in the United States.

Conflict soon erupted in one of the new school districts. The board hired new employees from outside the regular citywide personnel system. In addition, the same board tried to transfer some teachers out of its schools and bring in new teachers. Critics charged that the neighborhood board was exceeding its authority (a common complaint in federal systems, as noted in chapter 4), and teachers responded by going on strike. Various disorders followed.

At this point the New York state legislature intervened and ended the experiment. The three experimental districts were terminated and replaced by thirty-one local boards that, together, covered the entire city. The new boards had essentially no control over budgets, personnel, or programs, but did provide forums where citizens could voice their complaints.

Recent proposals for school voucher plans represent another attempt to reduce the power of public school bureaucracies, although the implications for neighborhood influence are not entirely clear. On the one hand, the increased competition that a voucher system could create should cause public schools to be more responsive to neighborhood or community concerns (or face the loss of students). On the other hand, if a voucher system leads to children from the same neighborhood going to several different schools and to students from many different neighborhoods going to any given school, the influence of neighborhoods on the schools might actually decline. If the choice of schools is no longer neighborhood or community-based, the neighborhood or community no longer has its "own" schools to influence.

The Case against Community Control

Critics of community control fear that the more drastic versions—those that would create neighborhood governments with genuine control over programs—would further fragment metropolitan areas where reaching agreement on areawide problems is already extremely difficult. If one hundred local governments in a metropolitan area rarely agree on a course of action, what will happen if that same area has one thousand or ten thousand local governments? United action will be impossible, say the critics.

In a related vein, critics charge that community control would lead to excessive parochialism, a criticism often levied against public choice advocates. Neighborhood governments would advocate neighborhood interests, which do not necessarily reflect the interest of the city or society as a whole. Although from an economic perspective, a city might benefit considerably from the presence of an industrial facility that is dusty, noisy, and generates considerable traffic, neighborhood organizations might not allow it in their respective neighborhoods. The same problem could erupt with mental health facilities, public housing, or many other projects.

Critics fear the neighborhood governments would neglect spillover effects that their decisions create. For example, if a neighborhood's residents believe that consumption of mind-altering substances is a sacred right and direct their police officers to ignore the sale and consumption of these substances, sale and consumption might spread from one neighborhood to the entire city and beyond. Affected people from outside the neighborhood would have little or no voice in the decision.

Some critics worry that creating more governments in a federal system that already has more than 80,000 will simply overwhelm voters, who already face a burdensome task in trying to monitor the activities of the governments now in existence. Voting surveys indicate that many citizens have only limited awareness of the activities of many public officials. Creating still more governments will only make the problem worse.

Some observers are concerned that neighborhood governments would encourage segregation. Some neighborhood governments in predominantly black (or nonwhite) neighborhoods emphasize strengthening the black (or nonwhite) community, while neighborhood governments in predominantly white neighborhoods may emphasize (implicitly or explicitly) the exclusion of blacks (Yates 1973: 161). Neither situation is conducive to integration. Moreover, as noted earlier, metropolitan fragmentation tends to foster residential segregation by race and by social class. Community control would certainly increase fragmentation and could reinforce existing segregation patterns.

A final problem with community control is a financial one. If neighborhood governments are located in poor neighborhoods, there will be very few financial resources available. Those governments will face a dilemma. Should they rely on their own resources, which will be too limited to support many programs, or should they seek aid from higher levels of government, in which case those higher levels will have financial leverage on the neighborhood governments? The fate of the Community Action Agencies is a powerful lesson in what can happen to small, financially dependent organizations with few allies. Their existence requires staying on good terms with their financial benefactors, which may limit their policy choices. Less dramatic but also important is the situation facing all governments dependent on funds raised by other governments: aid typically brings strings, regulations, and guidelines.

Bear in mind that these criticisms are primarily directed at the more drastic versions of community control, those in which neighborhood governments make policies and allocate resources. Milder versions, such as little city halls, pose fewer problems but also provide fewer benefits.

The Interlocal Dilemma

The problem facing interlocal relations is fundamental. How do we devise a system of local governments large enough to handle areawide problems and small enough to remain responsive to the needs and desires of neighborhoods and other small areas? In theory, federated local government seems a promising solution, but the political feasibility of this approach is exceedingly low. Instead we have a variety of local governments, some of which are small enough to approximate neighborhood governments, where areawide problems are dealt with, sometimes imperfectly, by a combination of special districts, interlocal agreement, and intervention by state and national governments. It is not a neatly organized system, nor does it always function effectively, but as both the public choice and class conflict perspectives indicate, it serves the interests of the wealthy relatively well. Consequently, adopting major changes in the system is very difficult.

Summary

The abundance of local governments in the United States has been a subject of interest for many years. The classical administrative perspective regards the large number of small local governments as a major problem because it leads to coordination problems, neglect of spillover effects, inequality of needs and resources, and a lack of economies of scale. By contrast, the public choice perspective emphasizes the benefits of multiple, small localities, including interjurisdictional competition as a stimulant to efficiency, more choices of government programs, and smaller, more accessible local governments. The class conflict perspective charges that a multiplicity of local governments promotes segregation by class and race; as a result, some local governments have abundant resources and few problems, but other local governments have limited resources and many problems. In addition, poor people are excluded from areas where economic opportunities are greatest. The intergovernmental perspective regards metropolitan fragmentation as, in part, a result of tensions between the states and large cities. Fragmentation, in this view, makes local resolution of problems difficult and reduces local influence over other levels of government.

A variety of responses to the problems of abundant local governments have been offered and tried. The solutions range from informal cooperation and service contracts to city-county consolidation and federated local government. In general, the solutions that would address more of the problems are also more difficult to enact.

Advocates of community control complain that large local governments are often inaccessible to neighborhood groups. Even if government is sympathetic to concerns, it is often unable to control large local bureaucracies, with the result that neighborhood viewpoints may have little impact on the actual operation of government programs. The community control solution is to establish mechanisms for increasing neighborhood influence over local programs. Critics charge, however, that the more extensive versions of community control would encourage parochialism and neglect of spillover effects. Moreover, neighborhood governments in poor neighborhoods face the dilemma of choosing between financial independence, which leaves them with very few resources, or financial dependence, which leaves them vulnerable to influence by the source of funds.

CHAPTER 9

Conclusions: Federalism as a Setting for Politics

Federalism sometimes appears to assume the form of a religion. Some observers contend that proper adherence to federal principles, or proper regard for the rights of states, or proper respect for local prerogatives, requires a particular course of action, apparently without regard to whether that course will yield disastrous policy consequences or enormous social costs. These observers give the impression that proper federal principles have been inscribed in stone by some divine messenger, and any reasonably intelligent person need only read the inscription to know the appropriate course of action.

In practice, of course, hardly anyone thinks about federalism in these terms. To do so would mean the triumph of the organization over the objectives it was created to pursue.[1]

In reality, federalism is like a game with multiple playing boards and very ambiguous rules. Players contest with one another over which playing boards will be used, what the rules will be, who will play the game, what teams (if any) players will form, and, *most important of all*, what the object of the game will be. Once a player determines the object to pursue, he or she looks for other potential players with the same goal and tries to persuade them to join the game. The player tries to select the playing board or boards where success is most likely, and interprets the rules in ways that further his or her goal. Once a player reaches one goal, pursuit of a new goal may require a switch to a new playing board,

---

1. On the general phenomenon of an organization triumphing over its objectives, see Michels (1962: 190, 338–39).

a new interpretation of the rules, an effort to include new players or exclude established players, and/or a reshuffling of teams. A large number of different games take place at the same time.

Participants in intergovernmental politics, then, try to use the federal system to achieve their policy goals. They look for allies, both in and out of government, and they look for governments receptive to their demands. They try to avoid decision-making arenas dominated by their opponents and to exclude supporters of the opposition (Schattschneider 1960; Michels 1962: 198–200; Nathan 1990: 241–56).They interpret the rules to maximize their advantages and weaken the opposition.

How, then, can we account for the prevalence of the federalism-as-religion rhetoric? While some of it is undoubtedly sincere, much of it is tactical. Few segregationists in the 1950s and 1960s believed that they would receive a favorable response nationally if they publicly asserted their beliefs in black inferiority, and their desire to deny blacks a constitutionally guaranteed right to vote. Consequently, segregationists emphasized the constitutional status of the states and their views regarding national-state relations. At the state level, their policy goals of segregation and subordination of blacks received a more sympathetic reception. Much of the rhetoric about federalism, then, is actually rhetoric about policy in disguise.

Complications arise, however, because discussions about federalism that begin as cloaks for policy views may take on an independent existence. People may initially formulate or adopt arguments about federalism to further their policy goals but may come to sincerely believe their arguments. John C. Calhoun, for example, was an ardent defender of the rights of states to conduct their affairs as they pleased in the period leading up to the Civil War. His position was used to defend the institution of slavery, which obviously did not protect the rights of blacks, yet he and many other people seemed to genuinely believe his contention that preserving states' rights was essential to the preservation of liberty.

Although arguments about federalism do at times take on lives of their own, they generally remain subordinate to policy views. The Reagan administration, therefore, was able to advocate a substantial reduction in national government involvement in both domestic policy-making and national influence over state and local governments. At the same time, the Reagan administration accepted legislation that cut federal highway aid to states not raising the legal drinking age to twenty-one, adopted regulations to require family planning clinics (many of which are run by state or local governments) to notify parents of minors receiving prescription contraceptives or face a cutoff of federal funds, and sought to gain access to private medical records to monitor treatment of handicapped infants. Examples of such inconsistency are widespread at all levels of government and among private groups and individuals. Abstract notions of federalism can rarely resist policy concerns.

Perennial Dilemmas

Federal systems face a number of dilemmas. Numerous efforts to resolve them have been attempted, and more attempts are certain to follow, but the dilemmas persist. In some cases the most that can be expected is that we live with them and try to make the best choices among conflicting goals.

Flexibility and Uniformity

One of the most fundamental dilemmas in federal systems is the choice between subunit flexibility, which enables subnational jurisdictions to respond to different policy views, and uniformity, without which there may be great inequalities in services and rights. In some instances the dilemma can be partially resolved, as in the case of the Supplemental Security Income Program, which provides for a nationwide minimum benefit level but permits states to provide higher benefits if they choose to contribute additional funds. That the resolution is only partial is due to two factors. First, establishing a minimum program reduces flexibility directly. Second, involvement by a higher level of government to establish a minimum program may bring additional regulations. National highway grants, for example, served as a basis for the twenty-one-year-old drinking age. Flexibility is lost in the process.

As a general rule, a more diverse country, if the diversity is geographically patterned—for example, one section of the country being primarily agricultural and another section primarily industrial—has a greater need for subunit flexibility. If opinions, needs, or conditions vary greatly from state to state, flexibility will be valuable in accommodating those variations. A homogeneous country or a country that is diverse but with a uniform diversity—that is, with many different views that are evenly distributed across the nation—will gain considerably less from subunit flexibility.

By contrast, as a society grows increasingly mobile and interdependent, uniformity gains appeal. People who remain home and are economically self-sufficient have limited grounds for concern regarding what other governments do. As people grow more mobile and interdependent, they are increasingly affected by decisions of jurisdictions within which they do not reside. Motorists are affected by the conditions of roads in any jurisdiction they enter. All travelers are affected by the crime rates of communities they visit. Residents of energy-importing states are affected by the decision of energy-exporting states. These situations produce demands for greater uniformity.

Innovation: Invention and Diffusion

A second fundamental dilemma centers on policy innovation. Federalism creates a variety of jurisdictions that can simultaneously test a number of policy approaches less expensively than nationwide policy experimentation.[2] However, once a successful program has been developed, the multiplicity of decision centers often slows adoption of the innovation. Federalism, then, may facilitate development of policy innovations but impede their adoption. Higher levels of government can offer inducements to speed up the diffusion of innovations, but these inducements risk creating inflexibility, which hampers development of future innovations.

Liberty and Unresponsiveness

A third dilemma involves the tension between federalism as a protector of liberty and federalism as a cause of unresponsiveness. The diversity of a large federal system limits the ability of any one group to exploit others, and the multiple decision centers give bases for opposition if any one government in the system fails to respect citizens' rights. These same features can produce policy deadlock. Divergent groups may be unable to agree on a policy. The many decision centers may adopt conflicting programs, a situation that often frustrates the development of a coherent approach to dealing with a problem. Reducing the autonomy of subnational governments would reduce their ability to obstruct needed programs but also reduce their ability to protect citizens' rights.

Interjurisdictional Competition

Interjurisdictional competition presents yet another dilemma for federalism. Competition among states or localities can stimulate innovation, efficiency, and responsiveness to public demands (Dye 1990b). Voters can compare the costs they pay and benefits they receive with the treatment of voters in other jurisdictions. If the comparisons are unsatisfactory, disgruntled citizens may remove the officials responsible from office or relocate to more responsive jurisdictions. Because the threat

2. Bear in mind that the national government can test a program in limited areas, which has occasionally been done.

Table 9.1: Citizen Satisfaction and the Level of Government

From which level of government do you feel you get the most for your money?

	Federal		State		Local	
Household Income	1982	1991	1982	1991	1982	1991
Under $15,000	42%	32%	15%	23%	21%	20%
$15,000 to $24,000	37	27	20	24	30	24
$25,000 or more	25	23	24	22	36	39

Sources: Advisory Commission on Intergovernmental Relations. 1982, 1991. *Changing Public Attitudes on Governments and Taxes.* Washington, DC.

of losing jobs, investment, and affluent citizens is much more compelling to officials than the threat of losing poor residents, and because poor people are effectively excluded from living in many localities, interjurisdictional competition also biases policy-making against low-income groups. The effect is most pronounced locally, where the affluent can relocate most readily and the poor are excluded most easily.

The greater responsiveness of smaller jurisdictions to the more affluent groups is reflected in surveys asking respondents to select the level of government that gives them the most for their money (see table 9.1). As respondents' incomes rise, the proportion responding that the national government gives them the most for their money declines, and the proportion responding that the state or local government gives them the most rises. Moreover, the increase is more pronounced and consistent for local government than for state government, a finding that supports the contention that the biasing effect is greater for smaller jurisdictions. Note, however, that while more affluent people consistently find local government to be the best value, the belief of poorer people that the national government is the best value declined considerably from 1982 to 1991. This shift undoubtedly reflects a growing recognition of the Reagan and Bush administrations' limited receptivity to the poor (Nathan 1990). Even in 1991, though, poorer people were more likely to regard the federal government as the best value.

The dilemma, then, is that increasing interjurisdictional competition may foster greater efficiency and innovation, as well as responsiveness to the affluent, but encourage neglect of low-income groups. Reducing competition places all income groups on a more equal footing but may encourage monopolistic tendencies in government. This dilemma can be partially resolved by assigning income redistribution programs to the national government (Musgrave and Musgrave 1980: 524–26), but it cannot be eliminated as long as some taxpayers are able to contribute more to the public treasury than others.

The Problem of Size

Federal systems confront the dilemma of choosing between units large enough to marshall sufficient resources—money, personnel, expertise, geographic reach—to attack major problems, and units small enough to be relatively amenable to citizen influence. Smaller units may be easier for citizens to reach and control but too small to cope with significant problems, especially in poor areas. Smaller units are not necessarily more responsive, as local governments in many parts of the South were notoriously unresponsive to the needs of black citizens in the 1950s. In addition, making jurisdictions smaller enhances the political leverage of affluent groups at the expense of poorer ones. Finally, the multiplicity of small governments may be more than citizens can readily comprehend. Larger units are better able to amass the funds, personnel, and expertise to carry out major programs, but may be less easily influenced by small groups.

The Problem of Administration

A final major dilemma results from the administrative effects of federalism. Creating a large number of governments diffuses the administrative burden and reduces the risk that any one unit will be overwhelmed by its administrative load. At the same time, the multiplicity of governments can create major coordination problems, duplication of effort, and a proliferation of reports, audits, inspections, and regulations.

These dilemmas assure that a federal system cannot perform ideally in all respects simultaneously. Actions designed to improve performance in some areas will worsen performance in others. This is not to say that improvements are impossible or that criticism should be ignored. Rather, the dilemmas indicate the need for keeping criticism in perspective and remembering that enhancing one capability may reduce another, a price that may be worth paying, but only after careful assessment.

Social, economic, technological, and political changes may alter the tradeoffs these dilemmas require. As a society grows increasingly mobile and interdependent, people are increasingly affected by decisions of subnational governments in localities other than their own. Greater uniformity and a larger role for higher level governments will be needed.

Regional disparities in wealth may create a need for intervention by higher levels of government to equalize resources. As those disparities decline (Break 1980: 26–27), national involvement for that purpose grows less necessary.

Technological changes may alter the responses to administrative dilemmas in many ways. A technological development such as the personal computer can greatly enhance the capabilities of smaller governments and increase their control over their environment. Other technological changes, such as the evolution from dirt paths to multi-lane expressways, can escalate the costs of some programs beyond the capacities of smaller jurisdictions. Rising educational aspiration, stimulated in part by countless technological developments, have exceeded the capacities of many small school districts and increased pressures for both school consolidation and state-supported university systems.

Ultimately the tradeoffs are based on political beliefs and judgements. An emphasis on equality may enhance the appeal of uniformity, while a concern for individualism may increase the appeal of flexibility. Whether interdependence exists is sometimes a political judgment as well. Were non-southern whites affected by discrimination against southern blacks? Is an easterner affected by the use of public lands in the West? Is a resident of Maine affected by the murder of someone in Arizona if the two people do not know each other? These questions can only be answered by the people involved, each of whom may provide a different answer.

The best responses to the dilemmas, in short, vary over time. Social, economic, technological, and political changes can render a formerly appropriate arrangement quite obsolete. One should, therefore, be wary of proposals that promise to "fix" the system once and for all. Permanent settlements are often poorly suited to impermanent conditions.

The Problem of Power

Public officials in a federal system face a difficult choice regarding their involvement in controversial policy decisions. If they vigorously and forthrightly address controversial policy issues, they risk antagonizing voters and campaign contributors.[3] Thus, they may conclude that letting other officials handle the difficult problems is safer. The catch, of course, is that if they do so, those other officials end up making the policy decisions.

Consider, for example, the complaint of local officials from smaller jurisdictions. They charge that the national grant system is too complex and confusing for them to comprehend. The commonly drawn implication is that the fault lies with the national grant system and the responsibility for fixing it, consequently, lies with national officials. An alternative possibility, which is rarely discussed in this context, is that those local governments might be too small to cope with certain conditions of life in the latter part of the twentieth century, and that they are in need of alteration. If some local governments are too small to deal with the

---

3. Research on presidential popularity seems to confirm that grappling with controversial issues reduces popularity. See Mueller (1970).

complexity of the national grant system, can they be much better equipped to face the complexities of criminal behavior, environmental protection, transportation, public health, and economic development?

This possibility is rarely mentioned by local officials from small jurisdictions because it places much of the responsibility on state and local officials. It calls for consolidation of small local governments into larger ones, a process that often provokes great controversy and powerful opposition, not to mention failure, as noted in chapter 8. It also would call for, in all likelihood, a reduction of the number of elected local officials, and an alteration of the political environments of the survivors. That the officials from small localities prefer to blame the national government is not surprising.[4]

In a similar fashion, there are periodic calls for national officials to exhibit more self-restraint in domestic policy-making in order to preserve a larger role for states and localities.[5] The likelihood of these calls being answered can be put into perspective by considering calls for self-restraint in a different arena. The increasing emphasis on publication as a criterion for salary increases and promotion in political science has led to a massive increase in research output. When someone observes that the increased volume is overwhelming our information-processing capabilities and is being accomplished in part by publication of many works that are of limited value, he or she might conclude that political scientists should use more self-restraint in publishing. That proposal would produce two predictable responses:

1. Many political scientists would claim, quite correctly, that a reduction in their research output would result in denial of promotion, smaller salary increases, and even unemployment.
2. Many would claim that they might produce valuable studies in the future. Self-restraint on their parts could, then, simply lead to publication of more marginal works by others.

Calls for self-restraint by national officials produce a similar response in many instances:

---

4. Reuss (1970) felt that revenue sharing should require local government reorganization. In a roundabout way, a very complex national grant system that would totally overwhelm local officials in small jurisdictions might accomplish a similar result; it would create incentives for reorganization. The current system is evidently not sufficiently complex for that.

5. This point is contained, explicitly or implicitly, in Walker (1981); Elazar (1984); Peterson et al. (1986); and Rivlin (1992).

1. National officials claim, often correctly, that many people expect them to address policy problems and that practicing self-restraint will anger those people and jeopardize the officials' careers.
2. National officials feel that they have useful ideas to contribute and fear that exercising self-restraint will lead to poorer public policies.

The chances that calls for self-restraint will be answered, given those perspectives, are no better than would be the case if an interest group were asked to exercise self-restraint for the benefit of other groups or the president were asked to practice self-restraint for the benefit of Congress.

Whether one believes national officials should exercise greater self-restraint is largely a matter of one's policy views. For people who believe they should exercise self-restraint, simply calling for it, may be less promising than other approaches. First, reducing the demands placed on Washington would leave national officials freer to practice self-restraint if they chose to. How this could be accomplished, however, is not at all clear. Second, electing more national officials opposed to the use of national government power in domestic policy-making would encourage a more modest national role, particularly if demands also fell. Third, strengthening the capacities of state and especially local governments to deal with policy problems, and filling them with officials who want to deal with those problems, would reduce the need for people to go to Washington. While a great deal of progress in increasing state capabilities has been made in recent years, many local governments in the United States are apparently designed to be as ineffective as possible in resolving major problems. When a metropolitan area contains a hundred different local governments, areawide problems of a controversial nature typically require state and/or national involvement. A rural county with four hundred residents has only modest capacity for dealing with substantial matters.

As the scope of conflict reminds us, many of the people who clamor for a reduced national role would not support the third approach because they are basically opposed to government action, regardless of the level. Many state and local officials are hesitant to reorganize local governments in a comprehensive way in order to increase local capacity. State and local officials may also hesitate to take actions that might drive away the affluent. People who are looking to government for help with a policy problem, however, are inclined to go to Washington if state and local officials do not respond because of unwillingness or inability. The accumulation of demands makes national self-restraint difficult to practice and, in the views of people looking for favorable responses, undesirable. At the same time, people want the option of appealing to state and local

officials for action on the same problem if the national government is
not receptive to their demands (Nathan 1990).

Restraint or Action?

What may be necessary, then, is to make state and especially local governments stronger rather than trying to make the national government
weaker, for weakening the national government does not necessarily
strengthen states and localities. If the entire national grant system were
abolished tomorrow, the national government's role in domestic policy-
making would be reduced, but would states and localities be stronger?
On balance many of them would not. They would be free of some of
the regulations and strings attached to grants, but they would also have
great difficulty replacing the lost resources, and poorer jurisdictions
would ultimately have far fewer dollars to spend.

Instead of clamoring for national government actions to enable
them to pursue their goals, state and local officials might do well to
devote more energy to state and local actions to reach their goals. We
may all wish to have someone provide us with a generous income that
would enable us to do as we please, but we probably do not have anyone
willing to enter into such an arrangement. In the same fashion, state
and local officials cannot realistically expect the national government to
hand over more than $100 billion without expecting some say in how
the money is used.

This is not to say that intergovernmental lobbying is pointless or
ineffective. However, if state and local officials want national officials
to play a more modest role, they must be willing to make controversial
decisions and coordinate their activities with those of other states and
localities. Most importantly, perhaps, states could avoid creating problems for one another, as when one state causes pollution that drifts to
another state or when one state acts to undercut the policies of another
state (as Florida did by banning its inheritance tax to lure wealthy retirees
away from other states). The prospects of this cooperation among states,
however, are not altogether encouraging.

Not all state and local officials are part of the clamor for a reduced
national role. Many support national involvement. Indeed, many national
grant programs were begun in part because of lobbying by state and
local officials. The Reagan administration's proposals to curtail a variety
of aid programs led to a storm of protest by state and local officials.
Complaints about national regulations, meddling, and intrusion should
often be taken with a grain of salt.

One final point in this regard: there is an enormous difference
between saying that the federal system is complex and saying that it is *too*

complex, or between saying that the national government is extensively involved in domestic policy-making and saying that it is *too* heavily involved in domestic policy-making. Most of us would agree that a modern airliner is complex, but is it too complex? Judgements about whether the system is too complex or the national government is too extensively involved cannot be made without reference to:

1. What do people want or expect the system to do?
2. What level of complexity or involvement is needed to satisfy those wants and expectations?

There is little doubt that we have the capacity as a nation to simplify the federal system and reduce national involvement in domestic policy-making if we choose.[6] There is a great deal of doubt regarding whether, given the many objectives the system is expected to pursue, the system would, on balance, perform better if simplification and reduction were to take place.

Bringing Order out of Chaos?

> Today . . . the Federal system is in complete disarray . . . It is long past time to dust off the Federalist Papers and to renew the debate commenced by Hamilton, Madison, and Jay. They would ask not only whether a proposal is a good program, but also "Is this a *Federal* function?" . . . If the states are to have a future, the process of sorting out and separating must begin now (Governor Bruce Babbitt, quoted in Glendening and Reeves 1984: 103).

> Jesus replied, "A man was going down from Jerusalem to Jericho, and he fell among robbers, who stripped him and beat him, and departed, leaving him half dead. Now by chance a priest was going down that road; and when he saw him he passed by on the other side. So likewise a Levite, when he came to the place and saw him, passed by on the other side. But a Samaritan, as he journeyed, came to where he was; and when he saw him, he had compassion, and went to him and bound up his wounds, pouring on oil and wine; then he set him on his own beast and brought him to an inn, and took care of him" (Luke 10: 30–34).

Morton Grodzins (1984: 3–10, 125–36, 334–36), in his classic work on American federalism, described much of the system as chaotic. Thou-

---

6. This reference is to capacity in a technological sense; we know what policies will simplify the system and reduce national involvement if we adopt them. Political willingness or feasibility is another matter.

sands of units of government, many of which overlap, provide a variety of services and make numerous policy decisions. Responsibility for many services and decisions is shared by officials at all levels of government.

More recently (Grodzins' book was originally published in 1966), some observers have expressed concern that the national government has intruded too much into state and local affairs and that the sharing of responsibility with a multiplicity of grants, regulations, and agencies is an administrative jumble that neither citizens nor officials can comprehend (Elazar 1984: 253–56; Rivlin 1992; Walker 1981). Governor Bruce Babbitt's comments, as well as the Reagan administration's New Federalism, reflected a desire for greater separation of governmental functions and a reduction of national involvement in domestic policy-making.

While some simplification of the grant system, with modest reductions in the attendant regulations and reporting requirements, could take place without major shifts in political power, any substantial changes in the allocation of powers and responsibilities are freighted with large policy implications. Indeed, this is generally the main reason people are interested in altering the federal system. Proposals to reduce national authority, regulations, involvement, and so forth, are proposals to alter the scope of conflict, although they may have other goals as well.

Consider the man who was robbed on the road from Jerusalem to Jericho. After two people passed by and ignored his plight, could we reasonably expect him to respond to the good Samaritan's efforts by saying, "Just a minute. I must ask not only whether your assistance is valuable to me; I must ask also whether this is a legitimate Samaritan function." The parable of the Good Samaritan contains a valuable lesson for the student of federalism: any proposals to exclude a level of government from a policy will encounter opposition (sooner or later) from people who believe that level might be the one to notice and respond to their problems.

When a child disappears, the parents are interested in government action that will aid in finding the child; which level of government will provide it is a trivial matter for them, unless one level is more likely to succeed. When an elderly couple with few assets and a limited income faces an astronomical medical bill, they look to any level of government for assistance; abstract theories of federalism will seem largely irrelevant. When concerned citizens wanted to preserve Yosemite Valley and the Grand Canyon, they were primarily concerned with finding a level of government willing and able to do it. Asking those people to consent to excluding a level of government that might be responsive to their needs from dealing with those needs is not likely to receive a positive response. Even if they agree today, because the officials currently in office are receptive to their demands, a newly elected group of officials may cause them to change their minds tomorrow.

Implications of Separation

Bear in mind that proposals to establish greater separation between levels of government are almost invariably proposals to reduce the influence of larger constituencies. If, for example, national and state responsibilities were completely separated, national political forces would lose influence over the responsibilities assigned to the state, but state influence over national policies would remain substantial. Members of Congress would still be sensitive to the needs and preferences of their states and districts. Presidential candidates, as well as presidents, would still be sensitized to state interests by the electoral college. The parties would remain decentralized; they would continue to emphasize candidates in tune with state or substate views rather than candidates loyal to national party programs. The separation would be largely one-sided.

Separation also runs afoul of the interdependence of programs and the multiple levels of effects that many policies have. If the educational system fails to produce enough competent scientists, the technological advances needed for defending the nation will not be forthcoming. An inadequate transportation system stifles economic development, and a faltering economy produces little revenue to support government programs. The performance of one program can affect the performance of other programs, regardless of which level of government is involved in each of them. Decisions by one level of government in one program can cause problems in other programs run by other levels of government. With separation, however, officials responsible for affected programs have no access to the program causing the problem.

In a related vein, most major government programs have multiple levels of effects—national, state, and local. The condition of the transportation system affects local traffic problems, prospects for economic growth at all levels, the cost of living (for the nation as well as regionally and locally), and the nation's dependence on foreign energy sources, not to mention the nation's ability to mobilize in an emergency. Pollution affects the local quality of life, can create health problems in a community, and may also spread to other localities, other states, or even other countries. The same can occur with infectious diseases. Much criminal behavior is local in nature, but some is organized on a regional, national, or even international scale. Moreover, criminals are mobile, and so are potential victims; a family on vacation or a business traveler has a legitimate interest in controlling crime in localities they visit as well as at home. Assigning any of these functions to a single level may result in effects at other levels, especially higher levels, being ignored.

Efforts to separate functions by level also encounter the problem discussed in chapter 4. How do we determine which level should handle each program? A number of key constitutional provisions are vague, and alternative mechanisms for allocating responsibilities all have shortcomings. Given that assigning responsibilities to a particular level determines the scope of conflict, the assignment carries important policy implications.

Finally, strict separation of levels of government in the federal system would greatly weaken the redundancy feature that helps to protect citizens' rights and prevent unresponsiveness. If a responsibility were to be handled poorly by the level of government to which it is assigned, other levels would not be permitted to intervene. The treatment of black Americans during the heyday of dual federalism, particularly from the 1880s to 1930s, is instructive in this regard. Under a system of shared responsibilities, failure by one level can prompt corrective action by other levels.

Federalism is, therefore, a system of government that is poorly suited to people with a penchant for neatness. A system with over 80,000 units of government and roughly half a million elected officials cannot be simple, orderly, or easily comprehended. As long as the fundamental structures of the system remain as they are, the system will continue to be very complex, as well as imperfectly coordinated. Moreover, proposals to simplify the system, such as consolidating some of the thousands of local governments, are voted down at the polls with great regularity, suggesting that many people do not feel greatly troubled by the system's complexity, at least relative to the cost of reducing the complexity.[7] Despite complaints of the complexity of national domestic programs and grants, public support for national involvement and grants remains (see table 9.2). Although people grew more concerned about excessive national government power in general in the late 1980s, they also saw national government as the most appropriate level for handling a number of specific policy problems. Moreover, they were as likely to feel that the national government gave them the most for their money as they

---

7. Research on voter participation has long established that less educated people and those who claim to have difficulty understanding politics are less likely to vote (Campbell et al. 1964; Verba and Nie 1972). People who are most troubled by the system's complexity, then, may be least likely to register that viewpoint at the polls.

Table 9.2: Citizen's Views on the Role of the Federal Government

The federal government	
Has too much power	38%
Has about the right amount of power	18%
Should use its powers more vigorously	30%
No opinion	14%

How necessary are these federal grant programs?

	Unnecessary	Indifferent	Necessary
For poor states	17%	26%	57%
For poor cities	21%	26%	53%
For states and localities to help poor people	12%	19%	69%
For states and localities to finance public service	13%	15%	72%
For states and localities to finance public facilities	17%	23%	60%

Source: Advisory Commission on Intergovernmental Relations. 1982 *Changing Public Attitudes on Governments and Taxes.* Washington, DC, pp. 6, 8.

were to feel that state or local governments gave them the most (*Changing Public Attitudes on Government and Taxes* 1987, 1989, 1990).

Future Prospects

If the preceding conclusions are correct, the future of American federalism will resemble its past half-century in a number of important respects. People in and out of government will continue to use the system to pursue their policy goals. They will seek out sympathetic policymakers without regard to which level of government these policymakers belong, and will seek to expand, maintain, or contract the scope of conflict to maximize their chances for policy success.

We can expect, at semi-regular intervals, proposals to streamline, overhaul, reorganize, or revamp the system in some relatively comprehensive way. These proposals can be expected to fail unless they are perceived to increase the system's ability to pursue the policy goals of policy coalitions. Proposals for major changes based solely on abstract notions of neatness, tidiness, or how federalism should work according to one model or another, generally will not be successful.

When changes do take place, they are usually based on individual policy needs, and they often emerge gradually. The intergovernmental grant system, for example, evolved over a period of many years in response to many different policy concerns: promoting vocational education, building highways, fighting poverty, and reducing pollution. The more abrupt changes in national-state and national-local relations that took place during the New Deal era were adopted primarily in an effort to combat a policy problem, the Great Depression. Even the drafting and adoption of the U.S. Constitution, one of the most far-reaching changes in the system since independence, was motivated in large measure by dissatisfaction with the policy performance of the system under the Articles of Confederation. The pursuit of policy goals emerges as the guiding force in much of the development of the system.

We can also expect the language of federalism, at least in the political arena, to continue to be used as camouflage. Advocates and opponents of a policy will talk about theories of federalism when they are really talking about policies. For example, "By turning this program over to the states and ending national involvement, we will significantly reduce bureaucratic red tape, increase flexibility, and improve program performance" may actually mean, "We're taking this program away from the national government, which won't do what we want, and giving it to the states, which will do what we want." Similarly, "The compelling national interest in this matter requires the national government to act and act now. The problem is too large for the states to handle on their own " may actually mean, "The states couldn't or wouldn't do what I wanted, but I think the national government will."

In a related vein, broad-ranging proposals about the federal system will be presented so as to make old ideas look newer and new ideas look older.[8] Creative federalism placed great emphasis on the role of local government but marked a major expansion of national involvement in domestic policy-making. The Reagan administration attached the label of New Federalism to an effort to, in large measure, return the federal system to a configuration that existed prior to 1933. George Bush continued the devolution of program responsibility to the local level but evidenced a greater faith than did Reagan in government at all levels to serve the needs of the public. While Reagan campaigned with an anti-government message, Bush emphasized "a thousand points of light." The Clinton administration's domestic agenda and emphasis upon innovation in policy development and delivery are certainly compatible with a creative federalism model. Some observers suggest that it is difficult to tell the difference between Clinton and Bush federalism because both advocate innovation in local government to address problems (Pagano

---

8. Wildavsky (1974: 108–109, 111–12) notes that agencies seeking funding for new programs often try to present them as parts of older programs. The private sector uses similar tactics. A product that is almost identical to its predecessors may bear a new name or be repackaged. A completely new item, by contrast, may emerge under the label of an old product to capitalize on an established reputation.

and O'M. Bowman 1993: 1–22). With federalism, things are not always as they appear.

We can expect periodic efforts to reorganize local governments, with the goal of reducing fragmentation, and we can expect most of these efforts to fail. If they do fail, local governments will retain their position as the weakest link in the system—the level of government most dependent on outside funds, least able to raise own-source revenue, and most vulnerable to regulation by other levels of government.

State and local officials will continue to complain about national grant inflexibility and regulations, even as many of these same officials lobby for national grants, including categorical grants, and for national standards. National grants will continue to be a major source of revenue for states and localities, and most of the funds will be distributed in ways that limit recipient discretion in the use of funds. At the same time, fungibility will enable recipient officials to, in effect, divert funds for one purpose to something else.

Finally, the federal system will, in all likelihood, continue to exceed the monitoring capabilities of many people. With over 80,000 governments and roughly half a million elected officials in the system, many citizens have great difficulty determining who is doing what. Only half of the public can recall the name of their member of Congress and far fewer can recall how he or she has voted on anything (Stokes and Miller 1962; Mann and Wolfinger 1980). Only one-fourth can recall the name of their state representative (Saffell 1982: 106), and one-third admit that they do not know whether their state has a constitution (*Changing Public Attitudes on Government and Taxes* 1988: 6). How informed are they likely to be regarding the personnel and activities of the thousands of local governments? Here, too, the scope of conflict is a factor: if the complexity of the system overwhelms some people, it also conveys advantage to groups and individuals capable of monitoring the activities of the governments they wish to influence.

REFERENCES

Adrian, Charles. 1976. *State and Local Governments,* 4th ed. New York: McGraw-Hill.

Adrian, Charles and Michael Fine. 1991. *State and Local Politics.* Chicago: Lyceum Books/Nelson-Hall.

Advisory Commission on Intergovernmental Relations. 1976. "The Mosaic of Metropolitan Governments." In *Political Power and the Urban Crisis,* 3d ed., edited by Alan Shank, pp. 345–64. Boston, MA: Holbrook.

Agranoff, Robert. 1972. *The New Style in Election Campaigns.* Boston: Holbrook.

———. 1976. *The Management of Election Campaigns.* Boston: Holbrook.

Albritton, Robert. 1990. "Social Services: Welfare and Health." In *Politics in the American States,* 5th ed., edited by Virginia Gray, Herbert Jacob and Robert Albritton, pp. 411–46. Glenview, IL: Scott, Foresman/Little, Brown.

Almy, Timothy. 1973. "Residential Location and Electoral Cohesion." *American Political Science Review* 67: 914–23.

Althaus, Paul and Joseph Schachter. 1983. "Interstate Migration and The New Federalism." *Social Science Quarterly* 64: 35–45.

Anderson, James, David Brady, Charles Bullock and Joseph Stewart. 1984. *Public Policy and Politics in America,* 2d ed. Monterey, CA: Brooks/Cole.

Anderson, Martin. 1964. *The Federal Bulldozer.* Cambridge, MA: M.I.T. Press.

Anderson, William. 1955. *The Nation and the States, Rivals or Partners?* Minneapolis, MN: University of Minnesota.

Anagnoson, Theodore. 1982. "Federal Grant Agencies and Congressional Election Campaigns." *American Journal of Political Science* 26: 547–61.

Anton, Thomas. 1989. *American Federalism and Public Policy.* New York: Random House.

Asher, Herbert. 1992. *Presidential Elections and American Politics,* 5th ed. Pacific Grove, CA: Brooks/Cole.

Axelrod, Robert. 1972. "Where the Votes Come From: An Analysis of Electoral Coalitions, 1952–1972." *American Political Science Review* 66: 11–20.

Bartels, Larry. 1985. "Resource Allocation in a Presidential Campaign." *Journal of Politics* 47: 928–36.

Barton, Weldon. 1967. *Interstate Compacts in the Political Process.* Chapel Hill, NC: University of North Carolina.

Beck, Paul and Frank Sorauf. 1992. *Party Politics in America,* 7th ed. New York: Harper Collins.

Beer, Samuel. 1976. "The Adoption of General Revenue Sharing: A Case Study in Public Sector Politics." *Public Policy* 24: 127–96.

——————. 1978. "Federalism, Nationalism, and Democracy in America." *American Political Science Review* 72: 9–21.

Berkley, George and Douglas Fox. 1978. *80,000 Governments.* Boston: Allyn and Bacon.

Beyle, Thad. 1989. "From Governor to Governors." In *The State of the States,* edited by Carl Van Horn, pp. 33–68. Washington, DC: Congressional Quarterly Press.

Bibby, John. 1987. *Politics, Parties, and Elections in America.* Chicago, IL: Nelson-Hall.

Bibby, John, Cornelius Cotter, James Gibson, and Robert Huckshorn. 1983. "Parties in State Politics." In *Politics in the American States,* 4th ed., edited by Virginia Gray, Herbert Jacob, and Kenneth Vines, pp. 59–96. Boston: Little, Brown.

——————. 1990. "Parties in State Politics." In *Politics in the American States,* 5th ed., edited by Virginia Gray, Herbert Jacob, and Robert Albritton, pp. 85–112. Glenview, IL: Scott, Foresman/Little, Brown.

Bickel, Alexander. 1980. "The Electoral College." In *Presidential Politics,* edited by James Lengle and Byron Shafer, pp. 382–86. New York: St. Martin's.

Bish, Robert and Vincent Ostrom. 1973. *Understanding Urban Government.* Washington, DC: American Enterprise Institute.

Blair, George. 1981. *Government at the Grass-roots,* 3rd ed. Pacific Palisades, CA: Palisades.

Bollens, John C. 1957. *Special District Governments in the United States.* Berkeley, CA: University of California Press.

Bollens, John and Henry Schmandt. 1975. *The Metropolis,* 3rd ed. New York: Harper and Row.

——————. 1982. *The Metropolis,* 4th ed. New York: Harper and Row.

Bond, Jon. 1985. "Dimensions of District Attentiveness Over Time." *American Journal of Political Science* 29: 330–47.

Book of the States, The. 1982. Lexington, KY: Council of State Governments.

Book of the States, The. 1990. Lexington, KY: Council of State Governments.

Book of the States, The. 1992. Lexington, KY: Council of State Governments.

Book of the States, The. 1993. Lexington, KY: Council of State Governments.

Bowman, Ann and Richard Kearney. 1986. *The Resurgence of the States.* Englewood Cliffs, NJ: Prentice-Hall.

Break, George. 1980. *Financing Government in a Federal System.* Washington, DC: Brookings.

Brock, Jonathon and Gerald W. Cormick. 1989. "Can Negotiation Be Institutionalized or Mandated? Lessons From Public Policy and Regulatory Conflicts." In *Mediation Research,* edited by Kenneth Kressel and Dean G. Pruitt, pp. 138–65. San Francisco, CA: Jossey-Bass.

Brudney, Jeffrey and F. Ted Hebert. 1987. "State Agencies and Their Environments: Examining the Influence of Important External Actors." *Journal of Politics* 49: 186–206.

Bullock, Charles and Charles Lamb. 1984. *Implementation of Civil Rights Policy.* Monterey, CA: Brooks/Cole.

Butler, David and Bruce Cain. 1992. *Congressional Redistricting.* New York: Macmillan.

Calvert, Randall and John Ferejohn. 1983. "Coattail Voting in Recent Presidential Elections." *American Political Science Review* 77: 407–19.

Cameron, David. 1978. "The Expansion of the Public Economy: A Comparative Analysis." *American Political Science Review* 72: 1243–61.

Campbell, Angus, Philip Converse, Warren Miller and Donald Stokes. 1964. *The American Voter*, abridged. New York: Wiley.

Campbell, Alan and Donna Shalala. 1970. "Problems Unsolved, Solutions Untried: The Urban Crisis." In *The States and the Urban Crisis*, edited by Alan Campbell, pp. 4–26. Englewood Cliffs, NJ: Prentice-Hall.

Caputo, David and Richard Cole. 1983. "City Officials and General Revenue Sharing: Attitudes, Perceptions, and Implications for Future Intergovernmental Policy." *Publius* 13: 41–54.

Caraley, Demetrios. 1976. "Congressional Politics and Urban Aid." *Political Science Quarterly* 91: 19–45.

_____. 1977. *City Government and Urban Problems*. Englewood Cliffs, NJ: Prentice-Hall.

Caro, Robert. 1974. *The Power Broker*. New York: Knopf.

Catalog of Federal Grant-in-Aid Programs to State and Local Governments; Grants Funded FY 1989, A. 1989. Washington, DC: Advisory Commission on Intergovernmental Relations.

Cater, Douglas. 1964. *Power in Washington*. New York: Random House.

Changing Public Attitudes on Governments and Taxes. 1982. Washington, DC: Advisory Commission on Intergovernmental Relations.

_____. 1987. Washington, DC: Advisory Commission on Intergovernmental Relations.

_____. 1988. Washington, DC: Advisory Commission on Intergovernmental Relations.

_____. 1989. Washington, DC: Advisory Commission on Intergovernmental Relations.

_____. 1990. Washington, DC: Advisory Commission on Intergovernmental Relations.

_____. 1991. Washington, DC: Advisory Commission on Intergovernmental Relations.

Chelf, Carl. 1981. *Public Policymaking in America: Difficult Choices, Limited Solutions*. Santa Monica, CA: Goodyear.

Chronicle of Higher Education. "High Court Ruling Transforms Battles Over Desegregation at Colleges in 19 States." XXXVIII 44 (July 8, 1992): A16–A21.

Chubb, John. 1985. "The Political Economy of Federalism." *American Political Science Review* 79: 994–1015.

Clarke, Gary and Charles Grezlak. 1975. "Some Obstacles to State Legislative Staffing— Real or Illusory?" Unpublished manuscript, cited in Alan Rosenthal. 1981. *Legislative Life*, pp. 206, 231. New York: Harper and Row.

Cohen, Jeffrey and David Nice. 1983. "Changing Party Loyalty of State Delegations to the U.S. House of Representatives, 1953–1976." *Western Political Quarterly* 36: 312–25.

Comptroller General. 1980. *Proposed Changes in Federal Matching and Maintenance of Effort Requirements for State and Local Governments*. Washington, DC: General Accounting Office.

Conlan, Timothy. 1988. *New Federalism*. Washington, DC: Brookings.

Converse, Philip. 1964. "The Nature of Belief Systems in Mass Publics." In *Ideology and Discontent*, edited by David Apter, pp. 206–61. New York: Free Press.

Cozer, Lewis, 1964. *The Functions of Social Conflict*. New York: Free Press.

Cronin, Thomas. 1977. "The War on Crime and Unsafe Streets, 1960–76: Policymaking for a Just and Safe Society." In *America in the Seventies*, edited by Allan Sindler, pp. 208–60. Boston, MA: Little, Brown.

Crotty, William. 1984. *American Parties in Decline*, 2d ed. Boston: Little, Brown.

Dahl, Robert. 1980. "The City in the Future of Democracy." In *Urban Politics*, edited by Harlan Hahn and Charles Levine, pp. 339–64. New York: Longman.

David, Paul and Ralph Eisenberg. 1961. *Devaluation of the Urban and Suburban Vote.* Charlottesville, NC: Bureau of Public Administration, University of Virginia.

David, Stephen and Paul Kanter. 1983. "Urban Policy in the Federal System: A Reconceptualization of Federalism." *Polity* 16: 284–303.

Davidson, Roger. 1969. *The Role of the Congressman.* Indianapolis, IN: Bobbs-Merrill.

Davidson, Roger and Walter Oleszek. 1981. *Congress and Its Members.* Washington, DC: Congressional Quarterly.

Deckard, Barbara Sinclair. 1976. "Political Upheaval and Congressional Voting: The Effects of the 1960s on Voting Patterns in the House of Representatives." *Journal of Politics* 38: 326–45.

Derthick, Martha. 1975. *Uncontrollable Spending for Social Services Grants.* Washington, DC: Brookings.

Derthick, Martha and Gary Bombardier. 1974. *Between State and Nation.* Washington, DC: Brookings.

Dilger, Robert. 1983. "Grantsmanship, Formulamanship, and Other Allocational Principles." *Journal of Urban Affairs* 5: 269–86.

Downs, Anthony. 1973. *Opening Up the Suburbs.* New Haven, CT: Yale University Press.

Dye, Thomas. 1964. "Urban Political Integration: Conditions Associated with Annexation in American Cities." *Midwest Journal of Political Science* 8: 430–46.

_____. 1965. "Malapportionment and Public Policy in the States." *Journal of Politics* 27: 586–601.

_____. 1981. *Politics in States and Communities,* 4th ed. Englewood Cliffs, NJ: Prentice-Hall.

_____. 1984. *Understanding Public Policy,* 5th ed. Englewood Cliffs, NJ: Prentice-Hall.

_____. 1990a. *Competitive Federalism.* Lexington, MA: Lexington.

_____. 1990b. *American Federalism.* Lexington, MA: Lexington.

Dye, Thomas and Thomas Hurley. 1978. "The Responsiveness of Federal and State Governments to Urban Problems." *Journal of Politics* 40: 196–207.

_____. 1981. "Rejoinder." *Journal of Politics* 43: 102–103.

Dye, Thomas, Charles Liebman, Oliver Williams, and Harold Herman. 1963. "Differentiation and Cooperation in a Metropolitan Area." *Midwest Journal of Political Science* 7: 145–55.

Education Grants Management. 1991. Washington, DC: General Accounting Office.

Eidenberg, Eugene and Roy Morey. 1969. *An Act of Congress.* New York: Norton.

Elazar, Daniel. 1962. *The American Partnership.* Chicago, IL: University of Chicago.

_____. 1972. *American Federalism,* 2d ed. New York: Crowell.

_____. 1984. *American Federalism,* 3d ed. New York: Harper and Row.

Eldersveld, Samuel. 1982. *Political Parties in American Society.* New York: Basic.

Enterprise Zones. 1988. Washington, DC: General Accounting Office.

Evans, Diana. 1986. "The Evolution of Regional Conflict Over Federal Aid to Cities in the House of Representatives." *Social Science Quarterly* 67: 108–17.

Fainstein, Norman and Susan Fainstein. 1976. "The Future of Community Control." *American Political Science Review* 70: 905–23.

Federal Formula Programs. 1990. Washington, DC: General Accounting Office.

Federal Influence on State and Local Roles in the Federal System, The. 1981. Washington, DC: Advisory Commission on Intergovernmental Relations.

Feig, Douglas. 1978. "Expenditures in the American States: The Impact of Court-Ordered Reapportionment." *American Politics Quarterly* 6: 309–24.

Fenno, Richard. 1978. *Home Style.* Boston, MA: Little, Brown.

Feiock, Richard. 1991. "The Effects of Economic Development Policy on Local Economic Growth." *American Journal of Political Science* 35: 643–55.

Field, Oliver. 1934. "State Versus Nation and the Supreme Court." *American Political Science Review* 28: 233–45.

Firestine, Robert. 1973. "The Impact of Reapportionment Upon Local Government Aid." *Social Science Quarterly* 54: 394–402.

Fisher, Roger and William Ury. [1981] 1983. *Getting to Yes: Negotiating Agreement Without Giving In.* New York: Penguin Books.

Fite, Emerson. 1932. *Government By Cooperation.* New York: Macmillan.

Follett, Mary Parker. 1924. *Creative Experience.* New York: Longmans, Green and Company.

Forman, Stephen C. 1989. "Community Problem Solving: There Are No Interjurisdictional Panaceas." *National Civic Review* 78 (January/February): 15–24.

Freeman, J. Leiper. 1965. *The Political Process,* rev. ed. New York: Random House.

Froman, Lewis. 1966. "Some Effects of Interest Group Strength in State Politics." *American Political Science Review* 60: 952–62.

Furniss, Norman. 1974. "The Practical Significance of Decentralization." *Journal of Politics* 36: 958–82.

Gates, John. 1987. "Partisan Realignment, Unconstitutional State Policies, and the U.S. Supreme Court." *American Journal of Political Science* 31: 259–80.

Gittell, Marilyn. 1971. "School Decentralization: The Ocean Hill-Brownsville Dispute." In *Politics in the Metropolis,* 2d ed., edited by Thomas Dye and Brett Hawkins, pp. 287–302. Columbus, OH: Charles Merrill.

Glendening, Parris and Mavis Reeves. 1977. *Pragmatic Federalism.* Pacific Palisades, CA: Palisades.

_____. 1984. *Pragmatic Federalism,* 2d ed. Pacific Palisades, CA: Palisades.

Grad, Frank. 1970. "The State's Capacity to Respond to Urban Problems: The State Constitution." In *The States and the Urban Crisis,* edited by Alan K. Campbell, pp. 27–58. Englewood Cliffs, NJ: Prentice Hall.

Gramlich, Edward. 1977. "Intergovernmental Grants: A Review of the Empirical Literature." In *The Political Economy of Fiscal Federalism,* edited by Wallace Oates, pp. 219–40. Lexington, MA: Heath.

Grant, Daniel and H. C. Nixon. 1982. *State and Local Government in America,* 4th ed. Boston, MA: Allyn and Bacon.

Grant, Daniel R. and Lloyd B. Omdahl. 1993. *State and Local Government in America,* 6th ed. Dubuque, IA: William C. Brown.

Grant Formulas. 1987. Washington, DC: General Accounting Office.

Graves, W. Brooke. 1934. *Uniform State Action.* Chapel Hill, NC: University of North Carolina.

_____. 1964. *American Intergovernmental Relations.* New York: Scribner's.

Gray, Virginia. 1973. "Innovation in the States: A Diffusion Study." *American Political Science Review* 67: 1174–85.

Griffith, Ernest. 1974. *A History of American City Government: The Progressive Years and Their Aftermath.* New York: Praeger.

Grodzins, Morton. 1966. *The American System,* edited by Daniel J. Elazar. Chicago, IL: Rand McNally.

_____. 1984. *The American System.* New Brunswick, NJ: Transaction.

Gulick, Luther. 1961. *The Metropolitan Problem and American Ideals.* New York: Knopf.

Hale, George and Marian Palley. 1981. *The Politics of Federal Grants.* Washington, DC: Congressional Quarterly.

Haider, Donald. 1974. *When Governments Come to Washington.* New York: Free Press.

Hamilton, Alexander, James Madison, and John Jay. 1937. *The Federalist.* New York: Modern Library.

Hamilton, Christopher and Donald Wells. 1990. *Federalism, Power, and Political Economy.* Englewood Cliffs, NJ: Prentice-Hall.

Handbook of the National Conference of Commissioners on Uniform State Laws. 1979. Chicago, IL: National Conference of Commissioners on Uniform State Laws.

Harmon, B. Douglas. 1970. "The Block Grant: Readings From a First Experiment." *Public Administration Review* 30: 141–52.

Harrigan, John. 1976. *Political Change in the Metropolis.* Boston, MA: Little, Brown.

_____. 1980. *Politics and Policy in States and Communities.* Boston, MA: Little, Brown.

_____. 1981. *Political Change in the Metropolis,* 2d ed. Boston, MA: Little, Brown.

_____. 1984. *Politics and Policy in States and Communities,* 2d ed. Boston, MA: Little, Brown.

Hawkins, Brett. 1966. "Public Opinion and Metropolitan Reorganization in Nashville." *Journal of Politics* 28: 408–18.

Hays, Steven and T. Zane Reeves. 1984. *Personnel Management in the Public Sector.* Boston, MA: Allyn and Bacon.

Heclo, Hugh. 1977. *A Government of Strangers.* Washington, DC: Brookings.

Hedge, David. 1983. "Fiscal Dependency and the State Budget Process." *Journal of Politics* 45: 198–208.

Hill, Melvin. 1978. *State Laws Governing Local Government Structure and Administration.* Athens, GA: Institute of Government, University of Georgia.

Hill, Richard. 1974. "Separate and Unequal: Government Inequality in the Metropolis." *American Political Science Review* 68: 1557–68.

Hinckley, Barbara. 1988. *Stability and Change in Congress,* 4th ed. New York: Harper and Row.

Ingram, Helen. 1977. "Policy Implementation Through Bargaining: The Case of Federal Grants-in-Aid." *Public Policy* 25: 499–526.

Interstate Child Support: Mothers Receiving Less Support From Out-of-State Fathers. 1992. Washington, DC: General Accounting Office.

Interstate Child Support: Need for Absent Parent Information. 1990. Washington, DC: General Accounting Office.

Interstate Child Support: Wage Withholding Not Fulfilling Expectations. 1992. Washington, DC: General Accounting Office.

Interstate Compacts, 1783–1977. 1977. Lexington KY: Council of State Governments.

Jewell, Malcolm. 1969. *The State Legislature,* 2d ed. New York: Random House.

Job Partnership Training Act. 1990. Washington, DC: General Accounting Office.

_____. 1992. Washington, DC: General Accounting Office.

Jondrow, James and Robert A. Levy. 1984. "The Displacement of Local Spending for Pollution Control by Federal Construction Grants." *The American Economic Review* 74: 174–78.

Jones, Charles. 1976. "Regulating the Environment." In *Politics in the American States,* 3d ed., edited by Herbert Jacob and Kenneth Vines, pp. 388–427. Boston, MA: Little, Brown.

Jones, Peter. 1976. *The U.S.A.,* vol. I, II. Homewood, IL: Dorsey.

Kammeyer, Kenneth. 1968. "A Comparative Study of Decision Making in Rural Communities." In *Community Structure and Decision-Making: Comparative Analyses,* edited by Terry Clark, pp. 383–91. Scranton, OH: Chandler.

Keefe, William and Morris Ogul. 1993. *The American Legislative Process,* 8th ed. Englewood Cliffs, NJ: Prentice-Hall.

Kettl, Donald. 1988. *Government by Proxy.* Washington, DC: CQ Press.

Key, V. O. 1937. *The Administration of Federal Grants to States.* Chicago, IL: Public Administration Service.

————. 1949. *Southern Politics*. New York: Vintage.

————. 1955. "A Theory of Critical Elections." *Journal of Politics* 17: 3–18.

————. 1956. *American State Politics*. New York: Knopf.

————. 1961. *Public Opinion and American Democracy*. New York: Knopf.

Landau, Martin. 1969. "Redundancy, Rationality, and the Problem of Duplication and Overlap." *Public Administration Review* 29: 346–58.

Lazin, Frederick. 1973. "The Failure of Federal Enforcement of Civil Rights Regulations in Public Housing, 1963–1971: The Co-optation of a Federal Agency by its Local Constituency." *Policy Sciences* 4: 264–71.

Leach, Richard. 1970. *American Federalism*. New York: Norton.

Leach, Richard and Redding Sugg. 1969. *The Administration of Interstate Compacts*. New York: Greenwood.

Levy, Frank. 1988. *Dollars and Dreams: The Changing American Income Distribution*. New York: W. W. Norton & Co.

Lineberry, Robert and Ira Sharkansky. 1978. *Urban Politics and Public Policy*, 3d ed. New York: Harper and Row.

Lipsky, Michael. 1980. *Street Level Bureaucracy*. New York: Russell Sage.

Lockard, Duane. 1971. "The Legislature as a Personal Career." In *Strengthening the States*, edited by Donald Herzberg and Alan Rosenthal, pp. 14–24. Garden City, NY: Doubleday.

Lord, William and Douglas Kenney. 1993. "Resolving Interstate Water Conflicts: The Compact Approach." *Intergovernmental Perspective* 19: 19–25.

Lowery, David. 1983. "Limitations on Taxing and Spending Powers: An Assessment of Their Effectiveness." *Social Science Quarterly* 64: 247–63.

Lowi, Theodore J. 1968. "Forward to the Second Edition: Gosnell's Chicago Revisited via Lindsay's New York." In *Machine Politics: Chicago Model*, by Harold Gosnell, pp. v–xviii. Chicago, IL: University of Chicago Press.

————. 1969. *The End of Liberalism*. New York: W. W. Norton.

————. 1979. *The End of Liberalism*, 2d ed. New York: W. W. Norton.

Lyons, W. E. and David Lowery. 1989. "Governmental Fragmentation Versus Consolidation: Five Public-Choice Myths About How to Create Informal, Involved and Happy Citizens." *Public Administration Review* 49: 533–43.

Macmahon, Arthur. 1972. *Administering Federalism in a Democracy*. New York: Oxford.

MacManus, Susan. 1981. "Special District Governments: A Note on Their Use as Property Tax Relief Mechanisms in the 1970's." *Journal of Politics* 43: 1207–14.

Mann, Thomas and Raymond Wolfinger. 1980. "Candidates and Parties in Congressional Elections." *American Political Science Review* 74: 617–32.

Marks, Thomas and John Cooper. 1988. *State Constitutional Law in a Nutshell*. St. Paul, MN: West.

Martin, Roscoe. 1965. *The Cities and the Federal System*. New York: Atherton.

Masters, Nicholas. 1961. "House Committee Assignments." *American Political Science Review* 55: 345–57.

Maxwell, James and J. Richard Aronson. 1977. *Financing State and Local Governments*, 3d ed. Washington, DC: Brookings.

Mayhew, David. 1974. *Congress: The Electoral Connection*. New Haven, CT: Yale.

McCarthy, David. 1983. *Local Government Law in a Nutshell*, 2d ed. St. Paul, MN: West.

McConnell, Grant. 1966. *Private Power and American Democracy*. New York: Knopf.

McDowell, Bruce. 1983. "Regional Organizations Hang On." *Intergovernmental Perspective* 8: 15.

McGregor, Eugene. 1978. "Uncertainty and National Nominating Coalitions." *Journal of Politics* 40: 1011–43.

McGuire, Martin C. 1978. "A Method for Estimating the Effect of a Subsidy on the Receiver's Resource Constraint with an Application to U.S. Local Government: 1964-1971." *Journal of Public Economics* 10: 25–44.

Michels, Robert. 1962. *Political Parties*. New York: Free Press.

Modernizing State Government, 1967. New York: Committee for Economic Development.

Morison, Samuel. 1972. *The Oxford History of the American People*, vol. 2, 3. New York: Mentor.

Mosher, Frederick and Orville Poland. 1964. *The Costs of American Governments*. New York: Dodd, Mead.

Moynihan, Daniel. 1970. *Maximum Feasible Misunderstanding*. New York: Free Press.

Mueller, John. 1970. "Presidential Popularity from Truman to Johnson." *American Political Science Review* 64: 18–34.

Murphy, Jerome. 1973. "The Education Bureaucracies Implement Novel Policy: The Politics of Title I of ESEA, 1965-72." In *Policy and Politics in America*, edited by Allan Sindler, pp. 160–99. Boston, MA: Little, Brown.

Musgrave, Richard and Peggy Musgrave. 1980. *Public Finance in Theory and Practice*, 3d ed. New York: McGraw-Hill.

Nathan, Richard. 1983. *The Administrative Presidency*. New York: Wiley.

_____. 1990. "Federalism: The Great 'Composition'." In *The New American Political System*, 2d ed., edited by Anthony King, pp. 231–61. Washington, DC: AEI Press.

Nathan, Richard, Fred Doolittle and Associates. 1983. *The Consequences of Cuts*. Princeton, NJ: Princeton Urban and Regional Research Center.

Neumann, Franz. 1962. "Federalism and Freedom: A Critique." In *Federalism: Mature and Emergent*, edited by Arthur Macmahon, pp. 44–57. New York: Russell and Russell.

"New Jersey Seizes Jersey School System." *Daily News*. (October 4, 1989) Pullman, WA: 2a.

Newton, Kenneth. 1975. "American Urban Politics: Social Class, Political Structure and Public Goods." *Urban Affairs Quarterly* 1: 241–64.

Nice, David. 1983a. "Representation in the States: Policymaking and Ideology." *Social Science Quarterly* 64: 404–11.

_____. 1983b. "Revitalizing the States: A Look at the Record." *National Civic Review* 72: 371–76.

_____. 1983c. "An Intergovernmental Perspective on Urban Fragmentation." *Social Science Quarterly* 65: 111–18.

_____. 1984a. "Cooperation and Conformity Among the States." *Polity*, XVI: 494–505.

_____. 1984b. "Teacher Competency Testing as a Policy Innovation." *Policy Studies Journal* 13: 45–54.

_____. 1987a. "State-Financed Property Tax Relief to Individuals: A Research Note." *Western Political Quarterly* 40: 179–85.

_____. 1987b. "State Participation in Interstate Compacts." *Publius* 17: 69–83.

_____. 1988. "Interest Groups and State Constitutions: Another Look." *State and Local Government Review* 20: 21–27.

_____. 1991. "The Impact of State Policies to Limit Debt Financing." *Publius* 21: 69–82.

_____. 1993. "The State Safety Participation Program." *American Review of Public Administration* 23: 43–56.

_____. 1994. *Policy Innovation in the States*. Ames, IA: Iowa State University Press.

Nie, Norman, Sidney Verba and John Petrocik. 1976. *The Changing American Voter*. Cambridge, MA: Harvard.

Orfield, Gary. 1974-75. "Federal Policy, Local Power, and Metropolitan Segregation." *Political Science Quarterly*. 89: 777–802.

O'Rourke, Timothy. 1980. *The Impact of Reapportionment*. New Brunswick, NJ: Transaction.

Ostrom, Elinor. 1972. "Metropolitan Reform: Propositions Derived From Two Traditions." *Social Science Quarterly* 53: 474–93.

Pagano, Michael. 1990. "State-Local Relations in the 1990s." *The Annals* 509: 94–105.

Pagano, Michael and Ann O'M. Bowman. 1993. "The State of American Federalism 1992–1993." *Publius* 23 (Summer): 1–22.

Palley, Marian and Howard Palley. 1981. *Urban America and Public Policies*, 2d ed. Lexington, MA: Heath.

Patterson, Samuel, Roger Davidson and Randall Ripley. 1982. *A More Perfect Union*, revised ed. Homewood, IL: Dorsey.

Pechman, Joseph and Benjamin Okner. 1974. *Who Bears the Tax Burden?* Washington, DC: Brookings.

Pelissero, John. 1984. "State Aid and City Needs: An Examination of Residual State Aid to Large Cities." *Journal of Politics* 46: 916–35.

Pelissero, John and David Morgan. 1987. "State Aid to Public Schools: An Analysis of State Responsiveness to School District Needs." *Social Science Quarterly* 68: 466–77.

Peltason, J. W. 1991. *Understanding the Constitution*, 12th ed. San Diego, CA: Harcourt Brace Jovanovich.

Penne, R. Leo and Paul Verduin. 1986. *State Government Associations: A Reconnaissance*. Washington, DC: National League of Cities.

Peterson, George. 1976. "Finance." In *The Urban Predicament*, edited by William Gorham and Nathan Glazar, pp. 35–118. Washington, DC: Urban Institute.

Peterson, Paul. 1981. *City Limits*. Chicago, IL: University of Chicago Press.

Peterson, Paul, Barry Rabe and Kenneth Wang. 1986. *When Federalism Works*. Washington, DC: Brookings.

Peterson, Paul and Mark Rom. 1989. "American Federalism, Welfare Policy and Residential Choices." *American Political Science Review* 83: 711–28.

Pierce, John, Kathleen Beatty and Paul Hagner. 1982. *The Dynamics of American Public Opinion*. Glenview, IL: Scott, Foresman.

Pilcher, Dan. 1983. "International Trade in the States." *State Legislatures* April: 16–20.

Polsby, Nelson and Aaron Wildavsky. 1980. *Presidential Elections*, 5th ed. New York: Scribner's.

Pressman, Jeffrey and Aaron Wildavsky. 1979. *Implementation*, 2d ed. Berkeley, CA: University of California.

Pritchett, C. Herman. 1977. *The American Constitution*, 3d ed. New York: McGraw-Hill.

Public Rangelands. 1988. Washington, DC: General Accounting Office.

Question of State Government Capability, The. 1985. Washington, DC: Advisory Commission on Intergovernmental Relations.

Ranney, Austin. 1965. "Parties in State Politics." In *Politics in the American States*, edited by Herbert Jacob and Kenneth Vines, pp. 61–99. Boston, MA: Little, Brown.

————. 1971. "Parties in State Politics." In *Politics in the American States*, 2d ed., edited by Herbert Jacob and Kenneth Vines, pp. 82–121. Boston, MA: Little, Brown.

————. 1976. "Parties in State Politics." In *Politics in the American States*, 3d ed., edited by Herbert Jacob and Kenneth Vines, pp. 51–91. Boston, MA: Little, Brown.

Reagan, Michael. 1972. *The New Federalism*. New York: Oxford.

Reed, B. J. 1983. "The Changing Role of Local Advocacy in National Politics." *Journal of Urban Affairs* 5: 287–98.

Reeves, Andree. 1992. "Enhancing Local Self-Government and State Capabilities: The U.S. Advisory Commission on Intergovernmental Relations Program." *Public Administration Review* 52: 401–405.

Reeves, Mavis. 1982. "The State Role and State Capability." In *State and Local Roles in the Federal System*, pp. 51–226. Washington, DC: Advisory Commission on Intergovernmental Relations.

Reuss, Henry. 1970. *Revenue Sharing: Crutch or Catalyst for State and Local Governments?* New York: Praeger.

Rich, Michael. 1989. "Distributive Politics and the Allocation of Federal Grants." *American Political Science Review* 83: 193–213.

Ridgeway, Marian. 1971. *Interstate Compacts: A Question of Federalism*. Carbondale, IL: Southern Illinois University.

Riker, William. 1964. *Federalism*. Boston: Little, Brown.

Rivlin, Alice. 1992. "A New Vision of American Federalism." *Public Administration Review* 52: 315–20.

Rohde, David and Kenneth Shepsle. 1973. "Committee Assignments." *American Political Science Review* 67: 889–905.

Rosenthal, Alan. 1971. "The Scope of Legislative Reform: An Introduction." In *Strengthening the States*, edited by Donald G. Herzberg and Alan Rosenthal, pp. 3–13. Garden City, NY: Doubleday.

_____. 1981. *Legislative Life*. New York: Harper and Row.

Sabato, Larry. 1978. *Goodbye to Good-time Charlie*. Lexington, MA: Lexington.

_____. 1983. *Goodbye to Good-time Charlie*, 2d ed. Washington, DC: Congressional Quarterly.

Saffell, David. 1982. *State and Local Government*, 2d ed. Reading, MA: Addison-Wesley.

Sanford, Terry. 1967. *Storm Over the States*. New York: McGraw-Hill.

Savage, Robert. 1978. "Policy Innovations as a Trait of American States." *Journal of Politics* 40: 212–28.

Savas, E. S. 1982. *Privatizing the Public Sector*. Chatham, NJ: Chatham House.

Schaller, Lyle E. 1966. *Community Organization: Conflict and Reconciliation*. New York: Abingdon Press.

Schneider, Mark. 1980. *Suburban Growth*. Brunswick, OH: King's Court.

_____. 1987. "Local Budgets and the Maximization of Local Property Wealth in the System of Suburban Government." *Journal of Politics* 49: 1104–17.

Schattschneider, E. E. 1960. *The Semisovereign People*. New York: Holt, Rinehart, and Winston.

Scholz, John, Jim Twombly and Barbara Headrick. 1991. "Street-Level Political Controls over Federal Bureaucracy." *American Political Science Review* 85: 829–850.

Schwarz, John. 1988. *America's Hidden Success*, rev. ed. New York: Norton.

Seidman, Harold. 1975. *Politics, Position, and Power*, 2d ed. New York: Oxford University.

Selznick, Phillip. 1949. *TVA and the Grass Roots*. Berkeley: University of California.

Sharkansky, Ira. 1970. *Regionalism in American Politics*. Indianapolis, IN: Bobbs-Merrill.

_____. 1978. *The Maligned States*, 2d ed. New York: McGraw-Hill.

Shin, Kwang and John Jackson. 1979. "Membership Turnover in U.S. State Legislatures: 1931–1976." *Legislative Studies Quarterly* 4: 95–104.

Significant Features of Fiscal Federalism, vol. 2. 1990. Washington, DC: Advisory Commission on Intergovernmental Relations.

_____. 1991. Washington, DC: Advisory Commission on Intergovernmental Relations.

_____. 1992. Washington, DC: Advisory Commission on Intergovernmental Relations.

_____. 1993. Washington, DC: Advisory Commission on Intergovernmental Relations.

Simon, Dennis. 1989. "Presidents, Governors, and Electoral Accountability." *Journal of Politics* 51: 286–304.

Simon, Dennis, Charles Ostrom and Robin Marra. 1991. "The President, Referendum Voting, and Subnational Elections in the United States." *American Political Science Review* 85: 1177–92.

Sokolow, Alvin and Keith Snavely. 1983. "Small City Autonomy in the Federal System: A Study of Local Constraint and Opportunity in California." *Publius* 13: 73–88.

Stanfield, Rochelle. 1976. "The PIG's: Out of the Sty, Into Lobbying with Style." *National Journal* 8: 1134–39.

Stanley, Harold W. and Richard G. Niemi. 1994. *Vital Statistics in American Politics*, 3d ed. Washington, DC: Congressional Quarterly Press.

State Laws Governing Local Government Structure and Administration. 1993. Washington, DC: Advisory Commission on Intergovernmental Relations.

State and Local Roles in the Federal System. 1982. Washington, DC: Advisory Commission on Intergovernmental Relations.

Statistical Abstract. 1985. Washington, DC: U.S. Census Bureau.

_____. 1990. Washington, DC: U.S. Census Bureau.

_____. 1993. Washington, DC: U.S. Census Bureau.

Stedman, Murray. 1975. *Urban Politics*, 2d ed. Cambridge, MA: Winthrop.

Stein, Robert. 1990. "Economic Voting for Governor and U.S. Senator: The Electoral Consequences of Federalism." *Journal of Politics* 52: 29–53.

Stein, Robert and Keith Hamm. 1987. "A Comparative Analysis of the Targeting Capacity of State and Federal Intergovernmental Aid Allocations." *Social Science Quarterly* 68: 447–65.

Stephens, G. Ross. 1974. "State Centralization and the Erosion of Local Autonomy." *Journal of Politics* 36: 44–76.

Stephenson, Jr., Max O. and Gerald M. Pops. 1989. "Conflict Resolution Methods and the Policy Process." *Public Administration Review* 49 (September/October): 463–73.

Stokes, Donald and Warren Miller. 1962. "Party Government and the Salience of Congress." *Public Opinion Quarterly* 26: 531–46.

Sundquist, James and David Davis. 1966. *Making Federalism Work*. Washington, DC: Brookings.

Sylvester, Kathleen. 1988. "Exporting Made Easy." *Governing* 1: 36–42.

Syme, Geoffrey J. and Elizabeth Eaton. 1989. "Public Involvement As a Negotiation Process." *Journal of Social Issues* 45 (Spring): 87–107.

Thomas, Kenneth. 1979. "Organizational Conflict." In *Organizational Behavior*, edited by Steven Kerr. Columbus, OH: Grid Publishing.

Tiebout, Charles. 1956. "A Pure Theory of Local Expenditure." *Journal of Political Economy* 64: 416–35.

Truman, David. 1962. "Federalism and the Party System." In *Federalism: Mature and Emergent*, edited by Arthur Macmahon, pp. 115–36. New York: Russell and Russell.

Ulmer, S. Sidney. 1985. "Governmental Litigants, Underdogs, and Civil Liberties in the Supreme Court: 1903–1968 Terms." *Journal of Politics* 47: 899–909.

U.S. Department of Agriculture: Farm Agencies' Field Structure Needs Major Overhaul. 1991. Washington, DC: General Accounting Office.

Verba, Sidney and Norman Nie. 1972. *Participation in America*. New York: Harper and Row.

Vincent, Jack. 1981. "Internal and External Conflict: Some Previous Operational Problems and Some New Findings." *Journal of Politics* 43: 128–42.

Vines, Kenneth. 1976. "The Federal Setting of State Politics." In *Politics in the American States*, 3d ed., edited by Herbert Jacob and Kenneth Vines, pp. 3–48. Boston, MA: Little, Brown.

Walker, David. 1981. *Toward a Functioning Federalism*. Cambridge, MA: Winthrop.

————. 1991. "American Federalism From Johnson to Bush." *Publius* 21 (Winter): 105–119.

Walker, Jack. 1969. "The Diffusion of Innovations Among the American States." *American Political Science Review* 63: 880–99.

————. 1971. "Innovation in State Politics." In *Politics in the American States,* 2d ed, edited by Herbert Jacob and Kenneth Vines, pp. 354–87. Boston, MA: Little, Brown.

Walters, Jonathon. 1994. "Reinventing the Federal System." *Governing* 7: 49–53.

Ward, Peter. 1981. "The Measurement of Federal and State Responsiveness to Urban Problems." *Journal of Politics* 43: 83–101.

Weber, Ronald. 1975. "The Political Responsiveness of the American States and Their Local Governments." In *People vs. Government,* edited by Leroy Rieselbach, pp. 189–226. Bloomington, IN: Indiana University Press.

Welch, Susan and Cal Clarke. 1973. "Interstate Compacts and National Political Integration: An Empirical Assessment of Some Trends." *Western Political Quarterly* 26: 475–84.

Welch, Susan and Kay Thompson. 1980. "The Impact of Federal Incentives on State Policy Innovation." *American Journal of Political Science* 24: 715–29.

Wheare, K. C. 1964. *Federal Government,* 4th ed. New York: Galaxy.

Wikstrom, Nelson. 1977. *Councils of Governments: A Study of Political Incrementalism.* Chicago: Nelson-Hall.

Wildavsky, Aaron. 1967. "Party Discipline Under Federalism: Implications of the Australian Experience." In *American Federalism in Perspective,* edited by Aaron Wildavsky, pp. 162–84. Boston, MA: Little, Brown.

————. 1974. *The Politics of the Budgetary Process,* 2d ed. Boston, MA: Little, Brown.

Wilensky, Harold. 1975. *The Welfare State and Equality.* Berkeley, CA: University of California.

Within School Discrimination. 1991. Washington, DC: General Accounting Office.

Wood, B. Dan. 1991. "Federalism and Policy Responsiveness: The Clean Air Case." *Journal of Politics* 53: 851–59.

World Almanac. 1988. New York: Newspaper Enterprise Association.

————. 1994. New York: World Almanac.

Wright, Deil. 1982. *Understanding Intergovernmental Relations,* 2d ed. Monterey, CA: Brooks/Cole.

————. 1988. *Understanding Intergovernmental Relations,* 3d ed. Pacific Grove, CA: Brooks/Cole.

————. 1990. "Federalism, Intergovernmental Relations, and Intergovernmental Management: Historical Reflections and Conceptual Comparisons." *Public Administration Review* 50 (March/April): 168–78.

Wright, Gerald, Robert Erikson, and John McIver. 1987. "Public Opinion and Policy Liberalism in the American States." *American Journal of Political Science* 31: 980–1001.

Yates, Douglas. 1973. *Neighborhood Democracy.* Lexington, MA: Lexington.

Yin, Robert and Douglas Yates. 1975. *Street-Level Governments.* Lexington, MA: Lexington.

Zampelli, Ernest. 1986. "Resource Fungibility, the Flypaper Effect, and the Expenditure Impact of Grants-in-Aid." *The Review of Economics and Statistics* 68: 33–40.

Zeigler, L. Harmon and Harvey Tucker. 1978. *The Quest for Responsive Government.* North Scituate, MA: Duxbury.

Zimmerman, Joseph. 1972. *The Federated City.* New York: St. Martin's.

————. 1991. "Federal Preemption Under Reagan's New Federalism." *Publius* 21: 7–28.

————. 1992. *Contemporary American Federalism.* New York: Praeger.

Zinn, Howard. 1980. *A People's History of the United States.* New York: Harper and Row.

INDEX